HOW TO
LISTEN SO PARENTS WILL TALK AND TALK SO PARENTS WILL LISTEN

HOW TO LISTEN SO PARENTS WILL TALK AND TALK SO PARENTS WILL LISTEN

JOHN SOMMERS-FLANAGAN

RITA SOMMERS-FLANAGAN

WILEY

John Wiley & Sons, Inc.

Library of Congress Cataloging-in-Publication Data:
Sommers-Flanagan, John, 1957-
   How to Listen so Parents Will Talk and Talk so Parents Will Listen / John Sommers-Flanagan and Rita Sommers-Flanagan.
      p. cm.
   Includes bibliographical references and index.
ISBN 978-1-118-01296-3 (pbk.)
ISBN 978-1-118-06799-4 (ebk.)
ISBN 978-1-118-06800-7 (ebk.)
ISBN 978-1-118-06801-4 (ebk.)
   1.   Counselor and client.   2.   Problem children—Counseling of.
3.   Parenting—Psychological aspects.   4.   Child psychotherapy—Parent participation.
5.   Parent-student counselor relationships.   I. Sommers-Flanagan, Rita, 1953- II. Title.
   BF636.6.S66 2011
   362.82'86–dc22   2011010998

*To all parents with whom we've worked and
who have worked with us — including our own.*

Contents

Case Examples   ix

Preface   xi

PART ONE: UNDERSTANDING AND BEING
WITH PARENTS

CHAPTER ONE
A Way of Being With Parents   3

CHAPTER TWO
Preparing Yourself to Work Effectively With Parents   17

CHAPTER THREE
What Parents Want: A Model for Understanding Adult Influence   33

PART TWO: STRATEGIES FOR WORKING
WITH PARENTS

CHAPTER FOUR
From Initial Contact to Assessment: Building and Maintaining
a Working Relationship With Parents   57

CHAPTER FIVE
Collaborative Problem Formulation   75

CHAPTER SIX
Creating and Providing Guidance, Advice, and Solutions   93

PART THREE: PRACTICAL TECHNIQUES FOR PARENTING CHALLENGES

CHAPTER SEVEN
Teaching Relationship-Based Interventions to Parents 113

CHAPTER EIGHT
Sharing Power to Gain Influence: Indirect and Problem-Solving
Interventions 133

CHAPTER NINE
A New-and-Improved Behaviorism: Child-Friendly but Direct
Approaches to Discipline 153

CHAPTER TEN
Ongoing Contact, Complications, and Referrals 177

CHAPTER ELEVEN
Dealing With Special Situations and Issues 195

Appendix A: An Annotated Bibliography of Parenting Books 209
Appendix B: Tip Sheets for Parents 217
Appendix C: Parent Satisfaction and Counselor Reflection Inventory 229
Appendix D: Master List of Attitudes, Strategies, and Interventions 233
Appendix E: Chapter Checklists 235
Appendix F: Parent Homework Assignments 241
References 261
Author Index 271
Subject Index 275

Case Examples

1. Emma the Great and Powerful   4
2. "Wanna Piece of *Me*?"   12
3. Chasing Malia: A Good Fitness Plan (*Not!*)   29
4. Walking on Eggshells   64
5. Caleb Gets Some Control   78
6. Understanding Jo Jo's Underachievement   84
7. Singing the Bedtime Blues   87
8. A Father in Precontemplation   95
9. "How About Now, Mom? Can I Have It Now?"   100
10. An Old-Fashioned Dad   103
11. "That Dog Don't Hunt"   114
12. "I Want to Spend More Time With You"   117
13. "I Think She Likes Yelling"   120
14. Addressing Step-Parenting Myths   125
15. Troy's Three Choices   135
16. Four Roads to Healthier Self-Esteem   138
17. Just Another Homework Battle   144
18. "We'd Like to Not Spank Travis"   158
19. A Visit to the Mall   161
20. An Emotionally Soothing Timeout   166
21. Terribly Tardy Tabitha   169
22. "Bully for You!"   186
23. "Can We Talk About Big Brother?"   188
24. Bedtime Is a Bad Time   189
25. Tobacco, Culture, and Addiction   196
26. Talking About Divorce   199

Preface

This book is about relationships.

In the midst of an electronic age where communication is fast and brief, this is a book about building positive, intentional, and influential face-to-face relationships between professionals and parents. It's also about how parents can build positive and influential relationships with their children. Even this paragraph is longer than a 140-character tweet.

This book is founded on our belief that counselors, psychologists, and other human services providers need specialized preparation and distinct skills to work effectively with parents. We see parents as different from other "clinical populations" and as deserving an approach designed to address their unique needs.

If you work with parents and caregivers (or have one yourself) you know their influence is wide and deep. Sometimes it's clear how powerfully we're affected by our parents and other times it's less clear, but their influence is nearly always at work.

Before jumping into Chapter One, we have a number of explanations, caveats, excuses, and acknowledgments to cover.

EXPLANATIONS

This book is designed for all professionals who work with parents. This might include school or mental health counselors, school psychologists, marriage and family therapists, counseling and clinical psychologists, clinical social workers, rehabilitation counselors, and other helping professionals.

While writing this book we were faced with many dilemmas, most of which we resolved in one way or another. However, we didn't fully resolve the question of what terms to use when referring to professionals who work with parents. In an effort to not offend anyone in particular, we alternatively use the words *human services professional* (or *provider*), *therapist*, *consultant*, *practitioner*, and *dude*. (Okay, so we never actually use *dude*, but we thought about it.) Our hope is that anyone who works directly with parents will feel comfortable using this book.

In the spirit of Carl Rogers, this book is about *a way of being with parents*. We consider much of what we write in the following pages to be a tribute to his person-centered philosophy and practice. However, to complicate things a bit, this book also follows many of the basic rules of B.F. Skinner's behavioral approach, and, in keeping with Insoo Kim Berg and Stephen de Shazer, includes a focus on solutions. Readers familiar with Alfred Adler will recognize his encouraging influence; there are also the logical consequences of having read Rudolf Dreikurs's explanations for why children misbehave. There is also much of William Glasser's choice theory woven throughout the book. Much like the Motivational Interviewing movement in counseling and psychotherapy, the approach advocated in this book has a person-centered foundation but moves into more active and directive strategies and techniques.

While this book is not a cookbook with specific recipes for working with parents, it does include detailed descriptions of 13 major interventions and less detailed descriptions of 14 others. It also includes 11 tip sheets for parents and 13 specific parent homework assignments. We include cases that focus on many different types of problems. Given this level of specificity, some readers may be disappointed that we don't link specific child problems (e.g., lying, bedtime, etc.) to specific interventions. We intentionally avoided this approach because we want to emphasize and embrace the uniqueness of every parent, every family situation, and every practitioner. The best guidance often springs from the co-creation of solutions generated by practitioner and parent. This is a collaborative and authoritative approach designed to represent not only a way for professionals to be with parents, but also a way that parents can be with their children. We encourage you to bring knowledge and expertise to your work with parents and to apply the ideas in this book with compassion and authenticity.

CAVEATS

Parenting can be controversial. Many people, including professionals, have rigid and emotional opinions about how to parent *right*. Often, taking any position on any parenting issue can start an argument. Not everyone will like this book or agree with its general philosophy or its recommended techniques, tip sheets, and parent homework assignments. However, regardless of your parenting perspective, we feel certain that this book can help make you better at reaching and teaching the many parents who are in need of professional guidance.

The parenting cases and stories in this book are an amalgamation and distillation of many parenting experiences. Some come from our own lives. Others come from the stories told to us in our work with parents. Still others were contributed by colleagues. Each "case" is generally a composite with identifying information removed, shifted, and changed and complex issues simplified and simple issues complexified (we love that particular neologism). These changes were made to protect the identity of parents with whom we've worked. Undoubtedly, anyone who sees themselves in these pages is resonating with a common or universal story that has been experienced by many parents and observed by many professionals.

EXCUSES

The approach to working with parents emphasized, repeated, and re-repeated in this book will not work with all parents in all situations. Sometimes parents will be perplexingly resistant, and other times our methods or strategies will not measure up to the substantial task of helping parents. In other words, if you plan to work with parents, you should be open to experiencing failure, learning from our mistakes, and learning from your own mistakes. Just as parenting is an art, a science, *and* an immense job where you never quite get it just right, so, too, is the job of helping parents.

ACKNOWLEDGMENTS

We have a list of many people to thank. We initially thought we should list every parent we've ever known, but then this would be a book of thanks, free from content. Instead, we're restricting ourselves to a short list of people who have provided inspiration, support, and knowledge.

That being the case, thank you to the Families First Missoula team: Diana Reetz-Stacey, Phillip Mamalakis, Tina Barrett, Andrew Peterson, Kerry Maier, Heidi Kendall, Sara Polanchek, Coco Ballew, Jana Staton, Amy Rubin, Barbara Cowan, Judy Wright, Sarah Mulligan, Danelle Danzer, Anya Vasquez, Amy Westering, and others. Thank you especially to Susan O'Connor whose immense generosity is matched only by her foresight into helping parents and families through gentle and respectful guidance. Thanks also to Linda Braun, co-founder and longtime director of Families First Boston.

Thanks to the University of Montana team of readers, reviewers, consultants, and colleagues, including, but not limited to, Cathy Jenni, Carol Roberts, Carrie Thiel, Crystal Tower, Joyce Mphande-Finn, Ty Bequette, and Deborah Maney. There are many others.

Finally, thanks to the Wiley team, especially Rachel Livsey, Sweta Gupta, Judi Knott, and Kara Borbely. Rachel, we appreciate your enthusiasm for and quick action on this project.

In closing, we'd like to acknowledge the many parenting writers and professionals who have come before us and influenced the way we work with and think about parents. We are particularly indebted to Adele Faber and Elaine Mazlish for the concept of "talking so children will listen and listening so children will talk." We love this idea so much that we've borrowed it, reversed it, and shifted its focus to fit our work with parents. It has become abundantly clear to us in recent years that our best ideas are always built on the good ideas of others who preceded us. With this in mind, we hope some readers of this book will join with and surpass us, writing books and offering workshops in an effort to create a better and more compassionate world. That would be most gratifying. However, for now, we simply wish you the best in your efforts to be of professional assistance to parents.

John and Rita Sommers-Flanagan
Missoula, Montana

PART ONE

Understanding and Being With Parents

These first three chapters focus on how practitioners can understand the challenges parents face and be with them in a way that facilitates therapeutic relationship development. Being with parents in an accepting, respectful, and positive manner, preparing specifically to work with them, and understanding what parents want are all crucial components to helping parents speak openly about their fears and hopes. And if parents don't speak openly, there's very little you can do to assist them in becoming better parents. As Carl Rogers might say, the initial goal for practitioners is to make psychological contact while holding an attitude of acceptance, empathy, and honest collaboration; this is the essence of the therapeutic relationship.

CHAPTER ONE

A Way of Being With Parents

Whether parents consider themselves to be "tiger" parents, collaborative parents, or find themselves feeling like doormat parents, parenting in the 21st century is stressful and demanding. According to recent epidemiological studies, 12 to 20 percent of children and adolescents in the United States meet the diagnostic criteria for mental disorders (Costello, Egger, & Angold, 2005; Costello, Mustillo, Erkanli, Keeler, & Angold, 2003; Merikangas et al., 2010). Although these extreme emotional and behavioral disorders are obviously of concern to parents, there are also many relatively mild parent–child problems that parents find puzzling and disturbing and for which they seek support and guidance. This helps explain why there are thousands of Internet websites, hundreds of popular press books, and dozens of magazines and newspaper columns—all with the primary aim of helping parents manage their parenting challenges. As Kohn (2005) stated in the opening of his book, *Unconditional Parenting*, parenting is no easy task:

> *Even before I had children, I knew that being a parent was going to be challenging as well as rewarding. But I didn't really know.*
>
> *I didn't know how exhausted it was possible to become, or how clueless it was possible to feel, or how, each time I reached the end of my rope, I would somehow have to find more rope. (p. 1; italics in original)*

This book is based on sound theoretical and empirical knowledge and is designed to help you give parents the help they want and need. This chapter describes how parents are unique. It also focuses on why adopting a particular way of being with parents will facilitate your ability, as a helping professional, to obtain positive therapeutic and educational outcomes.

WHY PARENTS ARE A DISTINCT AND UNIQUE POPULATION

Parents face many unique challenges. It's often impossible to know the magnitude of the parenting problem before the parents step into the consulting room.

Case: Emma the Great and Powerful

Imagine you're meeting with a mother and a father to talk about parenting. From the session's beginning, both parents speak bluntly about their situation. The father says,

> I don't know how much more we can take. Emma, our only child who just turned seven, has complete control of our household. I dread coming home from work. I've been staying longer at the office to postpone the inevitable series of angry confrontations that I know will start within 10 minutes of my arrival home. I know that's crazy. I know we need help. I mean, I know I need help. I feel like our family is about to disintegrate.

The mother is even more emotionally distraught. Between tears, she describes a recent walk to school with Emma.

> I knew it would be a struggle. She didn't want to wear gloves, but there's snow on the ground and it's below freezing and so she needed them. We argued for 10 minutes. She finally put them on. Then, partway through our walk to school she dropped them and kept walking. I asked her to pick them up. She refused. I told her, "If you don't pick up those gloves you won't get to watch TV after school." I knew that would get her. She bent down and slowly picked up her gloves and we walked the rest of the way to school. Because we were late, I was dropping her off in front of the teacher and her class and when I leaned down to kiss her on the cheek and wish her a good day, she reared back and slapped me across the face. I was so shocked and embarrassed and hurt that I just cried all the way home.

If you were meeting with these parents, you would easily recognize their pain, their distress, and their need for help. Most likely, your main question would be something like: How can I most efficiently support these parents and provide them with guidance and tools for dealing with Emma's challenging behaviors?

What Parents Want From Professionals

Emma's parents, and parents in general, are distinct from other clinical populations in several ways.

- When parents schedule an appointment, they're not seeking professional assistance for their own adult problems; they're usually seeking professional input or assistance for how to deal with their child or children.
- Parents tend to want immediate and direct guidance and advice. If you had spent an hour with Emma's parents and had not provided them with practical suggestions for how to deal with Emma's behavior, they most likely wouldn't return or recommend your services to other parents. On the other hand, as we will discuss below, they also want and need to feel respected, safe, and understood before any attempts at advice will be successful.
- Partly because of keen interest in their children's well-being and partly because of previous exposure to many different parenting ideas, parents can be

exceedingly critical of educational or therapeutic interventions. Emma's parents have most likely already talked to their friends and family and possibly consulted online resources or read books about how to deal with strong-willed children. This is one reason why parents want, and sometimes demand, experienced and competent professional helpers.

- Parents are often simultaneously defensive and vulnerable. Although they want help, if they don't feel respected and accepted by helping professionals, they can quickly become defensive and sometimes hostile. For example, if a helping professional immediately informed Emma's mom that Emma needs natural consequences and therefore should be allowed to go to school without gloves, that professional might be viewed as clueless and uncaring—and may get a harsh lecture on the dangers of frostbite during Montana winters.

Based on the preceding factors it's clear that parents constitute a unique clinical population and deserve individually tailored educational and therapeutic approaches.

THE MANY VENUES AND SETTINGS AVAILABLE TO PARENTS IN DISTRESS

In the preceding situation, Emma's parents had many potentially effective choices for how to deal with their family situation. They could have sought help from Emma's pediatrician; they could have taken Emma to a counselor or psychotherapist or attended family therapy together; they could have obtained a parenting consultation through a local community agency; they could have contacted Emma's school psychologist or school counselor; or they could have enrolled in a parenting education course or signed up for a more intensive and longer-term parent-training curriculum.

From the menu of options available, Emma's parents selected a two-session parenting consultation that was offered as a part of a research project in their community. Broadly speaking, the purpose of the research was to investigate what parents found most useful during their consultation experience (J. Sommers-Flanagan, 2007). Within the framework of this two-session protocol, Emma's parents completed a registration form and several standardized parenting questionnaires prior to their initial session. One month after their initial session, they returned for a second session. Following their second session they completed post-intervention questionnaires and a satisfaction measure. Twelve weeks later they were contacted via telephone to assess their perceptions of their two-session consultation experience.

Despite their dire initial presentation and an extremely brief intervention, Emma's parents experienced a remarkably positive outcome. During the second session, Emma's father spoke passionately about the changes they experienced following their first session:

> Everything is much, much better. It's not that Emma changed; we changed. What I remember most is that we decided to try the boring consequences and passionate rewards technique that you suggested and it was a life saver. We started talking about it in the car on the way home from our consultation. We discovered it wasn't so much

about our daughter, but it was about us and how we'd been responding to her. We'd been so angry and reactive and ready to jump on her whenever she misbehaved that the idea of being completely boring helped us let go and focus on her behavior rather than our reactions. And once we got more in control and became boring, Emma's behavior improved too. Everything is much better.

Emma's parents also reported significant positive changes on their post-session questionnaires and endorsed the highest satisfaction ratings possible. Twelve weeks later, in a telephone interview with an independent evaluator, they continued to articulate the benefits of their short parenting consultation experience.

USING THEORY AND EVIDENCE

Although Emma's parents chose a short parenting consultation intervention, they could have selected any of the other educational or therapeutic options mentioned previously—and possibly obtained similarly positive outcomes. Previous research and individual parent testimonials support the fact that many different treatment approaches and models can produce positive child behavior outcomes and parental satisfaction (Kaminski, Valle, Filene, & Boyle, 2008; Lambert & Barley, 2002; Lambert & Bergin, 1994; Wampold, 2005, 2010). Similar to clinical work with other populations, positive outcomes with parents are likely driven by four common factors (Lambert & Barley, 2002; Lambert & Bergin, 1994). These factors include:

1. Development of a positive working relationship
2. Implementation of specific psychological interventions
3. Positive expectations
4. Extratherapeutic factors

These four *common factors* and their implementation or activation form the foundation of modern evidence-based counseling and psychotherapy. Interestingly, when it comes to psychological interventions and behavior change, human services providers are able to directly implement only the first two common factors: (a) the *positive working relationship* and (b) the *specific psychological interventions*. Based on existing research and our previous experiences working with parents, when these two factors are addressed well, the third and fourth factors are activated: Positive expectations follow and parents are more likely to engage or utilize their extratherapeutic resources. In this way, the evidence-based common factors that lie at the heart of positive outcomes are maximized (Wampold, 2010).

For example, previous research on parenting consultation and parent training programs emphasizes that (a) parents work more effectively with professionals who employ collaborative and culturally sensitive strategies, rather than expert-oriented strategies (Hirschland, 2008; Holcomb-McCoy & Bryan, 2010; Sheridan et al., 2004; Sheridan & Kratochwill, 2008); (b) interventions that focus on improving the quality of parent–child relationships tend to produce more robust results (Erchul, 1987; Kaminski et al., 2008); and (c) positive educational and therapy outcomes are more likely when therapists and human services providers offer parents very specific and useful solutions, information, and resources (Dunst, Trivette, & Thompson, 1994; J. Sommers-Flanagan, 2007).

As a consequence, because this book is designed to help you work more effectively with parents, we will focus almost exclusively on addressing the following questions:

- What core attitudes and general strategies can help you develop positive working relationships with parents? In other words—how can you work collaboratively and effectively with parents?
- When working directly with parents, what specific interventions or techniques are most likely to contribute to positive educational and therapeutic outcomes?

A *Manualized* and *Person-Centered Approach*

We recognize that educational and therapeutic manuals are anathema to person-centered counselors or therapists. Nevertheless, we also recognize that therapists and educators can benefit from clear and direct assistance for how to work effectively with specific clinical and educational populations. Consequently, in the best spirit of a manualized approach to psychotherapy, this book offers concrete guidance to help you through the process of counseling, coaching, teaching, or consulting with parents. This guidance includes many examples of technical interventions with parents and descriptions of methods for helping parents implement developmentally sensitive and scientifically supported strategies for managing their children's behavior.

Of course, effective work with clients or parents requires much more than manual-based technical instruction (Norcross, Beutler, & Levant, 2006). So, correspondingly, in the best spirit of person-centered therapy and evidence-based relationships, this book also focuses on specific attitudes, strategies, and techniques that you can use to build positive and collaborative working relationships with parents. This *less technical*, more relationship-based approach highlights our belief that establishing collaborative relationships with parents facilitates their responsiveness to educational and therapeutic interventions.

BUILDING A THERAPEUTIC RELATIONSHIP WITH PARENTS: THREE CORE ATTITUDES

Our underlying assumption is that parents constitute a unique population that requires and deserves a specifically tailored treatment approach. Similar to person-centered therapy, this approach is characterized by three core therapist attitudes: (a) empathic understanding; (b) radical acceptance; and (c) collaboration.

Empathy for Parents and Parenting

As is well-known, empathic understanding is one of the three core conditions for psychotherapy originally identified by Carl Rogers (1942; 1961; 1980). Over the years, research has left no doubt that therapist empathy facilitates positive therapy outcomes (Goldfried, 2007; Greenberg, Watson, Elliot, & Bohart, 2001; Mullis & Edwards, 2001). As applied to parents, empathy involves:

> The therapist's ability and willingness to understand the parent's thoughts, feelings, and struggles from the parent's point of view and an ability to see, more or less completely, through the parent's eyes and adopt the parent's frame of reference. . . . It means entering the private perceptual world of a parent. (adapted from Rogers, 1980, pp. 85, 142)

When working with parents, counselors, psychologists, and other human services professionals must learn to sensitively enter into the parent's unique perceptual world. The practitioner needs to demonstrate empathy and sensitivity for specific parenting challenges. A person-centered perspective also implies that professionals who work with parents show empathy for the barrage of criticism, scrutiny, and associated insecurity that parents experience due to their exposure to social and media sources. Brazelton and Sparrow (2006) capture one way in which socially driven parental insecurity can manifest itself:

> When Mrs. McCormick held Tim in her lap at the playground, she sat alone on a bench across from the other mothers as if she were ashamed of Tim's clinging. She knew that if she sat by other mothers, they would all give her advice: "Just put him down and let him cry—he'll get over it." "MY little girl was just like that before she finally got used to other kids." "Get him a play date. He can learn about other children that way." (p. 8)

This example illustrates how parents anticipate criticism and work hard to avoid it. If you've been a parent or you work with parents, you know how easy it is for them to feel defensive about their children's behaviors and their parenting choices. This is partly because, like Mrs. McCormick, they're unable to measure up to narrowly defined parenting standards and cannot face the cascade of criticism or advice they're likely to receive when their child doesn't behave perfectly in social settings. To provide an optimally empathic environment, practitioners should have and show empathy or attunement with parents' sensitivity to perceived or actual criticism and counter this sensitivity by amplifying their support and acceptance (we cover therapeutic methods for amplifying support and acceptance in greater detail in Chapter 4).

Similar to the empathic attitude associated with person-centered therapy, it's crucial for professionals who work with parents to hold the attitude that parenting is naturally difficult and that making mistakes or having a child who publicly misbehaves is nothing to feel shameful about. By maintaining this attitude, practitioners provide a nonjudgmental and empathic space for parents to explore their personal doubts and fears. This is the way the theory works: By being nonjudgmental, compassionate, and openly supportive, parenting professionals provide an environment free from societal *conditions of worth*, which then stimulates parents to become more open and collaborative when examining their weaknesses with a trusted professional.

Radical Acceptance

Radical acceptance is a central therapeutic attitude held by practitioners who work effectively with parents. Radical acceptance is both an attitude and a clinical technique. This concept was originally articulated by Marsha Linehan (1993) and is a foundational component of dialectical behavior therapy. It involves a particular attitude that builds on Carl Rogers' core therapeutic condition of unconditional positive regard as well as Eastern (Buddhist) philosophy.

Radical acceptance enables helping professionals to approach each client or parent with an overarching, pervasive dialectic belief, which we translate as, "I completely accept you just as you are, *and* I am committed to helping you change for the better." When working with parents, consultants strive to simultaneously hold both of these beliefs or attitudes. On the surface, these attitudes may seem contradictory, thus the term *dialectic*. At a deeper level, in a helping relationship, each attitude is necessary to complete the other.

As a technique, radical acceptance serves two main functions. First, it can help you refrain from expressing negative personal reactions to statements by parents that inadvertently push your buttons (we'll focus more on button-pushing in Chapter 2). If you hear a statement that pushes an emotional button for you, having a radical acceptance attitude would help remind you that your job is to fully accept the person in the room with you—as is. In this situation, you don't have to say anything as you simply quiet your roiling reactions. You can just be present and nonreactive.

Second, beyond momentary silence, radical acceptance allows parenting professionals to actively embrace whatever attitudes or beliefs parents bring into the consulting room. As we've stated previously (J. Sommers-Flanagan & Sommers-Flanagan, 2007a):

> *The generic version or statement of radical acceptance is to graciously welcome even the most absurd or offensive . . . [parent] . . . statements with a response like, "I'm very glad you brought that [topic] up." (p. 275)*

Radical acceptance is especially warranted when parents say something you find disagreeable. This may include racist, sexist, or insensitive comments. For example:

PARENT: I believe in limiting my children's exposure to gay people. Parents need to keep children away from evil influences.

CONSULTANT: Thanks for sharing your perspective with me. I'm glad you brought up your worries about this. Many parents have similar beliefs but won't say them in here. So I especially appreciate you being honest with me about your beliefs. [Adapted from J. Sommers-Flanagan & Sommers-Flanagan, 2007a, p. 276.]

Rest assured, radical acceptance does not mean agreeing with the content of whatever parents say. Instead, it means moving beyond feeling threatened, angry, or judgmental about parents' comments and authentically welcoming whatever comes up during the session. The main purpose of welcoming disagreeable or challenging parent comments is to communicate your commitment to openness. If you don't communicate and value openness by welcoming all remarks, parents or caregivers may never admit their core underlying beliefs. And if parents cover up their true beliefs—especially disagreeable or embarrassing beliefs—there will be no opportunity for insight or change because the underlying beliefs will never be exposed to the light of personal and professional inspection.

Similar to person-centered therapy, one key to using radical acceptance effectively is genuineness or congruence. This means you should never falsely welcome parents' racist, sexist, insensitive, or outrageous comments. Instead, you should welcome such comments only if you really believe that hearing them is a good thing that can benefit the counseling or consultation process.

Radical acceptance also involves letting go of the immediate need to teach parents a new and better way. We must confess that we haven't always maintained an attitude of radical acceptance ourselves. During one memorable session, upon hearing the classic line, "I got spanked and I turned out just fine!" John, being in an impatient and surly mood, barely managed to suppress an extremely destructive impulse (he wanted to say, "Are you really so sure you turned out fine?"). Nevertheless, a judgmental and dismissive comment still slipped out and he said: "I can't tell you how many times I've heard parents say what you just said." Not surprisingly, that particular session didn't proceed with the spirit of empathy, acceptance, and collaboration we generally recommend.

This leads us to some obvious advice: Although you cannot be radically accepting all the time, you should always avoid radical judgment. There's no need to test the "How about I treat parents in a judgmental, dismissive manner?" technique. Outcomes associated with judgmental and disrespectful counselor behavior are quite undesirable.

Collaboration

Collaboration, as an attitude, requires that at least to some extent, parenting professionals come from a position of "not knowing" (Anderson, 1993; Anderson & Goolishian, 1992). As Anderson (1993) stated: "The not knowing position is empathic and is most often characterized by questions that come from an honest continuous therapeutic posture of not understanding too quickly" (p. 331).

Not knowing requires professionals to resist the ubiquitous impulse to be all-knowing experts. Resisting the impulse to demonstrate one's expertise is especially important when initially meeting with and working with parents.

Not surprisingly, it can be very difficult for parenting professionals to establish and maintain a collaborative attitude. This is partly because human services providers who work with parents also need to be *experts* and must demonstrate their expertise. Similar to radical acceptance, collaboration between professionals and parents is a dialectic where the professional embraces both the parents' expertness and his or her own expertise.

Some writers have emphasized that true collaboration between professionals and parents requires a form of leaderlessness (Brown, Pryzwansky, & Schulte, 2006; Kampwirth, 2006). In contrast, our position is that professionals who work with parents can and should bring the following knowledge, skills, and expertise to the consulting office:

- How to lead or direct a counseling or consultation meeting
- How to quickly form collaborative relationships and a working alliance with parents
- Knowledge of what contemporary research says about child development and child psychopathology
- A wide range of theoretically diverse and research-informed strategies and interventions to use with parents
- A wide range of theoretically diverse and research-informed strategies and techniques for parents to implement with their children

At the same time, *parents are also experts* who bring the following knowledge and expertise into your office:

- Their own personal memories and experiences of being parented
- Knowledge and experience of their children's unique temperament and behavior patterns
- Awareness of their personal parenting style and efforts to parent more competently
- Knowledge of their existing parenting strategies as well as the history of many other parenting ideas they have tried and found to be more or less helpful
- An understanding of their limits and abilities to use new or different parenting strategies and techniques

In a very practical sense, it would be inappropriate (and probably ineffective) to ignore the fact that parents come to human services professionals *expecting advice and guidance* about how to be and become better parents. This is the frame from which virtually all parenting interventions flow. Consequently, if the consultant or therapist behaves too much like an equal and doesn't act at all like an expert who offers concrete and straightforward advice, the meeting will likely fail because the basic assumption that the therapist is a helpful expert will be violated.

On the other hand, for many reasons, parents are in a vulnerable state and, consequently, if they feel their parenting consultant is acting like a judgmental or condescending expert, they will usually become defensive and antagonistic. To counter this possibility, the professional needs to hold a collaborative attitude that honors the parents' knowledge and experience. This collaborative attitude will help parents see themselves as respected and relatively equal partners in the therapeutic and/or educational consultation process.

Overall, the model we describe in this book emphasizes that, from a position of respect, interest, and curiosity, parenting consultants, counselors, and therapists work to quickly establish a partnership with parents. When therapeutic or educational work with parents is most successful, parents will likely perceive you as an empathic, accepting, and collaborative expert willing to offer a wide range of theoretically divergent, practical, meaningful, and simple suggestions for how to parent more effectively.

THEORY INTO PRACTICE: THE THREE ATTITUDES IN ACTION

In the following example, Cassandra is discussing her son's "strong-willed" behaviors with a parenting professional.

Case: "Wanna Piece of Me?"

CASSANDRA: My son is so stubborn. Everything is fine one minute, but if I ask him to do something, he goes ballistic. And then I can't get him to do anything.

CONSULTANT: Some kids seem built to focus on getting what they want. It sounds like your boy is very strong-willed. [A simple initial reflection using common language is used to quickly formulate the problem in a way that empathically resonates with the parent's experience.]

CASSANDRA: He's way beyond strong-willed. The other day I asked him to go upstairs and clean his room and he said, "No!" [The mom wants the consultant to know that her son is not your ordinary strong-willed boy.]

CONSULTANT: He just refused? What happened then? [The consultant shows appropriate interest and curiosity, which honors the parent's perspective and helps build the collaborative relationship.]

CASSANDRA: I asked him again, and then, while standing at the bottom of the stairs, he put his hands on his hips and yelled, "I said *no!* You wanna piece of *me*??!"

CONSULTANT: Wow. You're right. He is in the advanced class on how to be strong-willed. What did you do next? [The consultant accepts and validates the parent's perception of having an exceptionally strong-willed child and continues with collaborative curiosity.]

CASSANDRA: I carried him upstairs and spanked his butt because, at that point, I *did* want a piece of him! [Mom discloses becoming angry and acting on her anger.]

CONSULTANT: It's funny how often when our kids challenge our authority so directly, like your son did, it really does make us want a piece of them. [The consultant is universalizing, validating, and accepting the mom's anger as normal, but does not use the word *anger*.]

CASSANDRA: It sure gets me! [Mom acknowledges that her son can really get to her, but there's still no mention of anger.]

CONSULTANT: I know my next question is a cliché counseling question, but I can't help but wonder how you feel about what happened in that situation. [This is a gentle and self-effacing effort to have the parent focus on herself and perhaps reflect on her behavior.]

CASSANDRA: I believe he got what he deserved. [Mom does not explore her feelings or question her behavior, but instead, shows a defensive side; this suggests the consultant may have been premature in trying to get the mom to critique her own behavior.]

CONSULTANT: It sounds like you were pretty mad. You were thinking something like, "He's being defiant, and so I'm giving him what he deserves." [The consultant provides a corrective empathic response and uses radical acceptance; there is no effort to judge or question whether the son "deserved" physical punishment, which might be a good question, but would be premature and would likely close down exploration; the consultant also uses the personal pronoun *I* when reflecting the mom's perspective, which is an example of the Rogerian technique of "walking within."]

CASSANDRA: Yes, I did. But I'm also here because I need to find other ways of dealing with him. I can't keep hauling him up the stairs and spanking him forever. It's unacceptable for him to be disrespectful to me, but I need other options. [Mom responds to radical acceptance and empathy by opening up and expressing her interest in exploring alternatives; Miller and Rollnick (2002) might classify the therapist's strategy as a "coming alongside" response.]

CONSULTANT: That's a great reason for you to be here. Of course, he shouldn't be disrespectful to you. You don't deserve that. But I hear you saying that you want options beyond spanking, and that's exactly one of the things we can talk about today. [The consultant accepts and validates the mom's perspective—both her reason for seeking a consultation and the fact that she doesn't deserve disrespect; resonating with parents about their hurt over being disrespected can be very powerful.]

CASSANDRA: Thank you. It feels good to talk about this, but I do need other ideas for how to handle my wonderful little monster. [Mom expresses appreciation for the validation and continues to show interest in change.]

As noted previously, parents who come for professional help are often very ambivalent about their parenting behaviors. Although they feel insecure and want to do a better job, if parenting consultants are initially judgmental, parents can quickly become defensive and may sometimes make rather absurd declarations like, "This is a free country! I can parent any way I want!"

In Cassandra's case, she needed to establish her right to be respected by her child (or at least not be disrespected). Consequently, until the consultant demonstrated respect or unconditional positive regard or radical acceptance for Cassandra in the session, collaboration could not begin.

Another underlying principle in this example is that premature educational interventions can carry an inherently judgmental message. They convey, "I see you're doing something wrong and, as an authority, I know what you should do instead." Providing an educational intervention too early with parents violates the attitudes of empathy, radical acceptance, and collaboration. Even though parents usually say that educational information is exactly what they want, unless they first receive empathy and acceptance and perceive an attitude of collaboration, they will often resist the educational message.

To summarize, in Cassandra's case, theory translates into practice in the following ways:

- Nonjudgmental listening and empathy increase parent openness and parent–clinician collaboration.
- Radical acceptance of undesirable parenting behaviors or attitudes strengthens the working relationship.
- Premature efforts to provide educational information violate the core attitudes of empathy, radical acceptance, and collaboration and therefore are likely to increase defensiveness.
- Without an adequate collaborative relationship built on empathy and acceptance, direct educational interventions with parents will be less effective.

CONCLUDING COMMENTS

As a unique population, parents bring to therapy many distinct needs, goals, and quirks. Consequently, they deserve a tailored approach to treatment that addresses their particular educational and therapeutic needs.

This chapter focuses on theoretical and research-based principles underlying effective educational and therapeutic work with parents. Generally, human services professionals who work with parents should attend to the robust common factors associated with positive therapeutic outcomes. This requires a broad focus on building a positive therapeutic relationship and a more narrow focus on particular strategies and techniques for providing specific educational and therapeutic interventions.

Similar to person-centered theory and therapy, three core professional attitudes are identified as crucial to building a positive therapeutic relationship. These attitudes include: (a) empathic understanding; (b) radical acceptance; and (c) collaboration. You will be able to provide more effective educational and therapeutic interventions if they adopt these three core attitudes.

The three core attitudes discussed in this chapter translate directly into professional behaviors. In particular, although parents who come for help have a strong desire for specific educational information, you should work on strengthening the therapeutic relationship (using the three core attitudes) before providing directive educational interventions.

Checklist for Being With Parents

☐ Be aware that parents are a distinct and unique population.

☐ Recognize that parents typically want immediate and direct guidance to help solve their children's problems (and that it's important to listen and understand the parents and parenting situation before attending to that desire).

☐ Recognize that parents tend to be knowledgeable, critical, and demanding consumers.

☐ Recognize that, especially when seeking help, parents are often both defensive and vulnerable.

☐ Develop and hold an attitude of empathy for parents and the parenting challenges they face.

☐ Experience and to some degree express radical acceptance.

☐ Develop and hold a collaborative or "not knowing" attitude toward working with specific parents.

CHAPTER TWO

Preparing Yourself to Work Effectively With Parents

Take a moment to imagine you're walking into a waiting room to meet and greet a distressed parent or into a classroom to begin teaching parents a curriculum on effective discipline. Whichever setting you choose, what feelings come up for you? Do you feel anxiety or sympathy? What thoughts go through your mind? Do you have concerns about your readiness? Do you worry about being perceived as judgmental or not fully engaged or too domineering? Do your feelings change if you're preparing to meet with a mother, a father, a couple, or a smaller or larger group? What if the parents are mandated to see you for educational or counseling services? What issues would that situation bring up for you?

Even after having seen many parents over the years, individually and in smaller and larger groups, we still experience pangs of anxiety, self-doubt, and judgment. Depending on the day, the hour, and the parents, several competing thoughts may creep into our brains:

- I wonder what they'll think of me.
- How can I make the best first impression possible?
- Will I be able to help these parents?
- I hope this consultation is about a problem I'm familiar with.
- Will this parent be difficult?
- This is pointless; I'll never get through to these people.
- Will he believe I actually know a thing or two about parenting?
- Will she be more knowledgeable about parenting than I am?
- Am I ready for this?
- I can handle anything they throw my way . . . I hope.

We wish it were easy to walk into a therapeutic or educational setting and drop off our emotional baggage so that it wouldn't adversely affect the helping process. We also wish that displaying the three core attitudes detailed in

Chapter 1 (empathy, radical acceptance, and collaboration) could be quick and straightforward. If managing our emotional baggage and displaying the core attitudes were easier, then we could quickly and efficiently establish a positive working relationship with parents and immediately get to work on teaching practical and effective techniques that parents can successfully use with their children. Unfortunately, when working with humans in general, and parents in particular, everything is slightly more messy and complicated than neat and simple.

This chapter focuses on how to prepare to work educationally and therapeutically with parents. Preparing to be of help should be an integral part of every helping professional's routine. One part of preparation involves committing yourself to giving parents your undivided attention:

> *Being attentive to parents who are distressed is essential. Attending means giving people your undivided interest. It means using your body, your face, and especially your eyes, to say, "Nothing exists right now for me except you. Every ounce of my being and energy is focused on you."* (McEwan, 2005, p. 31)

But it takes more than good attending and undivided interest to work effectively with parents. Parents are complicated and working competently with them is challenging. Competence is central to any ethical professional practice: Not only is preparation a reasonable and practical part of working with parents, our ethical codes mandate that we prepare ourselves adequately to work with diverse populations (R. Sommers-Flanagan & Sommers-Flanagan, 2007). As one example, the American Psychological Association ethics code (American Psychological Association, 2002) states:

> *In those emerging areas in which generally recognized standards for preparatory training do not yet exist, psychologists nevertheless take reasonable steps to ensure the competence of their work and to protect clients . . . from harm.* (Standard 2.01e)

When it comes to working with parents, there are no "generally recognized standards for preparatory training." This makes it crucial for practitioners to take "reasonable steps to ensure" competence when working with parents.

We begin this chapter with an exploration of personal issues that can affect professionals who work with parents. These issues include (a) your attitude toward parents, (b) your reactions to parents who push your emotional buttons, and (c) general preparation tips. Then, we take a step back from examining personal issues and review four therapeutic strategies that will enhance your ability to work effectively with parents.

PREPARING FOR PARENTS

Preparation involves putting yourself in a state of readiness. This section focuses on personal issues to address as you ready yourself to work effectively with parents.

Exploring Your Attitude Toward Parents

Take a few moments to reflect on the following questions:

- How do you feel about working with parents?
- Do you usually look forward to meeting them?
- Do you sometimes dread meeting them? If so, what contributes to the dread?
- Have you ever had especially positive or negative experiences with parents?
- What are your beliefs and biases about what it takes to be a good parent?
- Do you have any personal baggage that might interfere with your ability to help parents? (Be brutally honest with yourself about this.)

We ask these questions because of the obvious fact that our own *personal parent baggage* directly affects our work with parents. When we first began working with parents, we tended to approach the sessions with feelings of fear and intimidation. Although we believed we had useful information, we weren't certain we could navigate through what we perceived as parental defensiveness. As time has gone by, and we have developed our model, gained experience, and seen some positive outcomes, we've grown much more positive and hopeful about working with parents. Nevertheless, we still occasionally experience strong (and sometimes surprising) negative thoughts and feelings about parents. For example:

> Not long ago I [JSF] worked with a mother who began referring to her young son as "evil." After hearing several references to the evil four-year-old who was making this mother's life miserable, I felt anger rising up within me. This was a familiar anger, an anger that arises when I begin thinking that parents are self-centered, acting against their children's best developmental interests. All I could think about was teaching this mother a lesson she wouldn't soon forget. I wanted to shame her into understanding the well-known phenomenon of self-fulfilling parental prophecy [Dreikurs & Soltz, 1964]. If she continued to think about and refer to her son as evil, obviously, her son would be damaged and would probably fulfill her parenting prophecy by showing his mother just how evil he could be. I had to use every bit of self-control I could muster to continue treating this mother with respect—instead of writing her off as an *evil* mother.

As we work with challenging parents, the speed and intensity with which negative judgments can overtake our consciousness is stunning. None of us is immune to lightning-fast judgment. And once we've made a negative judgment, it can be very difficult to repeal that internal verdict.

Like us, you may have memorable experiences that support your general attitude toward parents. Your attitude may be similar to our initial worries—that parents are defensive and not receptive to professional advice—or it may be much different. You may have discovered that you love working with parents and even found they quickly and eagerly follow your advice. If so, we hope this book helps you build on that positive experience (and we hope you'll share some of your insights with us!). But if you've had mixed experiences or fear engaging with parents, we hope to give you new direction and hope.

Similar to working with multicultural and diverse populations, one key to working effectively with parents is self-awareness: getting to know yourself and your personal vulnerabilities, places where you hold too much judgment about particular parenting behaviors (D. W. Sue & Sue, 2008). We encourage you to get to know that judgmental side of yourself and to work on it with your peer group, supervisor, or therapist. Eventually, this self-knowledge will help you become less judgmental and more compassionate. You will need this compassion as you listen to parents describing their parenting struggles—some of which you will find emotionally disturbing.

Dealing With Emotional Button-Pushing

Like teenagers, parents are excellent button-pushers. Even parents who schedule an appointment with you on their own volition will sometimes start sessions with a negative or provocative agenda.

Our Favorite Personal Buttons   As you read through the following list of our favorite emotional button-pushing statements, imagine how you might react or respond. Then consider making a list of your own personal buttons.

- I got spanked when I was a kid and I turned out just fine.
- Homosexuality is wrong. If my son decides to be a fag, I'll disown him.
- What I want is for my five-year-old daughter to choose which parent she'd like to stay with and for how long.
- I have old-fashioned family values. Children should be seen but not heard.
- This stuff you're telling me is a bunch of touchy-feely crap. It's plain and simple—children should obey their parents.
- I believe in Bible-based parenting. If you spare the rod, you spoil the child.
- I don't believe in bribing my kids to do what they should be doing anyway.
- How long have you been doing this?
- Do you have any children?

Getting your emotional buttons pushed by parents is inevitable. If you think you're button-free, check your pulse. If you're alive and human, you have tender spots, bad memories, unfulfilled dreams and hopes, and many other experiences and attributes that contribute to certain vulnerabilities we all have. Given the need to stay calm, accepting, and compassionate when working with challenging parents, consider the following guidelines for coping with emotional button-pushing.

Guidelines for Coping With Emotional Button-Pushing

- Explore your emotional buttons *before* working with parents so you're prepared for when they might arise. This requires a professional consultation group, frank discussions with friends and family, personal therapy, journaling, long walks, or whatever other means necessary to look within.

- Before meeting with parents, take a moment or two to clear your mind, and using language or imagery, tell yourself that your next task in life is to be completely available to the parent you'll be working with. Smile. Relax. And conjure up a picture of yourself being kind, empathic, and wise.
- Use radical acceptance (see Chapter 1).
- Get your ego out of the way and respond with support and validation (see Chapter 4).
- Remember that when parents get defensive or push your buttons, the best process involves seeking understanding while avoiding retribution or counter-defensiveness.
- Collaboratively lower your educational and therapeutic expectations (e.g., say something like, "It sounds like you're already pretty knowledgeable about parenting. I'm not sure if I can offer much help, but would you be willing to give it a try?").

These guidelines are neither perfect nor exhaustive. We provide them to stimulate your thinking about how you can cope with emotional button–pushing situations. We encourage you to expand on these ideas and to develop new strategies of your own.

Tips for Creating a Positive Experience With Parents

Based on our experiences working with parents and the research literature, we offer you the following preparation tips.

Be Familiar With the Popular Parenting Education Literature   During your formal academic training you undoubtedly learned about child and adolescent development as well as child and adolescent psychopathology. Although this knowledge will serve you well, when working with parents it's also important to be familiar with the popular parenting literature. That's the literature parents are most likely to have read and are most likely to ask you about.

Parents will notice and value the fact that you've read or have in your office popular or classic parenting books. For example, when sibling rivalry issues arise, it helps considerably to have read *Siblings without Rivalry* and to be able to recite Faber and Mazlish's (1987) opening story designed to increase empathy for sibling conflict and jealousy. Similarly, if divorce and shared parenting is the topic, quoting from Isolina Ricci's *Mom's House, Dad's House* (1997) will improve your credibility.

The sheer volume of parenting books in print makes it impossible for anyone to have comprehensive knowledge of the area. At some point, parents will ask about books you've never heard of. In such situations, you can take one of two approaches, both of which involve directly apologizing to parents for your limitations:

1. "I'm sorry, but because there are so many books out there, I have to plead ignorance. I've never heard of *Raising a Sensory Smart Child* [Biel & Peske, 2009]."

2. "I'm sorry, I don't know the books in the area of sensory integration and so if you give me a few days, I'll do a little research and then email you [or call you] with a recommendation."

To help with your basic knowledge about parenting books, Appendix A provides an annotated bibliography of common parenting books published in the United States.

How to Respond to Questions About Your Credentials or Status as a Parent   Parents seeking your professional assistance will naturally wonder whether you're a parent yourself. This is perfectly normal and you should work hard to avoid seeing it as either a threat to, or potential endorsement of, your credibility.

We'd like to emphasize that non-parents can serve as competent and helpful parenting consultants. The central issue is whether you have knowledge and expertise that might be helpful, not whether you've directly experienced parenthood. In fact, not having children can make you more objective because you won't always be comparing the parents who come to see you with yourself and their children with yours.

If a parent you're working with asks whether you have children, always answer the question directly and honestly. There's no need to rationalize, justify, or equivocate to prove yourself. Especially, never offer other experiences you've had as if those experiences were a direct substitute for parenting. (In other words, don't say "Well, I don't have any kids, but I've got a dog!" unless you laugh uproariously after saying it, and even then, you may be in trouble.) After you've answered the question directly and honestly, gently paraphrase the parent's underlying concern. You might say:

> No, I don't have children. And sometimes, that can be an important dimension of our work. But what I hear underneath your question is some concern about whether I can really understand what you've been going through and whether I can be of help.

Most parents will appreciate this direct summary of their concerns and others will deny any concerns and overtly reassure you that, of course, they *totally* believe you can help them. At that point you can either move on or try to address their concerns by saying something like:

> I know I don't have children of my own and that can be a problem for some parents. But I've been studying child development and parenting for a number of years, and I think I might be able to be of some help. Otherwise, I wouldn't be meeting with you. Of course, you'll be the best judge of whether I'm helpful, but I hope you'll give me a chance.

In nearly every case, handling parent questions directly and honestly will at least temporarily allay parent concerns about your competence. If not, your best strategy is to offer referral options.

Parents also will sometimes ask directly about your credentials. When this happens, honesty is again the best policy. Never inflate your credentials. If you're a graduate student in psychology, counseling, or social work, say so with clarity and confidence: "I'm in my second year of graduate school and I'm studying to be a school counselor." There's no need to apologize for the fact that you don't have an advanced degree. This means you should avoid saying, "I'm *just* a graduate student" or "I only have a bachelor's degree." In several cases we've paired parents who have doctoral degrees with graduate students and the outcome has been fine. Interestingly, many individuals with extensive and specialized education know next to nothing about parenting and child development, and they're hungry to hear from someone like you—someone who has taken time to obtain special expertise in the area.

Talking About Yourself or Your Own Children   If you have children, it can be tempting to mention them during your work with parents. This might be appropriate, but only in small doses. Specifically, we recommend to students and workshop attendees that they limit themselves to two comments or stories about their own children or parenting experiences for each hour they spend with parents. In our practice we often tell one or two brief stories about our own children to illustrate a parenting technique or as a way to express empathy (you'll see evidence of this in forthcoming chapters). However, because it is surprisingly easy to talk far too much about yourself and your own children, be sure to limit yourself to two brief self-disclosures. Parents generally appreciate it when therapists exercise self-discipline over their need or desire to talk about themselves.

WORKING EDUCATIONALLY AND THERAPEUTICALLY WITH PARENTS

Most parents seek professional help for educational purposes; they seek knowledge, information, and advice to help them parent more competently. Brief approaches to working with parents generally embrace this educational focus by providing parents with detailed "prescriptions," advice, or tips to take home and immediately try out (Battino, 2007; Bitter, Christensen, Hawes, & Nicoll, 1998; Conroy & Mayer, 1994). Prescription specifics vary based on the parents' presenting problems and their openness to examine their own contributions to their children's problems. For example, prescriptions might include anything from step-by-step directions for holding a family council to methods parents can use to put their children or themselves into an emotional timeout.

However, as emphasized in Chapter 1, effective work with parents requires more than just educational interventions; it also involves a therapeutic process. This therapeutic process flows from a strong emphasis on empathy, acceptance, and parent–therapist connection/collaboration. Also, because of the intense nature of parenting and strong tendency toward parent self-scrutiny, it's not unusual for parents to quickly report remarkable insights about how their parenting behaviors are being driven by their childhood experiences (Zuckerman, Zuckerman, &

Siegel, 2005). For example, one mother started a brief educational consultation with the following statement:

> I grew up in a house with parents who yelled all the time. They yelled at each other, and they yelled at me and my brothers. I vowed that I'd never yell at my kids, but the past few weeks, I've started to feel my mother's voice pushing itself into my head. I know *I don't want* to be like her. Now I need to know how to stop that from happening.

When working with parents, many layers and levels of reflection and insight are possible. It's possible for insights to emerge quickly and forcefully—even within an extremely short-term individual or group format. This is one reason why the following therapeutic strategies are critical for facilitating parent insight and preparing parents for educational interventions.

Four Therapeutic Strategies

In Chapter 1 we reviewed three core attitudes for practitioners who work with parents. These attitudes form a foundation for working with parents. However, similar to most therapeutic approaches, practitioners need to move beyond therapeutic attitudes and use specific therapy strategies and techniques. Many techniques for influencing parents during consultations are reviewed in future chapters and many of these techniques involve direct educational processes (e.g., teaching, providing advice, explaining how to implement parenting interventions). For now, we focus on four general therapeutic strategies that practitioners can use to facilitate educational interventions. These therapeutic strategies are woven into the parent counseling and consultation process and therefore constitute competencies necessary for working effectively with parents.

General Strategy 1: Focus on Parent Strengths Using Compliments and Validation   When listening to parents describing their family situations, parenting professionals will hear an assorted mix of positive and negative parenting behaviors and attitudes. This is very similar to what most parents observe in their children—a mix of desirable and undesirable child behaviors and attitudes. What, then, should professionals focus on when working with parents—the positive or the negative behaviors and attitudes?

Dreikurs and Soltz (1964) offer advice for how parents should approach positive and negative behaviors in children, and this advice is useful for all practitioners and educators who work with parents.

> . . . *anyone who stops to think will realize that we really do follow our noses. If our nose points at mistakes, we arrive just there. If we center our children's attention on what they do well, express our confidence in their ability, and give them encouragement, the mistakes and faults may die from a lack of feeding. (p. 107)*

Dreikurs and Soltz's advice also applies to working with parents. If we let our noses lead us toward negative parenting behaviors, we grow resistance. If, instead, we focus on positive parenting behaviors and offer sincere compliments on their efforts, parents will usually respond by directly asking for advice on how to improve their parenting. Additionally, parenting mistakes and faults may wither and die from lack of feeding.

From a constructive or solution-focused theoretical perspective, positive and affirming comments from practitioners should stimulate parent motivation toward self-improvement (Berg & DeJong, 2005). Consequently, parenting professionals should avoid criticism, focus on the positive, and trust parents to lead them to where the work needs to be done. For example, in the case described at the close of this chapter, a parent articulates her negative behavior very clearly by stating:

> She's engaged me, and I've engaged her; and it's not a good situation. And, you know, she's eight years old. The time for spanking is definitely, you know, getting to be over. Plus, at this point, she knows how to move and duck so she doesn't get spanked. And so I'm running around the house chasing her. And I'm like, *this is not good.*

Despite the very clear negative images provided in this parent's narrative, to be true to a strength-based approach, the practitioner must avoid criticism and instead focus on the mom's positive intentions as well as her awareness and self-evaluation that her current behavior "is not good."

General Strategy 2: Parallel Process—Therapists as Active Role Models   Parallel process is a theoretical construct that is also an amazing phenomenon to experience. Originally noted in the psychoanalytic literature, it was described as a process occurring between a psychotherapy supervisor and supervisee. Writers reported that the interactions or other aspects of relationships between supervisor and supervisee somehow begin to mimic or parallel the process occurring between the supervisee and his or her client (Searles, 1955). Searles stated, " . . . processes at work currently in the relationship between patient and therapist are often reflected in the relationship between therapist and supervisor" (p. 135).

We've frequently observed parallel process dynamics at work during educational and therapeutic sessions with parents. These observations fit with the psychoanalytic model because in many ways the therapist is acting as supervisor or even as a parent for the parent. The fact that parents begin acting a bit like their children and therapists have an opportunity to act like positive parenting role models is a natural dynamic. After working with parents and children for 30 years, Rice (2006), acknowledged the same phenomenon:

> *I have come to see my reactions to the parent and child as similar to the reactions the parents and child are having to each other. My feeling that I am not a competent therapist mirrors the parents' feelings that they are not competent parents. My feeling of exasperation parallels the parents' feeling of not knowing what to do when their children continue to be oppositional.* (Rice, 2006, "Making Use of the Therapist's," para 2)

Several years ago, Rita was conducting a parent consultation with Barb, a mother who had a master's degree in psychology. Barb had scheduled the consultation to talk about the growing disconnection she felt between herself and her 15-year-old daughter, Kim. On several occasions during the session, Barb emphasized her academic and employment background, stating things like, "Well, I have twenty years of experience in behavior modification and psychology." It took significant self-discipline for Rita to restrain herself from becoming defensive, responding with something snippy like, "Well, that's pretty good, but I have twenty-*two* years' experience and a doctorate!"

Instead of getting into an authority contest, Rita simply kept listening, acknowledging Barb's substantial knowledge and experience. At the same time, Rita used her awareness of parallel process to formulate a hypothesis about what might be happening between Barb and Kim. "Could it be," she wondered aloud, "that your education and experience are a bit intimidating for Kim? Maybe now that she's fifteen, she recognizes that you're an expert in psychology and so it makes her more insecure or even resistant about being open with you."

Barb found Rita's problem formulation intriguing. However, it wasn't necessarily Rita's ability to articulate her case formulation that helped make her eventual intervention acceptable. Instead, Barb was able to accept Rita's ideas because Rita had offered support and validation of Barb's competence. Of course, while validating Barb, Rita was also hoping that Barb could learn to offer support and validation for Kim's growth toward independence and adulthood.

Near the end of the session, Rita and Barb collaboratively developed a plan. Barb would consistently acknowledge Kim's competence, while at the same time restraining her own impulses to tell Kim that she should "listen to her mother" because of her mother's superior education and experience. They talked specifically about how Barb could watch for spontaneous opportunities to acknowledge Kim's intelligence and experiences without expressing negative judgment and without adding advice. Further, Rita coached Barb that, when possible, it might help to tell Kim things like, "You are so smart" and "That's a great idea."

In this situation, Rita developed an awareness of parallel process (Barb may have been feeling insecure in Rita's presence and needed to prove herself to feel respected). If Rita hadn't developed awareness of parallel process, she might have more actively expressed her own authority in the session (causing Barb to grow more competitive and defensive) and missed the similar process that had developed between mom and daughter (daughter felt dominated by mom and needed to have her own growing competence supported and affirmed).

When working with parents, we don't recommend interpreting the process to parents as you might with a supervisee. Instead, it's best to observe it happening and to take mental notes; this will help you understand what might be happening between parent and child at a deeper level. Then you can use the concept of parallel process to inform yourself on how to best behave like a positive role model within the therapy or consultation session.

General Strategy 3: Therapist–Parent Goal Alignment   There is a long history of both theory and empirical research attesting to the importance of goal-setting for positive behavior change (Latham & Locke, 2007; Locke & Latham,

2006). In particular, for decades, Adlerian theorists and practitioners have emphasized that therapists should work to closely align their goals with their clients' goals (Sweeney, 2009). Additionally, empirical research clearly indicates that goal-setting contributes to the positive behavior change process (Locke & Latham, 2006). With these findings in mind, parenting professionals should work collaboratively with parents to develop goals for their work together (Anthony, 2003).

With many parents, goal alignment is simple and straightforward and several illustrations are included in subsequent chapters. Simplicity in goal alignment mostly arises from the fact that most parents want the same things: They want respect; they want their children to be healthy, happy, and to grow up with a reasonable amount of self-discipline; they want to be a positive influence in their children's development. Attending to the following five-step process will help with goal alignment:

1. Listen to what parents want from their children and from their relationship with their children (sometimes this involves listening for themes below the surface of what parents are saying).

2. Use active listening techniques to reflect back to parents what you hear they want from their children (e.g., "You want your son to respect you" or "You want your daughter to be successful at school").

3. Transform the general goal into a more specific and workable goal within the parents' control (e.g., "We could work on ways you can gain your son's respect" or "We can develop a list of techniques to give you the best chance possible to be a positive influence on your daughter's school performance").

4. Ask permission to include the goal on a goal list (e.g., "May I write this down as one of your possible goals for today?").

5. Provide a caveat or two. This involves saying something that captures both the fact that parents cannot control their children and the experimental nature of parenting interventions (e.g., "Of course, because your son is in charge of his own behavior and beliefs, there's no guarantee we can get him to respect you. But I'm sure we can come up with a list of strategies that have a decent chance of success . . . and all we can do is have you try them out and then see if they make a difference").

Goal alignment or mutual goal-setting is part of creating a collaborative working relationship; for parents, there's nothing quite like the feeling of being on the same page with their counselor or consultant, working together from the same perspective.

General Strategy 4: Embracing the Primacy and Power of Social Interaction   Counseling sessions, consultations or small-group classes with parents are all psychosocial interventions. It would be even more accurate to describe them as *social-psycho* interventions, in that the emphasis is on the primacy of social interactions in generating and influencing behavior (J. Sommers-Flanagan & Campbell, 2009). The focus is on modifying social interactions between parent and child with the hope of influencing internal psychological processes in parents and children. In other words, if parents and children interact differently—with more empathy, encourage-ment, positive affect, and effective communication—they may begin to think differ-ently and cognitive structures could be modified in a positive direction. A substantial research literature exists suggesting that social relations and interventions can have powerful effects on biological processes (J. Sommers-Flanagan & Campbell, 2009).

Embracing the primacy of social interactions is mostly a practitioner mindset or strategy and not a particular technique. Many parents who seek help will have been exposed to and perhaps even indoctrinated into the biomedical model as a means of explaining children's misbehavior (Glasser, 2003; Whitaker, 2010). In practice, consistent with radical acceptance, we accept and never argue with bio-medical formulations. If parents label their children as "ADHD" or "bipolar" or as being on the "Spectrum," we accept these labels, but eventually try to break them down to specific behaviors. This is because it's easier to intervene with a specific behavior emanating from a unique child than it is to intervene with a general label that, on occasion, can seem carved in stone. Additionally, when parents use nega-tive labels to describe their children's behaviors, we eventually teach them about character feedback and other positive ways to influence their children's behaviors and identity formation (see Chapters 7 through 9). For example, although we're jumping ahead a bit and the following monologue about psychiatric diagnosis is more wordy and one-sided than we'd recommend, a discussion that emphasizes the primacy of social interaction might include some of the following:

> As you probably know, it's perfectly natural for us, as parents, to comment on our children's negative behaviors more than their positive behaviors. And, of course, our words and what we tell our children about themselves are very powerful! For example, even though using the term "bipolar" to describe your daughter helps convey impor-tant information to physicians and mental health providers, it might give her a negative message about herself. Even though she has that diagnosis, focusing on it too much could make her label herself as emotionally out of control.
>
> As we've discussed in here, sometimes she controls her emotions better than other times. So we want to help her focus on exactly what she's doing when she has more control. It's like when you have to go to the bathroom. Even though it's a biological process and it needs to happen, we still have some control over when, where, and how it happens. The same is true for your daughter. We need to help her focus on when, where, and how she's managing to control her emotions and expand on that.
>
> Instead of using the term "bipolar" with your daughter, we'd like you to try using posi-tive language to help her move past this negative way she thinks about herself. For example, you might say something like, "I've noticed that in the past you've had big mood swings, but they seem to be getting smaller." Or you could just notice and com-ment on times when she doesn't have a mood swing, "Hey, I noticed we just had a great discussion and we both stayed in a nice mood." Or, at any point when her mood seems under control, you could ask, "What are you doing right now to help you have control over your mood?" These positive statements and questions will help your daughter focus more on how she's improving and controlling her moods and less on how she's a defective girl with a "bipolar" label.
>
> What do you think of these ideas?

Although labels can be useful and informative and medications can occasionally have a positive impact on children's behavior (although usually only in the short term), counseling or consulting with a parent is a unique opportunity to focus on social and psychological factors that may be contributing to, maintaining, or exacerbating problem behaviors in children.

The Three Core Attitudes and Four Therapeutic Strategies in Action

The following example further illustrates the three core attitudes and four therapeutic strategies. As you read this excerpt, notice how the parenting consultant:

- Expresses empathic understanding
- Intentionally skips over opportunities to judge the parent and instead engages in radical acceptance
- Shows an attitude of collaboration
- Focuses almost exclusively on the parent's strengths and positive qualities
- Is sensitive to parallel process dynamics (the mother is very verbally active and dominating and complains that her daughter is similarly "strong-willed" and dominant) and is acting as a positive behavioral role model
- Clearly and explicitly aligns his consultation goals with the parent's goals by initiating a goal list
- Avoids biomedical-psychiatric diagnostic language, focusing instead on parent–child interactions and psychological factors

Prior to the beginning of this excerpt, the mother had already discussed a variety of issues including (a) her daughter's psychiatric diagnoses and (b) resources she had solicited to help her daughter. During the following excerpt, the mother initially focuses on her child's misbehavior. However, by the end, she is focusing more on herself and she and the consultant-practitioner have aligned themselves to focus on her goal to become a better mother.

Case: Chasing Malia: A Good Fitness Plan (Not!)

MOTHER: She's not as compliant at home, but I can certainly deal with her being more compliant at school. I feel like at times and she's told me, too, that she's trying to be so good at school and to listen to her teacher and do what she's supposed to do at school so that when she gets home she just cannot. . . .

CONSULTANT: She can't hold it together any more. [The consultant is using empathic reflection to focus on the parent's compassion or empathy for her daughter's struggles at school; it's almost always good to use reflection when parents express empathy for their children.]

MOTHER: She can't handle it and I'm like, you know what, that's fine, we can do that. But when it comes to her and my relationship, I'll tell her to do something and she'll come up with sixteen different reasons why either she can't get it done, she can't get it done now, it'll be done in a minute. It'll be done tomorrow. And all I want her to do is to spend the five seconds or five minutes to do it and we can move on. And, it, it always, nine times out of ten it turns into an argument. And here's her and here's me and then here's her and here's me. [Mom motions her hands upward to signal step-by-step escalation.]

CONSULTANT: Okay. [Rather than stopping the mom and focusing on anything about the obviously difficult parent–child dynamic, the consultant just continues listening to the mom's outpouring of frustration.]

MOTHER: I'll yell at her and she yells right back. Which is good, well . . . I guess it's not good, but, um, I guess I'm glad. . . . [Mom recognizes that the yelling matches are not so good, but is trying to focus on something positive about them, anyway.]

CONSULTANT: You're not crushing her spirit. [The consultant ignores the potential negativity associated with yelling matches and instead uses nonpathologizing language (i.e., "spirit") to describe the daughter while attuning to the mother's effort to come to a positive conclusion about her daughter's "yelling back."]

MOTHER: Thank you. Yeah. I don't think it would work if she was a very mild-mannered child because as soon as I would start yelling, you know, she would . . . but instead she just hands it right back to me. [Mom clearly appreciates that the consultant "gets" her positive spin on the yelling matches.]

CONSULTANT: Yeah.

MOTHER: Which is kind of good, because she keeps me in shape. But, there are times when I feel like I'm just absolutely losing it with her and she's losing it right back. It's just not a good situation. I know it's not a good situation. When we get into it, we are completely butting heads and it gets to the point where, I'm just, I am *not* gonna lose this argument. [Mom is now beginning to acknowledge her own stubbornness.]

CONSULTANT: Well, I just want to comment on, it sounds like you've garnered a whole lot of resources to help with Malia and I'm really impressed with all that you've done. Now . . . when you talk about that [head-butting], it sounds to me like one of your goals, one of your main goals would be to take an edge off those kinds of interactions. [The consultant hears the mom's negative self-evaluation, but still begins this intervention with a reflection of the mom's hard work at gathering resources for her daughter mentioned earlier in the session; then, he reframes her negative self-appraisal and stubbornness as a consultation goal—a goal stated in a positive way that includes an improvement in parent–child interactions.]

MOTHER: Oh, yeah, oh, yeah. Just kind of, just kind of dial it down. I don't know. I know we get in these situations; I can see myself in the midst of it and I'm trying to figure out a way to dial it down. And it's like I can't see the forest through the trees because . . . she's engaged me and I've engaged her and it's not a good situation. And, you know, she's eight years old. The time for spanking is definitely getting to be over. Plus, at this point, she knows how to move and duck so she doesn't get spanked. And so I'm running around the house chasing her. And I'm like, *this is not good*. We need to come up with some better situation. My husband seems to think I expect too much from her. I worked in child care before we had Malia. I have a Master's degree in child development.

I'm very used to if I tell a child to do something, they would pretty much do it or I could get them to do it. But being a parent, it's, it's . . . [The mom is getting more comfortable describing her negative behavior patterns and her doubts about herself.]

CONSULTANT: It's a new world, huh? [The consultant chooses not to focus on the negative image of this mom running around the house chasing her daughter and instead stays with an empathic response to the mom's disclosure of her amazement at how difficult parenting is.]

MOTHER: It *is* a new world. I swear you can be in childcare or early childhood for years and you have your own kid and the roof just caves right in. That's probably the biggest struggle I have. Working with other people's kids was fine, but having my own is just tough. [Mom continues to reflect on the fact that, despite her education and experience in child behavior management, raising her own child is very difficult.]

CONSULTANT: And I hear you saying, and I saw that you wrote [on the registration form] that you feel like you're a failure at this point. You feel you're not doing as well at parenting as you could be. [The consultant finally starts focusing in on the mom's negative feelings about herself.]

MOTHER: I'm not doing good by her. I'm not doing good by me. I know I could be doing better. [Mom slows down in her verbal output and acknowledges her deep unhappiness with her current parenting.]

CONSULTANT: That's another goal. For you to feel better about your parenting. [The consultant continues the goal list and alignment of goals, staying positive, but this time framing a goal designed to relieve mom of her feelings of disappointment and guilt about herself as a parent.]

MOTHER: I know I could be doing better. [Mom continues to resonate with her motivation to become a better parent.]

This excerpt illustrates how parents, with the help of the three core attitudes and four therapeutic strategies, can quickly begin admitting negative feelings and begin a personal goal-setting process. If negative feelings are gently accepted as a natural byproduct of parenting a challenging child and the practitioner continues to weave in references to the parent's positive qualities, the parent's motivation is nurtured and educational work can begin and move forward rapidly. In essence, the practitioner is doing the therapeutic work up front to get to the educational work later.

Approximately 12 weeks after completing her second and final consultation session, Malia's mother was contacted and completed a telephone interview. In response to several questions, she made the following statements:

- "I remember the friendliness and not feeling judged [during the consultation]."
- "I just used the skills ten minutes ago!"
- "I found it helpful to put myself in my daughter's shoes—special time."
- "It was helpful to learn to not engage when my daughter is upset."
- "My stress level is better."

- "My daughter's behavior is better; her temper tantrums happen less frequently and end quicker."
- "I feel I'm not so quick to fly off the handle; I'm not so quick to react."

As noted in Chapter 1, our research data supports the possibility that brief collaborative therapist–parent contacts can have a positive effect on parent and family outcomes (J. Sommers-Flanagan, 2007). Similar to Malia's mother, based on data from follow-up interviews at three months post-contact, most parents directly attribute positive parenting outcomes (e.g., "My children's tantrums have decreased") to their consultation experience.

CONCLUDING COMMENTS

This chapter emphasizes that to work effectively with parents, practitioners should engage in an intentional preparation process and learn to implement four general therapeutic strategies. Preparation for working with parents is essential because of the many ways parents can activate or push our emotional buttons. Additionally, competent and ethical human services providers should always prepare themselves to work with unique or diverse populations—like parents. If you take the time to prepare for working with parents and develop skills associated with the four general therapeutic strategies, not only will you feel more comfortable stepping into the room with parents, but you're very likely to have more positive treatment outcomes.

Checklist for Preparing to Work With Parents

- ☐ Explore and examine your attitudes toward parents.
- ☐ Prepare to deal with emotional button-pushing.
- ☐ Know the literature on child/adolescent development, child/adolescent problems, and parenting.
- ☐ Prepare to respond nondefensively to questions about your competence.
- ☐ Create an informed consent form, and work out an informed consent process for working with parents.
- ☐ Take time to mentally and emotionally prepare for each session.
- ☐ Practice describing child problems without using diagnostic terms.
- ☐ Prepare to practice using the four therapeutic strategies: (a) focusing on parent strengths, (b) parallel process and role modeling, (c) goal alignment, and (d) acknowledging and embracing the primacy of social interaction.

CHAPTER THREE

What Parents Want

A Model for Understanding Adult Influence

In this chapter we're asking (and trying to answer) a big question: "What do parents want?" As you mull over this question, consider your own parenting experiences. If you've not been a parent, put yourself in the shoes of parents you know or have known. Contemplate, for a moment, what you'd guess are the most basic and essential desires of nearly all parents. Consider both immediate and longer-term parental desires.

After providing a frame for what parents want, this chapter moves to a second big question: "What do parents do (and what should they do) when they're trying to get what they want?" Given that this book is about how to work effectively with parents, it's especially important for professionals to be able to think about and resonate with what parents want and then to understand how parents are going about trying to achieve their goals.

As you read this chapter keep in mind that we're presenting a model for how to understand adult efforts to influence children. For now, we're not focusing on how professionals can influence parents—because we're emphasizing the importance of understanding parents first—and intervening later.

What Do Parents Want?

At the risk of overgeneralization, we believe the basic desire or fundamental goal of nearly all parents boils down to wanting to *exert a positive influence* on their child (or children) *now and into the future*. This desire includes the implicit wish to keep children safe from potentially dangerous forces in the world. When we talk to parents, they tell us things like:

- "I just want her to grow up happy."
- "I want him to make good decisions now and for the rest of his life."

- "She's a good girl. If she can just be healthy and follow her passions—that's all I want."
- "I'd like him to feel good about himself. And it would be great if he could stay out of prison, too!"

Virtually every parent we've ever met wanted to exert that *positive influence* in their child (or children)'s lives. This desire leads parents to seek very specific advice and guidance from professionals on exactly what they should say and do to help their children lead safe, happy, and healthy lives. They want children who follow their talents and passions, make good decisions, develop positive self-esteem, and avoid jail time. Unfortunately, many, and perhaps most parents try to be a positive influence using direct guidance. Gottman & DeClaire (1997) describe the general inadequacy of this approach:

> . . . *it's not easy to ignore your parental agenda in the face of misbehavior—especially when you can feel the sermon on the tip of your tongue. But moralizing about a misdeed without addressing the feelings behind it is usually ineffective. It's like putting a cold compress on your child's fevered brow without treating the infection that's causing the fever in the first place. (p. 115)*

In the late 1990s, we attended a workshop that applied a social power model to teacher-student influence (Alderman & Craver, 1999). This model, originally described by Mary Wood (1996), identified four ways in which individuals use their social power to influence other individuals. Over the past decade, we've used this model to describe parent–child influence dynamics, modified it based on feedback and experience, and now present to you the *Parenting Influence Model (PIM)*.

How Parents Influence Their Children: A Parenting Influence Model (PIM)

Although some individuals might suggest that adults *always try to control* children— and children (especially adolescents) *always try to rebel* against generational pressure and oppression—we see the world of adult–child relationships through a much rosier lens. In particular, we believe most adults don't really want to control and oppress children and that most children, though striving for individuation and independence, are not automatically rebellious or oppositional. Instead, we believe most adults want to shape or influence children's (especially *their* children's) thoughts, feelings, and behaviors and most children feel the need to rebel only when their parents slip into an excessively controlling style.

As we move forward with this explanation of the PIM, we're aware that some professionals and some parents may have negative reactions to the idea of using power or being an authority figure. Nevertheless, our rationale for describing a parent influence model is based on the reality of parent–child power differences. In this regard, we're in agreement with the sentiment in the following passage by Grosshans & Burton (2008), who stated:

When you become a parent, you take on not only an unprecedented responsibility, but you are immediately imbued with an unparalleled dimension of power in relationship to another human being. Whether you philosophically agree with it, want it, or feel prepared or equipped to exercise it, when you are a parent, you've got it. In fact, you are the most powerful person in the world to your child, because she depends on you for everything. (p. 17)

Let's face the reality that parents automatically have power—and focus on how they can use it appropriately, humanely, and respectfully.

Based on the PIM, parents have four *power sources* (Wood, 1996, original social power labels are in parentheses):

1. Direct power (coercion)
2. Problem-solving power (expertness)
3. Indirect power (manipulation)
4. Relationship power (likability)

These power sources are presented in an order such that, if you were to overlay a triangle on this list, *direct power* would be at the tip and *relationship power* at the base. This is because relationship power functions as the foundation for all other power and influence approaches or strategies. We begin our discussion at the tip of the pyramid (or triangle) and work our way down.

Direct Power

Direct power is simple and straightforward. It involves directly informing children what to do and what not to do. It's bossy and often manipulative but not necessarily tyrannical. As we all know, it's possible to have a benevolent boss, someone to look up to as a respected authority. Alternatively, many of us know or have experienced a tyrannical boss. For many reasons, well-established through parenting research and child development, when direct power is needed, parents should enact that power in a wise and benevolent manner—rather than behaving as a controlling tyrant (Baumrind, 1975). A parent we once worked with articulated this practical principle when she told us her philosophy of parenting. She said, "Rules without relationship equals rebellion."

Direct power can be communicated through voice tone (an extremely firm voice, or even snarling), voice loudness (a raised level, even yelling), body posture (standing and pointing), eye contact and facial expression (a hard stare, serious face, or even an unpleasant grimace), and other physical means. Spanking, hitting, and all physical approaches to discipline are classic efforts at exerting direct power. Similarly, when parents use threatening words or verbal abuse with their child, usually they're trying—somewhat desperately—to directly influence their child's emotional state or behavior. When things get desperate, verbal efforts to influence children often end up sounding rather absurd. For example, we've heard parents saying things like,

- "I'll give you something to cry about."
- "I brought you into this world and I can take you out."

Table 3.1   Direct Power Strategies

Physical or corporal punishment
All forms of behavioral psychology, including:
   Punishment or aversive consequences
   Positive reinforcement
   Response cost
   Negative reinforcement
   Ignoring behavior (extinction)
Grandma's Rule
Giving commands or prompts and limit-setting
Preset rules

Obviously, yelling, hitting, and verbal abuse are threatening and extreme means of trying to exert parental influence or control.

All forms of behavioral psychology are direct power strategies. Glasser (1998) makes this clear by referring to behavioral psychology as *external control psychology*. Similarly, Dreikurs (1958) has described all reward and punishment systems as inherently authoritarian. No matter how compassionately administered, punishment, positive reinforcement, response cost, negative reinforcement, and extinction programs are direct efforts to exert outside control over child behavior. The bottom line is that if parents are offering rewards (or taking them away), they own the rewards. And if the parents own and control the rewards, then they're using direct power. Following Glasser's ideas, we consider most behavioral parenting interventions as external or "outside-in" influences. Although it's very important for parents to occasionally manipulate behavioral contingencies or physically intervene with misbehaving children, we advise against overusing direct power strategies. Overusing direct power strategies will usually and eventually elicit rebellion or opposition in children (Kazdin, 2008).

The most common forms of direct power are listed in Table 3.1 and described next.

Physical or Corporal Punishment   Physical or corporal punishment can involve hitting, pushing, slapping, washing children's mouths out with soap, holding children down, and other physical encounters designed to obtain behavioral compliance. Corporal punishment always involves using direct power to reduce undesirable behavior.

Spanking is a particularly controversial topic with parents and when entering into a discussion about spanking practitioners are warned to use substantial sensitivity and tact (which we will discuss later). For now, we want to emphasize that our professional position on spanking and physical or corporal punishment is straightforward and based on psychological research and common sense. Kazdin (2008) provides an excellent description of what the research says about using punishment (including spanking):

. . . study after study has proven that punishment all by itself, as it is usually practiced in the home, is relatively ineffective in changing behavior. . . .

Each time, punishing your child stops the behavior for a moment. Maybe your child cries, too, and shows remorse. In our studies, parents often mistakenly interpret such crying and wails of I'm sorry! as signs that punishment has worked. It hasn't. Your child's resistance to punishment escalates as fast as the severity of the punishment does, or even faster. So you penalize more and more to get the same result: a brief stop, then the unwanted behavior returns, often worse than before. . . .

Bear in mind that about 35% of parents who start out with relatively mild punishments end up crossing the line drawn by the state to define child abuse: hitting with an object, harsh and cruel hitting, and so on. The surprisingly high percentage of line-crossers, and their general failure to improve their children's behavior, points to a larger truth: punishment changes parents' behavior for the worse more effectively than it changes children's behavior for the better. And, as anyone knows who has physically punished a child more harshly than they meant to—and that would include most of us—it feels just terrible. (pp. 15–17)

For those of you who work with children and are familiar with the behavioral literature on punishment, Kazdin's position on punishment is probably not new information. Virtually all child development and child behavior experts agree that punishment is ill-advised (Aucoin, Frick, & Bodin, 2006; Eisenberg, Spinrad, & Eggum, 2010; Gershoff, 2002). And if you've tracked the rationale for avoiding punishment closely, you may have noticed that we—and Kazdin—haven't even mentioned two of the main reasons why punishment is inadvisable: (a) Punishment generally models aggression and (b) punishment involves paying substantial attention to negative behavior—which is why it often backfires and becomes positively reinforcing.

In the end, however, Kazdin's position and all the research data in the world probably won't convince many parents to stop using punishment. This is no big surprise: Using too much punishment can be habitual, irrational, and cultural—which is why we almost always avoid trying to engage parents in a rational argument regarding the merits and disadvantages of spanking (see Appendix B, Tip Sheet 1: The Rules of Spanking).

At this point we're simply noting that as a tool for parental influence, punishment occupies a very small space at the very tip of the pyramid described earlier. It should be used sparingly, if at all. In Chapters 4 and 8 we'll discuss how professionals can engage parents in productive discussions about discipline, including corporal punishment.

All Forms of Behavioral Psychology   Although all forms of behavioral psychology are by definition direct power strategies, these strategies are not necessarily bad. They're just good examples of direct power and direct power shouldn't be overused.

As noted in our discussion of physical punishment, *punishment* involves the administration of an aversive or negative consequence when an undesirable behavior—as defined by the adult—occurs. Negative consequences are employed in an effort to decrease the frequency of undesirable behavior.

Most parenting experts emphasize that, in contrast to corporal punishment, consequences work best if they're naturally and logically connected to the child's misbehavior. Unfortunately, most parents have a terrible time identifying natural and logical consequences for their children's negative behaviors.

One father we spoke with had wracked his brain for a reasonable consequence to use when his son broke a toy in our office. The father insisted that his son apologize, but the son refused. Finally, the father told his son: "Either you can apologize and we'll go home and everything will be fine, or I'll apologize for you and you'll have to scrub the toilet with a toothbrush when you get home." The son, having a PhD in stubbornness, just stared straight ahead.

Although this father managed to come up with a reasonably sized consequence, the natural or logical link was stretched or absent. This difficulty identifying natural and logical aversive consequences is so typical that we address it with examples and dialogue in later chapters.

Positive reinforcement involves giving a "reward" when a behavior defined by the adult as desirable occurs. The hope is that the reward will increase the frequency of the desirable behavior and research attests to the fact that this is usually, but not always, the case (Kohn, 1993). For all its power and utility, positive reinforcement is not without its detractors. The downside is that too much external reinforcement can reduce children's natural and internal motivation (Kohn, 1993). Then, the child ends up dependent upon (and demanding) positive reinforcement for positive behavior and the parent is left wondering who's really in charge. Our position, presented in more detail in Chapter 9, is that natural reinforcements, sometimes amplified and sometimes taking on a surprising spontaneity, constitute the most reasonable use of positive reinforcement.

Response cost involves taking away something positive from the child that she or he already had or naturally has in her or his environment. This *taking* occurs when the child engages in undesirable behavior—again, as defined by the adult. Examples include putting the child in timeout or taking a toy away from a child or grounding a teenager.

For many of us professionals, there is an important distinction between punishment (the application of an aversive stimulus) and response cost (the withdrawal of a positive stimulus). Response cost is the original intent of timeout (timeout from reinforcement). However, despite our theoretical hairsplitting, most children are likely to respond to excessive response cost in a manner similar to their response to punishment.

For example, years ago, John used a response cost system with an after-school group (when undesirable behaviors occurred, he took away baseball cards he had given group members earlier). The vivid part of the memory was when John was showered with ripped-up baseball cards by a young girl who "knew" she was going to end up losing them all anyway. For this girl, giving up something positive was a very aversive event. Consequently, we should remember that response cost can feel very disappointing and painful to children and recognize that inside the mysterious domain of children's emotions, it's not far removed from Skinner's original punishment paradigm.

Negative reinforcement, an often-misunderstood term, actually involves *taking away* something aversive or negative when the child engages in a desirable behavior. As always, the desirability of any given behavior is defined by the adult. Examples of negative reinforcement include (a) letting a teenager off early from grounding for good behavior or (b) stopping nagging when a desired behavior occurs.

Negative reinforcement for specific child behaviors has not been a major focus of research. Nevertheless, to avoid backward behavior modification it's important to be aware of this behavioral principle (see Chapter 9 and Parent Homework Assignment 9-1 for more detail).

Negative reinforcement holds particularly good explanatory power for substance use and abuse (J. Sommers-Flanagan & Sommers-Flanagan, 2004a). Specifically, based on a negative reinforcement model, addiction occurs, at least in part, because individuals experience a lessening of physical or emotional pain when using drugs or alcohol. As the lessening of physical or emotional pain becomes more and more associated with substance use, the individual becomes more likely to crave the substance as an escape from the pain. This is a very important concept for parents of teenagers to understand, because teenagers can begin to drink alcohol or use drugs in an effort to moderate or modify feelings of sadness, insecurity, anger, or isolation.

Ignoring behavior (or extinction) is a direct power technique designed to reduce or extinguish inappropriate or undesirable behaviors. Although many parents naturally pay far too much attention to negative behaviors and far too little attention to positive behaviors, ignoring undesirable behavior—or at least not paying too much attention to it—is a very strong behaviorally based intervention.

If you think about what it's like to *really* ignore someone or to *really* be ignored, you'll quickly recognize the power behind this behavioral principle and technique. Not many people like to be ignored and the emotional pain of being ignored can contribute to powerful efforts to gain attention. Prolonged ignoring can also contribute to a learned helplessness scenario where the child completely quits trying to get attention. When we talk about using this type of extinction plan with children in later chapters, we also emphasize that parents must make their ignoring response very behaviorally specific. For example, parents might choose to systematically ignore whining. At the same time, parents need to let their children know how they can obtain positive attention ("When you use your big-girl [-boy] voice"), which will end the ignoring process.

Grandma's Rule is a language-based intervention that clearly spells out the sequence of desired or required behaviors and optional or reinforcing behaviors. Grandma's Rule always follows a "When you/then you" format. For example, a parent might say to her child, "When you finish the dishes, then you can call your friends." Using Grandma's Rule is a clear and concise way to communicate parental authority by letting the child know exactly what he or she needs to do before engaging in a fun and positively rewarding activity. If you'd like to experience how Grandma's Rule feels, try this out on yourself: "When you finish reading this chapter, then you can check your Facebook."

When working with parents who sometimes use ambiguous language with their children, or with parents who are ambivalent about exerting authority, Grandma's Rule can be very helpful. In particular, parents may need to be coached on avoiding the use of *if* instead of *when*. For example, parents who say, "If you do the dishes, then you can call your friends," convey a sense of uncertainty as to whether their children really will be doing the dishes. Children who have oppositional or defiant tendencies will quickly latch onto the *if* and begin a debate over whether that behavior will ever occur. Grandma's Rule always involves using "*When* you/ then you" language.

Parents frequently give commands or prompts, directing their children to engage in specific behaviors. This technique involves directing children to perform or stop performing a particular behavior. Examples include: "Stop what you're doing right now!," "Keep your hands to yourself," and "Go put away your toys."

Obviously, giving out instructions or commands to children is absolutely necessary. However, too much of this technique will soon become tiresome for most children, who may be inclined to complain: "You're not the boss of me!" If this interaction develops, parents then often feel obligated either to give up and give in to their powerful child or to prove to their children that they are in fact "the boss of them." Neither of these scenarios have happy endings.

Preset rules can be established by parents in an effort to manage or influence child behavior. When using this approach parents (or adults) establish rules in the home that children are expected to comply with. If children do not comply with the rules, they usually receive punishment or disapproval. Examples include:

- "We do not hit or hurt each other."
- "You may not go outside without asking permission."
- "When I'm on the telephone and you ask me for something, the answer is always no."

As you might expect, it can be both useful and important for parents to establish preset rules to help govern children's behavior. This is an excellent illustration of why direct power is not inherently bad or inherently good. Direct power is just one of many strategies parents can use to influence their children.

Some direct power is always necessary. Parents may need to keep their young children from running into the street or from hitting or biting. In such cases, using a mild physical means to redirect children or obtain compliance may be appropriate. Occasionally, a sharp, scolding "*No!*" can help keep children from engaging in dangerous or very undesirable misbehavior.

The important thing to remember is that parents should use direct power only when necessary. Direct power should not be overused, because it can become abusive or oppressive. It should never constitute the primary or default parenting strategy. When parents use scolding or other negative means to influence child behavior excessively, they're violating a basic scientific truth that regular punishment becomes ineffective. Renowned developmental psychologist Jerome Kagan (1998) articulated this point very well:

> *Surprises motivate interpretations, and interpretations are the critical determinants of what will be felt, remembered, and done. The child who is scolded continually for [a particular behavior] . . . becomes accustomed to the punishment; the child who is not scolded most of the time will react with considerably more feeling when a parent unexpectedly chastises him for [a particular behavior]. (p. 8)*

Most parents instinctively realize that direct power should not be their first and best parenting strategy. However, because direct power is often immediately very effective, many parents will claim, "They only listen when I yell" or "Spanking works." Nevertheless, in addition to being poor long-term strategies, yelling and corporal punishment also can activate a natural developmental force in children. Too much direct power often eventually results in child opposition or rebellion.

Helping parents become more aware of their use of direct power strategies gives them a choice. They can begin to recognize how to use direct power appropriately and choose preferable alternatives the rest of the time.

Problem-Solving Power

Problem-solving power refers to a group of parent influence strategies designed to activate, within children or teenagers, a problem-solving or solution-focused mental state. This strategy is best illustrated with an example:

> Sonya is busy at her laptop reading an online newspaper while her 6-year-old son plays in the living room. She notices her son working hard on a small puzzle and after he gets a piece into place, she says: "How did you figure out where that piece went?" Her son looks up and replies, "I don't know. It just fit there."

This interaction may seem trivial, but the mother, whether she knows it or not, is using problem-solving power to encourage her son to reflect on how he's getting his puzzle together. This particular approach is based on constructive or solution-focused principles. The underlying belief is that the more we can get our children thinking about how to solve problems, the better they'll become at problem-solving. Further we are helping them become more optimistic, focusing on solutions and successes instead of pessimistically focusing on failures and problems.

The polar opposite of problem-solving power occurs when parents, in frustration, ask their child something like, "What's wrong with you?" or after a sequence of misbehavior, "What were you thinking!?" When parents ask these problem-oriented questions, it encourages children to focus on their failures, what's wrong with them, or on their negative thoughts and behaviors.

Just like solution-focused therapy, problem-solving power is indirect and leading (Murphy, 2008; Steenbarger, 2004). It's also something we have to train ourselves to do. For some reason, it seems more natural to ignore our children when they are behaving, and to give them attention when they are not. Many parents

Table 3.2   Problem-Solving Power Strategies

Mutual problem-solving
Solution talk
Generating behavioral alternatives
Consequential thinking
The Four Big Questions of Choice theory
Active problem-solving and role-playing
Child-generated rules

remain silent and even detached while children play quietly (savoring the silence). This, of course, is the equivalent of ignoring good behavior, which we know from our basic behavioral principles is a great way to extinguish behavior.

The most common forms of problem-solving power are listed in Table 3.2 and described next.

Mutual Problem-Solving   Unlike some problem-solving strategies, mutual problem-solving is a straightforward procedure designed to help children take at least partial ownership of family problems and begin contributing to solutions. Due to its strong collaborative flavor, mutual problem-solving is one of our favorite parent consultation interventions (see Chapter 8). We often use it when problem polarization is occurring within the family (i.e., the parents are overly invested in a specific child behavior and the child is underinvested; see the Dear Abby example later in this chapter, as well as Chapter 8).

Solution Talk   This approach, illustrated in the previous example with Sonya and her laptop, involves using questions to help children focus on solutions and successes, rather than problems and failures (Metcalf, 2008; Zimmerman, Jacobsen, MacIntyre, & Watson, 1996). Typical solution-focused questions include: "How did you manage to finish all your homework tonight?" or "What were you thinking to yourself when your friend got mad at you, but you stayed so calm?" Parents can also focus on the positive when talking with their children by asking their children to reflect on what has worked for them in the past (e.g., "Do you remember when you used to just cruise through your homework? What were you doing back then to be so successful?").

Generating Behavioral Alternatives   When stressed, angry, or sad, humans become less capable of generating solutions to their problems (Shneidman, 1996). When children are stuck and unable to come up with ideas for how to solve a problem, it can be helpful for parents to say things like, "Let's just make a list of every possible way you might handle this situation." This is a brainstorming approach during which critical analysis is suspended until a wide range of potential ideas are generated.

Consequential Thinking   Consequential thinking is an evidence-based strategy that many therapists employ with children and teens (Shure, 1992; Spivack,

Platt, & Shure, 1976). The purpose of consequential thinking is to help young people (as well as some of us older people) stop and think about potential negative and positive consequences associated with specific behaviors. This approach is often used along with the generating behavioral alternatives (or brainstorming) procedure described above. For example, after a parent and child discuss a range of possible ideas for how to deal with fighting or bullying at school, together they can then analyze what might happen in response to each potential idea. Typically, parents don't take the problem-solving process quite that far, but some may be interested in taking this next step.

The Four Big Questions of Choice Theory   William Glasser (1998) and Robert Wubbolding (Richardson & Wubbolding, 2001; Wubbolding & Brickell, 2000; Wubbolding, Brickell, Loi, & Al-Rashidi, 2001) have written extensively about four key questions that can help parents, children, consultants, and mental health professionals focus on consequential thinking. These questions provide an excellent foundation for parents as they think about how to move toward their parenting goals (and might have been a good framework for CEOs, government officials, and others who contributed to problems within corporations, banks, the investment industry, etc.). The four big questions of choice are: (a) "What do you want?"; (b) "What are you doing?"; (c) "Is what you're doing helping you get closer to what you want?"; and (d) "Should you make a new plan?" (See Parent Homework Assignment 8-1 and 9-6 and Appendix B, Tip Sheet 2, for more information on using choice theory with children.)

Active Problem-Solving and Role-Playing   The goal of problem-solving power is to actively engage children in a problem-solving process. Especially with young children, this process can be directly discussed and practiced. For example, with a child who bites or hits, consequential thinking questions can be asked: "What will happen if you bite (or hit) Mommy?" The answer can be both stated and enacted: "Mommy will say, 'No' and move away from you." With older children, it's always important to have them demonstrate that they know the household rules: "Hey, Bobby, before you go out tonight, tell me what time you need to be home."

Parents can engage their children in active problem-solving and role-playing in many venues. For example, family discussions with teenagers over dinner can include everything from discussions about how to take advantage of college scholarship opportunities to how to say "no" when offered alcohol or drugs. With younger children, many interesting scenarios can be introduced using play with dolls or action figures.

Child-Generated Rules   As noted previously, parent-generated family rules are an example of direct power. In contrast, when using problem-solving power, parents try to hook their children into generating rules themselves. Interestingly, as family members discuss what they want for themselves and for the family, children often become motivated to contribute to very positive and reasonable

family rules. Many authors have written about family meetings or the family council (Croake, 1983; Dreikurs, Gould, & Corsini, 1974).

Problem-solving power is an excellent way to help children reflect on and
contribute to family solutions. It's a method for helping children learn solutions
and rules from the inside out—instead of the external or outside-in behavioral
approach. Problem-solving power can be used liberally but sometimes parents
need to take charge and solve family problems themselves. This is especially
true with younger children. As family therapist Carl Whitaker once said (we're
paraphrasing), "Two-year-olds cannot take over leadership within a family unless they're standing on the shoulders of a parent." In the end, things go better
if parents are the primary leaders in the home who not only allow their children
to voice opinions, but also engage their children in the family problem-solving
process.

Indirect Power

Indirect power involves a strategy or process whereby parents obtain compliance
through an indirect means. In contrast to direct power, this particular strategy generally doesn't activate rebellion and therefore power struggles are minimized.
Indirect power strategies include some of the most important parenting strategies
of all time, as well as a few strategies that are somewhat playful and, some might
say, manipulative.

The most important indirect parenting strategy is modeling. If parents don't
want their children to swear, they should avoid swearing (at least in their children's presence). Children are strongly inclined to model their behavior after
their parents' behavior, especially if they respect their parents. There is scientific
truth in the old saying, "Imitation is the sincerest form of flattery" (Bandura, Ross,
& Ross, 1963; Bandura & Walters, 1963).

Modeling highlights the perpetual 24/7 aspect of parenting. If you tell your
child, "Don't lie," but then you call in sick so you can go skiing instead of going to
work, or sit home on a night when you turned down a social invitation because you
were "too busy," you're role-modeling the opposite of what you're preaching.
In essence, you're asking your children to do as you say, but not as you do. And
we all know how well that works. Parental behavior is often closely scrutinized by
children, even when they don't let on that they are watching.

John recalls a particularly uncomfortable situation with his younger daughter
when she was four years old. As he hurried on his drive home with her beside him
in a child's seat, they were forced to stop at a railroad crossing. Frustrated, John
muttered under his breath a particular four-letter word generally associated with
fecal matter. Much to his horror, his sweet 4-year-old instantly picked up the beat,
repeatedly letting fly with the dung word until, finally, John came up with the
bright idea of correcting her by compounding his mistake: "Oh no sweetheart,
you've got that wrong. What Daddy really said was, 'shoot!' Try saying that,
'shoot.'" When his daughter finally was able to satisfactorily mutter "shoot" under
her breath, John felt a mixed gratification. He had lied to his daughter to stop her

Table 3.3 Indirect Power Strategies

Modeling
Encouragement
Character feedback
Giving choices
Storytelling
Wagering, racing, and giving audience

from using profanity. Clearly, this was only a marginal parenting success and one that illustrates the complex burden of parental modeling.

The most common forms of indirect power are listed in Table 3.3 and described next.

Modeling   As implied in the preceding discussion, the words and actions we use as our children watch and listen are arguably the most powerful shaping influence we have with children. When working with professionals, parents often spontaneously begin scrutinizing their own behavior and will mention concerns about what their children may be learning from them. This usually results in productive discussions and an opportunity for helping professionals to reassure parents that because no one is perfect, part of a good parent's job is to model how well-intentioned humans can admit mistakes and work on imperfections.

Encouragement   When it comes to parenting, encouragement is usually defined in at least two ways. The first is more general and is captured by the phrase "You can do it." Parents can give this message both directly (by saying "I know you can do it") or indirectly (by giving children tasks to accomplish).

The second form of encouragement involves a *reflection or reflective process*. This form of encouragement is best captured by phrases that begin with "I noticed . . . " and then a focus on a positive behavior. For example, after a child has had a pleasant play date with a friend, a parent might say, "I noticed you and Angelina had a very nice time together playing and you shared your toys with each other." The purpose of this encouragement statement is to help the child see her positive behavior and then, in contrast to praise, come to an independent conclusion about whether the particular behavior was desirable or undesirable. This technique is further illustrated through a therapist–parent dialogue in Chapter 8.

Character Feedback   In contrast to praise and encouragement, character feedback suggests that a child has a positive character trait. The statement: "You're the kind of girl who knows how to finish her homework on her own" is an example of character feedback. Character feedback is also illustrated in Chapter 8 and is the topic of a tip sheet (see Appendix B, Tip Sheet 3).

Giving Choices   It should come as no big surprise that many children respond better to choices than to ultimatums. Unfortunately, ultimatums are easier, and provide another example of how parents often, quite naturally and instinctively, use ineffective strategies. Giving choices is harder than giving an ultimatum. Giving choices requires parents to think through a situation and offer reasonable alternatives, alternatives designed to empower the child's growing decision-making abilities. Rather than engaging in this extra effort, parents easily fall back to relying on directives and ultimatums.

Several relatively easy choice-giving strategies are available. For example, parents can give choices that have to do with

- *Timeliness:* "Would you like to do the dishes now or at eight P.M.?
- *Work alternatives:* "Would you rather put the dishes in the dishwasher or take out the garbage?"
- *Play activities:* "I've got some free time this afternoon. Would you like to go to the park or the pool?"

In each example the parent is in control of the choices and yet gives his or her child limited freedom to choose. And for some strong-willed children, freedom to choose is what life is all about.

Storytelling   As you will likely observe throughout this book, we're big believers in the power of storytelling. In many cases, children learn and respond to stories much more easily and perhaps more deeply than they do to lectures or direct information. This makes storytelling an excellent indirect influence strategy. Several storytelling examples are provided in Chapter 8.

Wagering, Racing, and Giving Audience   These indirect strategies are usually playful. For example, parents might say, "I bet I can eat up my broccoli before you do" (wagering) or "Let's race and see who can get dressed and ready to go out to the car and to school the fastest" (racing) or "I heard you're really good at your times tables. How about if you do a set for me and I just watch and listen?" (giving audience).

To be honest, wagering, racing, and giving audience are manipulative ploys. They involve enticing children into compliance using techniques framed as fun and competitive. As a consequence, some parents don't like these particular parenting strategies.

Nevertheless, these techniques can be useful and are often employed effectively by some parents. For example, as described previously, with children who are slow at dressing themselves, an indirect intervention might involve a competition or race:

Okay, sweetheart, let's see who can get ready the fastest. I'll run to my bedroom and see if I can get dressed and ready to go before you're all dressed. I think I'm the fastest, but you might be. I don't know. Are you ready? Ready, set, go!

The problem with this form of indirect power is not so much that it's manipulative (almost everything is manipulative in one way or another), but that *it can begin to feel manipulative* to children. Consequently, although parents should use positive role-modeling whenever possible, these more playful and manipulative indirect approaches should be used only occasionally.

Relationship Power

Relationship power is the foundation of all parental power. Having a high-quality, respectful parent–child relationship is the fuel that naturally drives children *to want to please their parents*. However, there is a serious problem associated with creating and sustaining relationship power.

In the 21st century, perhaps more than previously, parents have tended to over-emphasize the "friendship" dimension between parents and children (Grosshans & Burton, 2008). The worst consequence of this friendship-oriented parent–child relationship is that sometimes parents hesitate to set limits on their children's behavior, fearing their children will not like them. Although wanting our children to like us is a perfectly natural impulse, it can become problematic if parents become frozen and unable or unwilling to set limits due to fears of rejection. When this happens, a very destructive pattern can emerge. This pattern is characterized by an imbalance of parent–child power. Unfortunately, often the consequence of this pattern is a child who is too free and too much in charge and a parent who feels impotent and disrespected. In extreme situations, the parent–child power relationship and the roles associated with that relationship are so twisted that the parent may begin inappropriately involving his or her child or children in adult matters, adult relationships, and even adult partying, including exposure to many adult issues and problems (e.g., sexual information or relationships and/or substance use).

The parent–child relationship that works best is characterized by respect, interest, caring, love, and kindness. It is not an egalitarian relationship between peers, but it is a central and all-encompassing relationship that entails love, sacrifice, and the willingness to be there, no matter what. Call us idealists, but we believe this is the foundation upon which parental authority and influence should be built.

Stephen Covey articulates the foundational quality of relationship when he discusses the *relationship bank account*, both in his book, *The Seven Habits of Highly Effective People* (Covey, 1990), and online. In the following excerpt from his website, he discusses the concept of the emotional bank account as a means of rebuilding trust—and rebuilding trust can be especially relevant for parents of teenagers. The concept is equally important with regard to building and maintaining trust and respect:

> *Examine your Emotional Bank Account with this person; it's most likely strained because of withdrawals. Make a commitment to start making deposits that matter most to that person, and do it. Little by little, even with small deposits, you will find that the account will grow. It may take time. But over time you will find the cumulative effect of the deposits. Slowly, depending on the severity of the broken trust, you can find trust being rebuilt and restored, and a new relationship will be born. Of course, this also depends on the other person, but you can choose to do your part regardless of the other person—to focus on your circle of influence. And you will find some peace, knowing that you've done your part. (http://www.stephencovey.com/blog/?tag=emotional-bank-account; accessed February 18, 2009)*

Table 3.4 Relationship Power Strategies

Everyday connection
Spontaneous and genuine statements of loving, liking, and affection
Special time
Asset flooding
Favors and IOUs
Shared teaming
Honest and measured expressions of anger and disappointment

Like modeling, relationship power is part of the 24/7 parenting role. Consequently, relationship power activities can and should be integrated into the parent–child relationship on a daily basis. Common forms of relationship power are listed in Table 3.4 and described next.

Everyday Connection   Most parents and children spend many hours and many days together building up or breaking down their relationship. According to most parenting and marriage experts, families work best when there are five positive behaviors or comments or interactions to every negative interaction (Kazdin, 2008). In Covey's terms, this means five deposits into the emotional bank account for every withdrawal. For whatever reasons (we suspect it's a human design flaw), children and adults tend to remember and dwell on negative and critical comments much more intensely than positive and empowering comments. Sometimes even after a substantial string of compliments, we might find ourselves lingering on the one critical comment we heard, instead of delighting in all the nice things someone said to us.

Parents can consciously take advantage of their everyday interactions and connections with their children. The key is to focus energy on noticing and creating positive interactions. A few examples include: brief shoulder massages, moments where parents listen to their children without judging them, playing music or sports together, singing together at home or in the car, and cooking a special meal together.

Spontaneous and Genuine Statements of Loving, Liking, and Affection   As children grow older, more independent, and sometimes, more challenging, it can become complicated for parents to express their positive feelings of affection and love. Nonetheless, expressions of affection should never stop. Even in tense and difficult situations, we've helped parents focus on their positive feelings and express them. A simple question like, "What are you doing to express your positive feelings to your children?" can be transformative for families with entrenched negative communication patterns.

Special Time   As noted and discussed throughout this book, but especially in Chapter 7, special time can be viewed as a specific activity to use with younger children and as a concept to act on with older children.

Asset Flooding   We initially learned about asset flooding during a public lecture by Daniel Hughes, a clinical psychologist who specializes in attachment theory (Hughes, 1998). During his lecture, Hughes emphasized that for children with attachment issues (caused by early disruption in the parent–child bond or relationship), criticism activates a fear of abandonment. As we imagined ourselves living inside an insecurely attached child's world, this idea made perfect sense and so we began thinking about it in reverse and came up with asset flooding.

Asset flooding is a specific technique designed to help children feel valued. This is especially important for children with attachment issues, because often they don't have an internalized sense of their positive attributes. Asset flooding is an informal, set-aside time when parents (and perhaps siblings, aunts, uncles, and grandparents) sit around with a child and give positive feedback. The adults might begin by saying something like, "It's been a while since we've talked about all your good qualities, so let's do that now." Each adult then takes turns making positive statements (e.g., "I love your sense of humor," "I appreciate your kind heart," "You have a smile that lights up the room" etc.). Most children enjoy the feeling of being on the receiving end of an asset-flooding experience and it may deepen the parent–child bond.

Favors and IOUs   Parents and children can and should do favors for one another. These favors can involve explicit requests ("Could you pick up some milk on your way home?") or thoughtful gestures ("I noticed you left your lunch on the table, so I dropped it off at school").

Some writers and experts emphasize that parents should be careful about excessive caretaking of their children (Cline & Fay, 1992). They explain,

> . . . *these kids keep breaking the speed limit because they know Dad will pay the fine, or they engage in promiscuous sex because Mom will get the birth control pills. A few years later, they flunk out of college, mishandle what little money they have . . . . The real world, these young adults discover, doesn't offer a grand helicopter parent in the sky to heal their diseases, pay for their bounced checks, save them from irresponsible people, or literally bail them out of jail. (pp. 31–32)*

We might add to these excellent points that, in the real world, families often function best as a team. On the family team, parents and children recognize their human weaknesses and, within reason, support each other and do each other favors.

This is an important distinction. Cline and Fay's (1992) "helicopter parent" gets in the way of natural consequences and therefore children have trouble learning personal responsibility. We don't advocate helicopter parenting. However, we do advocate the family team, where family members stick up for each other and occasionally pick up for each other. Another way of describing this relationship-building quality is to say, "If your children forget to take their homework to school three days a week, stop helping and enabling their irresponsibility. But, if your children forget their homework once or twice a month, provide them the help and support you'd want if you forgot some important business at home and needed your teenager to pick it up and bring it to you at work." On the family team, both parents and children support each other (but do not enable repeated acts of irresponsibility). This teamwork, asking for and granting favors, builds up the emotional bank account and helps family members feel useful.

Natural Teaming   Sometimes parents and children get into a pattern of chronic disagreement. This is especially common during the teen years. Natural teaming is not an antidote to parent–teen disagreement. Instead, it's a relationship-based technique that helps balance the positives with the negatives when negative interactions are increasing.

Although our society tends to focus on differences between parents and teenagers, it's just as natural for parents and teenagers to agree or to feel similarly about things. To use natural teaming, parents intentionally (and sometimes with great effort) focus on and highlight times when there is agreement. Statements such as, "It's nice that we both like *American Idol*" or "I agree with you when you say it's very hard to go out without drinking or partying" highlight similarities and agreements. This is important balancing information if negative interactions are becoming the norm.

Honest and Measured Expressions of Anger and Disappointment   We venture into this particular relationship power-based technique with great reservations, but do so because parents should sometimes directly express their emotions to their children—even when these emotions are negative.

Parental anger and disappointment serves as important feedback to children. If parents are never angry and never disappointed, children may not adequately develop an internal emotional compass. Of course, if parents are constantly angry and disappointed, children quickly learn to disinvest or distance themselves from their parents. As usual, the key is to be balanced and honest and consistent.

For some children, a raised brow or frown will elicit tears and remorse. For others, clearer and more calculated emotional expressions are necessary. Families operate in an emotional environment wherein all parties are naturally exposed to love and acceptance as well as criticism and disappointment. As noted previously, exceptional or infrequent emotional expression or negative feedback carries with it much greater significance than continual negative feedback (which eventually loses its power as it fades into a general sea of negativity).

THE PIM IN ACTION

Many cultures focus excessively on using direct power to get children to comply with parental authority, and our dominant American culture is certainly among them. This may be in part because of the powerful influence of behavioral psychology and partly due to a historical white-European devaluing of children identified by some authors (Breggin, 2000; Glasser, 1998). Fortunately, the Parenting Influence Model (PIM) provides parents with effective alternatives to simply using direct power over and over again.

As an American icon, "Dear Abby" regularly provides guidance for parents who face specific parenting challenges. However, for better or worse, Abby usually offers advice based almost exclusively on direct power. While you read through the following summary of a Dear Abby column, consider the PIM. In particular, think about which indirect, problem-solving, and relationship power strategies you might suggest for the parenting dilemma described in this column.

In her February 17, 2009 column, Abby responded to a letter written by a mother described as Tanya of North Lima, Ohio. Tanya described a challenging situation with her 9-year-old son. She reported that he refused or made excuses when asked to take a shower after his wrestling practice and that she was at her "wits' end." She noted other personal hygiene problems, including difficulty getting him to brush his teeth and change his underwear. She ended her letter with a plea: "Please give me some advice."

Abby responded with clear and direct guidance. She instructed Tanya to:

1. Establish rules and enforce them.
2. Consider asking the wrestling coach to "impress upon him the importance of personal hygiene."
3. Refuse to serve the son dinner until he has showered.
4. Require him to "brush his teeth before coming to the breakfast table."
5. If the problem continues for over six months, consider a consultation with a "child psychologist."

The problem that Tanya of Ohio presented to Abby was typical. Tanya has an agenda and she wants her child to comply with her agenda. She has tried direct power strategies, failed miserably, but is still unable to think outside the direct-power paradigm. For example, she states: "I tell him to take a shower," "I have had to personally bathe him," and "I don't know what to do to get him . . . ." Each of these phrases articulates at least two things: (a) she has taken on the primary responsibility for her son's hygiene (and so he is free to not care much at all about hygiene; we refer to this as *problem polarization* and discuss it at length later); and (b) she is focused, as far as we can tell, exclusively on direct power strategies.

Using the PIM as a guide, in an educational or therapeutic setting, the first step would be for the parenting professional to model an attitude reflected in the short phrase, developed by a parenting organization in Boston: "Get curious, not furious." The professional would empathize with the parent's frustration ("It *is* hard when your nine-year-old smells bad!") while gently exploring the roots of the problem ("What do you suppose is going on that makes it so your son really doesn't seem to care about showering and brushing his teeth?"), and gathering concrete information about exactly what the parent has tried and how it has worked. In the end, the professional might provide the parent with a collaboratively generated list of parenting strategies. For Tanya and her son, the list would likely, but not inevitably, include an individualized combination of the following:

- Mutual problem-solving
- Solution questions
- Character feedback
- Giving choices
- Asset flooding
- Expressing anger and disappointment

In contrast, as Abby articulated so well, our popular cultural advice for parents who face problem child behavior is something like:

You need to force that boy to comply with your parental authority.

Abby's solution advocates parental over-control: She recommends withholding food. She recommends usurping the boy's privacy by consulting with his wrestling coach (apparently behind the boy's back). She doesn't seem to understand the powerful force of encouragement—or even positive reinforcement. Although the mom may win this battle using direct power, her withdrawals from her joint emotional bank account with her son may be immense. Their relationship will suffer and their conflicts may continue to grow. Eventually, the mom's power-plays may become significantly less effective as he heads into his teenage years.

Overall, the purpose of this parental influence model (the PIM) is to help parenting consultants to become more aware of specific influence strategies parents are using in their daily lives. Practitioners can then use this awareness to help parents expand their influence repertoire, and hopefully help parents become more successful in really getting what they want: being and becoming a positive and guiding influence in their children's lives.

CONCLUDING COMMENTS

To summarize, we offer the following rules when it comes to using the four approaches to adult influence:

- Use direct power when absolutely necessary.
- Use problem-solving power when there are specific problems and it's a reasonable strategy.
- Use indirect power, especially modeling and encouragement, often (although some of the more manipulative indirect power strategies should be used sparingly).
- Make deposits into your relationship bank account whenever you can.

This chapter includes four general strategies and many specific techniques that parents can use to get what they want. The purpose of the PIM is to help consultants (and parents) become more aware of the different approaches to influencing children and teenagers. With this model, the overall goal is to influence young people while at the same time building a positive relationship for the future.

Checklist for Thinking About What Parents Want

- ☐ Recognize that to some extent most parents want to be and to exert a positive influence on their children.
- ☐ Develop an understanding of the four approaches to parental influence or social power.
- ☐ Recognize that all behavioral approaches to influence and change are forms of direct power where a person in authority is in control of rewards and punishments.
- ☐ Recognize that problem-solving power is a strategy for helping children activate their inner personal problem-solving skills.
- ☐ Recognize that indirect power involves modeling or manipulating and framing situations so that parents can indirectly get children to comply with parental wishes.
- ☐ Recognize that without relationship power, parents will often be unsuccessful in being a positive influence with their children.
- ☐ Do your best to help parents be aware that they should use direct power only when necessary and the other forms of power more often.

PART TWO

Strategies for Working With Parents

Because parents frequently want immediate and direct guidance regarding how to influence their children's behavior, practitioners need to move beyond developing a therapeutic relationship with parents. Part Two of this book includes three chapters focusing on informal approaches to assessment, collaborative problem formulation, and methods for providing guidance, advice, and solutions in ways that bypass parental resistance.

CHAPTER FOUR

From Initial Contact to Assessment

Building and Maintaining a Working Relationship With Parents

This chapter is about the initial or early contact between helping professionals and parents. This early contact primarily focuses on specific relationship building but also includes informal (or formal) assessment procedures and possibly even the introduction of intervention strategies and techniques. If all goes well, as you establish a connection and gain understanding of the parents' situation, parents will begin seeing you as a trustworthy and credible adult with whom they can openly discuss their parenting struggles and challenges. As Rogers (1942) describes in the following quote, when a trusting connection within an accepting environment is established between parent and counselor, insight and change become possible:

> . . . when the mother is allowed to talk out her feelings in an accepting situation, insight begins to develop . . . It is her own attitude which she begins to see as a part of the problem, and her own adjustment which she recognizes as difficult to make. Having once become conscious of this as an integral part of the total problem, her own behavior in regard to the situation is bound to undergo change. (pp. 175–177)

STEPS AND STRATEGIES FOR MAKING INITIAL CONTACT AND ESTABLISHING CONNECTION

Initial interactions between parents and professionals are powerful and set the stage for more or less smooth educational and therapeutic interactions. This section begins with an analysis of first contact and ends with a description of how therapists can collaboratively explore what interventions parents have tried on their own to address their parenting concerns. Initial contact and connection involves establishing a relationship foundation for effective therapeutic and educational work while simultaneously gathering assessment information to aid your case formulation.

First Contact

Parents who come to an initial educational or therapeutic session may enter the waiting room with a wide range of thoughts, expectations, and emotions. These might include:

- "What in the world am I doing *here*?"
- "I wonder if there is any chance this will help."
- "I can't wait to learn something that might solve the problems with my son."
- "This is hopeless. My daughter is impossible."
- "What can these 'experts' give me that I don't already know?"
- "Finally, I'm about to get the help I need."
- "Maybe no one will notice if I slip back outside and skip out on this whole thing."
- "This person will see right through me and know what a horrible parent I am."

Given that it's impossible to know for certain what parents are thinking, your job is to meet, greet, normalize, and comfort as appropriate. This is true whether you're meeting with a parent individually or beginning a small-group class. In an individual situation, you may have already met the parent(s) over the telephone when the appointment was scheduled—or the parent may be a stranger whose appointment was scheduled by your receptionist. Either way, we recommend a standard, polite, and low-key beginning, characterized by your own personal version of one or more of the following:

- "Hello. I'm Rita Sommers-Flanagan. It's very nice to meet you."
- "Were you able to find the office easily?"
- "How was parking?"

If the parent expresses frustration or appears grumpy and if your waiting room is relatively private, consider using a feeling validation statement that focuses on whatever negative feeling or frustration the parent is expressing:

- "It *is* very hard to get parking around here. I'm sorry about that."
- "Sometimes parents aren't thrilled about coming for this type of appointment, so I really appreciate you being here."

Depending on your circumstances, you might also include a statement that reflects enthusiasm for what you do and what's to come:

- "I'm happy we were able to work out a time to meet."
- "It can be challenging to come by the school after hours (or during the school day)."
- "Welcome to (insert agency name here). This is a great place and I'm glad you're here."

Discussing Confidentiality and Providing a Collaborative Role Induction

For individual appointments, once a parent is seated in your office, you have several important opening tasks. If you don't get to these tasks right away, parents may jump in and immediately begin telling you about an intense, immediate, or emergent parenting problem. We advise that after the initial pleasantries, you graciously keep control of the verbal airspace, and quickly shift to providing basic professional information. Otherwise, you may end up having to cut off a verbose or agitated parent to talk about confidentiality and other issues that need to be mentioned up front. Put something like the following into your own words:

> Thanks for coming. Let me start by talking a bit about some basics. First, what you say here stays here. It's private. However, there are a few legal exceptions to your privacy. If you tell me anything that leads me to suspect there is abuse or neglect going on in your home, then, of course, I can't keep the information private, but I would work with you to get the right people involved to make the situation better. I'm saying this because it is important for you to know about the limits of your privacy, not because I suspect we'll be talking about abuse or neglect today. I know you also probably filled out a bunch of forms about this in the waiting room, but I like to go over it with people to see if you have any questions.

At this point, parents may ask about confidentiality of records or make a joke about not being a child abuser. Whatever the case, practice reflective listening and provide whatever pertinent information is needed. Be sure to know your agency, school, and/or state laws and policies regarding confidentiality, the parent's access to you and your time, and related matters.

After discussing confidentiality, tell the parent about the usual format and flow of how you work with parents. This information is for clarification purposes. By providing a short description of your typical educational or therapeutic process, you will help develop clear, shared expectations, which is an important component of effective counseling or psychotherapy (Duncan, Miller, Wampold, & Hubble, 2010). When offering time-limited parent consultations, we generally use a statement similar to the following:

> I can see from the paperwork that you have three children, but that you mostly want to talk about your oldest child, your thirteen-year-old, Lucy. Before we begin, I'd like to tell you a bit about how our parent consultation process works. I'll start off asking you to tell me about the biggest challenges you face as a parent. This usually involves you describing for me exactly what's going on with you and your child at home or at school—whatever you're concerned about. While you talk about this, mostly I'll just listen, take a few notes, and ask a few questions. As I get more information, I'll probably

ask even more questions. Finally, after about twenty or thirty minutes of listening and questions, I'll start offering you ideas for what might help with Lucy.

But I want to emphasize that this is your consultation. If it seems like I'm talking too much, just tell me to be quiet and listen and I will. Or, if you start feeling like you want more advice and suggestions, let me know that as well. At the end of our session I'll write down the specific ideas we come up with and give you a copy.

The last portion of this opening statement explicitly offers parents control over their consultation process. Parents usually respond by saying something like, "Oh, I want advice!" This interaction deepens your collaborative agreement and gives you permission to be an expert. Even if parents say nothing in response to your offer to share power, the invitation can contribute to a sense of collaboration. Also, consistent with research in social psychology, parents are more likely to accept advice when they've declared they want it (Goldstein, Martin, & Cialdini, 2008).

This opening statement can be modified to describe whatever approach you may use when working with parents and their children. For example, if you use a child therapy model where the parents are present along with the child for an initial session and then attend later family meetings (J. Sommers-Flanagan & Sommers-Flanagan, 2007b), you might describe your process in the following manner:

This first meeting is a lot about getting to know each other. So to start with, I'll be asking you all questions about your goals or wishes for therapy. I'm very interested in what you want from our time together and what, for you, would make this a positive experience. We'll talk together as a group about this for twenty minutes or so. Then, Mom and Dad will take a break and go into the waiting room to fill out some question-naires and you and I [therapist looks toward young client] will spend some time to-gether getting to know each other and talking more about what you want from our time together. Finally, at the end, your mom and dad will come back in and, as a group, we'll agree on one or two or maybe three goals we'd like to accomplish.

Some researchers refer to these opening statements as a "role induction" or so-cialization process because it helps educate clients about their role and clarifies expectations (Luborsky, 1984). As professionals, we need to directly and clearly demystify the counseling or consultation process. The best way to accomplish this demystification is to directly communicate with the parent about what to expect and to invite questions at the beginning and throughout. Not surprisingly, most parents find this direct approach comforting (J. Sommers-Flanagan & Sommers-Flanagan, 2007b). Research on counseling cultural minorities also suggests using a direct approach is preferable, so the client doesn't have to wonder who you are or where you're coming from (D. W. Sue & Sue, 2008).

Honoring the Parent as Expert

Consistent with a solution-focused framework (de Shazer et al., 2007; Murphy, 2008), if you're working with parents independently in a parenting consultation or parent training format, from the first contact onward you should honor parents as being the best experts on their family and children. This position and belief should be expressed verbally and should remain an abiding attitude underlying your behavior throughout your educational or therapeutic intervention. A simple statement acknowledging the parent's expertise can begin this process. You can say something like the following:

> Now that we've taken care of the red tape [confidentiality stuff], I want to hear from you about your concerns because, obviously, you're the best expert on what's going on in your family and with your child.

Again, if you're working with parents and children together, you would modify this statement to include the child or children as having similar expertise in helping you understand the family.

Providing Compliments and Reassurance

As discussed in previous chapters, most parents who come for professional help feel vulnerable and insecure. It's important to address that vulnerability by providing reassurance, sincere compliments, and other forms of support. One way to do this is to let your attention focus on the parent's underlying positive motivations. This requires a very upbeat solution-focused or person-centered attitude. For example, you might need to say to yourself: "I'm listening for how this parent loves her child" or "I will try to notice how much he seems to know about his child." Remember that if you get caught focusing on what the parent is doing wrong, your negative attitude toward the parent will increase, and at some point or other you'll find yourself going down a road you didn't intend to travel: (a) Your negativity will leak out, (b) the parent will perceive it, (c) the parent will feel more defensive, and (d) your work together will be adversely affected.

There are many natural places to notice and appreciate positive parent qualities. For example, even though your focus is positive, you still might intentionally listen as a parent goes on and on venting anger and frustration. If so, it's possible to move beyond the surface frustration and anger in the parent's voice and use an interpretive feeling reflection to resonate with the parent's underlying concern (J. Sommers-Flanagan & Sommers-Flanagan, 2009):

PARENT: That damn kid of mine has a smart mouth. That's why I'm here. He'll talk back to me about anything. If it's a beautiful day and I say the sky is blue, he'll tell me it's gray. There's something seriously wrong with that kid.

CONSULTANT: Wow. He sounds really tough.

PARENT: That's not half of it. He's in trouble at school for the same thing, and I've tried talking with him about it and nothing works. He'll just tell me, "Dad, you don't know shit" and swear at me and walk away.

CONSULTANT: I hear loud and clear that your son is really strong-willed and it's hard to get him to listen. But I also notice how much feeling I hear in your voice and in your words. He's causing you a huge amount of frustration and anger. But I'm guessing you wouldn't feel as much frustration if you didn't care about him so much.

PARENT: Damn right. It would be easier if I just didn't care. That's what I've been thinking.

CONSULTANT: Sometimes it seems like our kids are just trying to get us to not care and so I'm really impressed that even though your son is being very, very difficult, you're here and you obviously still care a whole lot about him and his future.

PARENT: [Silence]

CONSULTANT: Another thing I hear is how much you wish your son would respect you. And so, if it's okay with you, I'm going to write down two possible goals that we might work on together. One is to figure out ways to let your son know how much you care, and the other is to figure out how we might get him to be more respectful of you as a parent and as a person. Is that okay with you?

PARENT: Um. Yeah. That would be great.

This exchange between a father and parenting professional provides an excellent example of a common process that occurs in therapy or consultation with parents. First, the consultant uses validation to honor the father's experience of his son as strong-willed, and disrespectful. Second, although the father expresses his *surface* anger and frustration, the consultant reflects the *underlying* positive emotion. In fact, the depth of the frustration illustrates that this father cares a great deal. In some ways, the consultant is just articulating the obvious. Third, the consultant compliments the father for managing to care about his son—even though the son seems to be trying to distance himself from his father. Fourth, the consultant notices and mentions that what the father really wants is what many fathers and mothers want: *respect*. Fifth, the consultant transforms this emotional discussion and interpretation into the beginning of parenting goals. Sixth (and this is a key collaborative piece of the intervention), the consultant *asks permission* from the parent to write down "two possible areas for us to work on."

Overall, this example also illustrates how service providers can use the right attitude and good listening skills to avoid getting caught up in parent negativity. For example, if you're not prepared in advance for things parents are likely to say, it would be easy to have a negative reaction to this father. The consultant avoids this by intentionally concentrating on *underlying* positive motives instead of stepping into the murky waters of reactivity or even succumbing to full-blown countertransference. Additionally, the professional also avoids attending to (and thus increasing or highlighting) the father's negativity and instead, in a somewhat leading but compassionate way, acknowledges positive wishes that underlie the father's frustration and anger. From some theoretical perspectives, this would be considered a cognitive reframe (Beck, 1976). From the common-sense perspective, it would be considered a smart move.

INFORMAL AND FORMAL ASSESSMENT

Some practitioners, especially psychologists, may be inclined to use formal assessment instruments and structured interviews in their work with parents and children (Sharp, Reeves, & Gross, 2006). Although we occasionally use formal assessment protocols, this section focuses on less formal assessment approaches and less structured interviewing approaches. This emphasis is not because we're disinterested in diagnostic issues or formal assessment protocols, but because we're more interested in using interactive and informal procedures to simultaneously gather information and make interpersonal connections with parents.

In the preceding example, the parenting professional quickly initiated a goal-setting process without having obtained a full problem description. Although this involves getting the intervention (cart) before the assessment (horse), it's possible to do so because many parents seek help for similar reasons. They want love, connection, and respect, and they want to see the behaviors that reflect these relationship values.

Parents also want and need concrete guidance and problem-solving—the sort of problem-solving that can lead them forward and backward. Parents generally want to get *back* to the amazing love, connection, and respect they felt when they initially held their baby in their arms. They also want to move *forward* toward family tranquility and toward being the parents of healthy offspring they can feel proud of and connected to. This leads us to an essential assessment component of working directly with parents, which involves obtaining a problem description.

Obtaining a Problem Description

As we describe how to obtain a problem description, we're aware that although this procedure will make our behaviorist friends very happy, it will make our family systems friends stammer in protest. To honor our family systems friends, we should note that the child may not really be the *owner or source* of the problem. In fact, as we hear details, we often recognize that the parent is contributing just as much (and perhaps more) to the problem as the child. Although this is true (family systems friends smile and relax), we also need to deal with the reality sitting in front of us. That is, most parents describe family problems as residing within their child's behavior or attitude. Therefore, despite our reservations about blaming children for having or being problems, we believe it remains essential to think like a good behaviorist (behaviorist friends nod enthusiastically) and obtain a clear, concrete, and detailed problem description—based on the parents' perceptions.

Often, parents will launch into their problem description without much prompting, but rarely do they spontaneously provide nitty-gritty details. Instead, most parents will identify a problem (see the following list), but the description will be general and in need of much elaboration before you can offer reasonable guidance. Here are several sample problem statements we've heard from parents:

- "I can't get her to use the toilet."
- "He's disorganized, his room is a mess, and he always forgets to turn in his homework."
- "She bites other kids. She'll be kicked out of her daycare the next time she bites."
- "He constantly picks on his sister."
- "She has terrible tantrums. I'm always worried she's going to lose it and melt down and ruin everything."
- "He'd play computer games all day if I let him and when I try to get him to stop he throws a living fit."
- "She wakes up ten times a night."
- "He doesn't have any friends because he's so bossy."

As you can see, in each case, the parent states a problem in such a way that you have a good general sense of what might be going on but you have little or no information on the details that lead to, maintain, or stop the problem. Unless you gather more specific information, you won't be able to provide helpful recommendations.

In the first example from the preceding list, it may be tempting to quickly recommend that the parent begin a behavioral contingency program designed to get her child to use the toilet. Although this is a good first try at a potential solution, in this real-life case we listened carefully first, and discovered that the 3-year-old girl was not your typical bedwetter or enuresis sufferer, but that she was deathly afraid of toilets! Obviously, obtaining that information was critical and led us down a completely different intervention road.

Case: Walking on Eggshells

After the parent states the problem or concern, it's the consultant's job to get a very specific and complete example or two of the problem.

PARENT: It's my six-year-old. She has terrible tantrums. I'm always on edge, afraid she's going to lose it and melt down and ruin everything.

CONSULTANT: That can be very stressful—especially in public, but at home too. Tell me about the last time or some very memorable time when she had a big tantrum or meltdown.

PARENT: *Hmm.* Just the other morning as we were getting ready to leave, she threw a huge fit. She became completely limp and I had to drag her out of the house

This is an excellent example of how parents initially respond to a behavioral interview. Despite a request for specifics, the parent provides another general problem description. Although there's slightly more information, it's not nearly enough to begin understanding the behavioral contingencies. The consultant must persevere.

CONSULTANT: So, just the other morning, you were getting ready to leave and your daughter had a meltdown. What exactly happened? Walk me through the scene just like I was a mouse in the corner watching the whole thing.

PARENT: I just said, "It's time to go," and she hit the floor and was a quivering lump. And I had to get to work.

CONSULTANT: What exactly was happening before you said, "It's time to go?"

PARENT: She was dressed and ready to go. And it wasn't easy getting her to get dressed, either, and she was playing with her Legos and I finished getting ready and then I told her, "It's time to go."

CONSULTANT: How did you manage to get her to get dressed?

PARENT: We have this routine where I lay out the clothes the night before and then when she gets up she stays in her pajamas and tells me I picked out stupid clothes and we fight and struggle, and finally I let her pick what she wants to wear and she'll eventually get dressed.

CONSULTANT: It sounds like you're not all that thrilled about this routine, but once you give in and let her pick the clothes, your daughter is willing to get dressed.

PARENT: Yep.

CONSULTANT: [Smiling] So . . . how is she with her fashion choices?

PARENT: [Smiling back] Absolutely terrible. Sometimes I'm completely embarrassed about what she wears to school.

CONSULTANT: It's funny how kids will make wild clothing choices but be so totally convinced that our ideas are horrible. It can really be embarrassing.

At this point, if you're reading closely and have a behavioral mindset, you may be getting nervous because the consultant is clearly and willingly being drawn off course. However, the consultant has already obtained some very important information (e.g., the fact that the 6-year-old very much likes control) and is now attending to the therapeutic relationship. By giving the parent a knowing smile about the daughter's clothing choices and expressing validation and empathy, the collaborative relationship is deepened. But the consultant eventually returns to the task of behavioral assessment.

CONSULTANT: And so there you are, all dressed and ready to go, and you tell your daughter you're ready and then your daughter just instantly collapses. Is there anything else you notice?

PARENT: Well, she collapses onto the floor and screams *"Nooooo!"* in a terrible, high-pitched whine.

CONSULTANT: Then what happens?

PARENT: She lays on the floor and I tell her if she doesn't get up she'll be late for school and I'll be late for work and she doesn't move and I say it again and then I probably yell at her and then I just pick her up and drag her outside to the car, which is completely humiliating.

CONSULTANT: It sounds very frustrating and it's the sort of thing that every parent I've ever spoken with considers miserable and humiliating.

The problem description process should continue until you have a clear picture and understanding of the beginning, middle, and end of the problem process. This may require continued prompting. Some interviewers recommend repeatedly asking, "What happened next?" or "What else happened?" (Sklare, 2005). Similarly, we find it useful to ask a question that focuses on the eventual passing of the problem, such as: "How did this all finally end?" or "How did your daughter get into a better mood?"

The purposes of obtaining a problem description are threefold. First, this process provides a perfect opportunity for you to join with the parent by expressing empathy and validation, and sometimes, by universalizing the problem (Yalom & Leszcz, 2005; *universalization* is a technique where the therapist gives the client the sense that she or he is not the only person suffering from a particular problem). Second, the problem description provides you with a foundation for developing goals and potential solutions (or interventions). Third, the problem description gives you a chance to listen for what we call "backward behavior modification." We describe each of these three purposes next.

Expressing Support, Empathy, and Universalizing the Problem   As parents begin describing the problem, and sometimes even disclosing how they might contribute to their child's problem, it's essential for the professional to provide empathy and validation. In the case of the mom and her tantrum-prone daughter, the mom acknowledged, "and then I probably yell at her." At some point after this disclosure the consultant should make an empathic-validating-universalizing statement like:

> I noticed you mentioned that sometimes you end up yelling at your daughter. One thing I can tell you is that pretty much every parent on the planet sometimes yells. . . .
> and pretty much none of us ever feels very good about it. I guess what I'm saying is that it's totally normal and natural to yell, but that we usually all want to yell less.

This statement is helpful because, as noted in Chapter 1, it provides radical acceptance (M. Linehan, 1993a; Linehan & Schmidt, 1995; J. Sommers-Flanagan & Sommers-Flanagan, 2007a). It gives parents the message: "I completely accept you for who you are, even when you tell me you yell at your child. Yet, at the same time, I'm committed to helping you change and become an even better parent who yells less."

It is important to be wise about universalizing a parenting problem. On one hand, it can be comforting for parents to know they are not the first parents to face their particular problem. On the other hand, be careful not to offer universalizing statements that seem to discount or minimize what the parent is describing.

Goals and Solutions   Underlying every parenting problem is a parenting goal and somewhere, linked to the parenting goal, there are potential solutions. Your job, in part, is to transform the problem into a goal, or a set of goals, and to begin identifying possible solutions. This process is both simple and complex. First, you need to attend to the problem and express empathy with the parent's emotions—the emotions that the parent currently experiences as linked to or caused by the problem. In this situation, one of the fundamental interventions will be to help the parent develop a new and different attitude toward and emotional reaction to her daughter's meltdowns (see Appendix B, Tip Sheet 4: I've Got a *New* Attitude).

For this parent, the initial problem is her daughter's tantrum behavior, both because the tantrums are undesirable and because they seem to come at very inopportune times. Naturally the goal is for the child to stop her tantrums. Or is it?

There are many fundamental truths about being human, and the process of identifying goals reveals one of these basic truths. For many good and natural reasons, the parent fervently wishes that her daughter would stop engaging in embarrassing, destructive tantrums. If this wish came true, it would undoubtedly improve the mother's quality of life, and in all likelihood her daughter would be happier, too. However, what the mother probably doesn't understand (yet) and what the consultant will eventually teach her (directly or indirectly) is the difference between wishes and goals.

There is a vast difference between fond wishes and attainable goals. People can wish, hope, and pray for outcomes beyond their direct control. Wishes are in the realm of magic or faith. In contrast, *goals should be primarily built with components that are within parental control.* Unless parents want to experience repeated and agonizing frustration, their goals must focus primarily on their own behavior. If the mom sets a goal for her daughter to stay calm and stop her tantrums, she'll likely experience the misery, frustration, and anger of not consistently attaining her goal because, as currently stated, her goal is completely dependent upon her daughter's behavior. This is one of the first lessons that parents need to learn because, like it or not, children are separate entities and therefore don't always want the same things their parents want.

This way of conceptualizing goal-setting is consistent with choice theory and reality therapy (Glasser, 1998, 2000). Glasser's first choice theory axiom is: *The only person whose behavior we can control is our own.* Although Glasser's axiom is stated in the extreme, and in fact sometimes parents can and should control or manage their children's behaviors, his main point is important and relevant for parents. That is, when parents focus too much on directly controlling their children's behavior, the parent–child relationship may suffer and unhappiness may ensue. Glasser stated:

> *The seeds of almost all unhappiness are planted early in our lives when we begin to encounter people who have discovered not only what is right for them—but also, unfortunately, what is right for us. (1998, p. 4)*

This leaves us with a conundrum. Obviously, the mom wants and needs her daughter to stop melting down and making her late for work, but to set that as her primary goal will lead to frustration. The solution is straightforward but difficult. The mom needs to recognize that her best strategy is to focus on modifying her own behavior, using an experimental mindset and maintaining an attitude of respect toward her daughter. Then as she changes her behavior and approach, she

can watch to see what happens. The following excerpt shows the consultant beginning with a traditional child-based goal (or wish) but shifting to a parent-based
goal.

CONSULTANT: So, one goal is to get your daughter to have fewer and shorter
tantrums?

PARENT: Yes! That would be great. I'd like her to have none at all, but I'd settle for
fewer and shorter tantrums.

CONSULTANT: As you've discovered, one truth about kids is that other than picking them up and dragging them somewhere, they're very difficult to control.
And so even though your goal is to get your daughter to have fewer and shorter
tantrums, all we can do is come up with ideas for what you might do differently
and then see how she responds. It's like an experiment, you try something and
then watch to see if her behavior changes.

Listening for Backward Behavior Modification   Parenting can be difficult
because in many situations the parent's natural impulse is to do exactly the opposite of what's appropriate and likely to be effective. For example, the most natural
parental urge in response to child misbehavior is to yell, scold, or hit. Kazdin
(2008) recently remarked on this phenomenon:

> . . . *when it comes to shaping and changing a child's behavior, what comes most easily and natu-
> rally to parents is often the opposite of what works best . . . It's not that we're bad parents; rather,
> when it comes to behavior, most of us share some basic instincts and assumptions as parents that
> don't do us or our children much good. We turn instinctively to punishment as option one for
> changing behavior. We nag. We clutter the airwaves with ineffective talk. We endlessly explain to
> our children why they should behave better. We concentrate so intensely on the behavior we want to
> eliminate that we forget to praise and reinforce the behavior we do want. (p. 14)*

Instead of long-term effectiveness, punishment typically results in future rebellion,
defiance, fear, and/or disrespect. Further, research is clear that no matter how
quickly it can suppress a particular behavior, corporal punishment has a number
of negative side effects and all too often can deteriorate into harsher and harsher
punishment and sometimes physical abuse (see Gershoff, 2002, 2008 and our prior
discussion in Chapter 3).

As Kazdin (2008) suggested, parents naturally tend to pay attention to negative
or *bad* child behaviors and to ignore positive or *good* child behaviors. We refer to
this strong and almost instinctive tendency as *backward behavior modification*, because
parents so frequently do the opposite of what behavior modification research indicates is effective.

The most common backward behavior modification pattern that parents engage
in is paying attention to negative child behavior through yelling, scolding, and
spanking. Unfortunately, this is usually in combination with the tendency to ignore
positive child behavior. Generally, it doesn't take long for parents to become habitual providers of negative attention for negative behavior and excellent ignorers of

good behavior. Even worse, sometimes parents begin to act surprised in response to their children's positive behaviors. For example, it's not unusual for parents to communicate, "Who are you and what have you done with my son?" when their son is engaging in positive and desirable behavior. As you can see, this response implies to the son that when he acts in a positive and desirable manner, he's not really acting like his true self.

The good news is that it usually doesn't take long for parents to recognize and understand backward behavior modification. This is true as long as the service provider describes it in a sensitive and compassionate manner, emphasizing that it's quite normal for parents to instinctively do the wrong thing. Most parents can grasp the fact that although this pattern is very natural, it often gets them the opposite of what they really want.

There are many ways to teach parents this behavior modification principle. In every case, however, feedback about backward behavior modification should be imbedded within an empathic-validating-universalizing statement. If you forget to be compassionate and empathic, you may alienate the parent and provoke defensiveness. In fact, you may do that even if you deliver the feedback with as much grace and kindness as you can muster. One excellent strategy for teaching about backward behavior modification is storytelling. Here's one example:

CONSULTANT: I noticed you mentioned that sometimes you yell at your daughter and I want to make sure you know that I know that's totally normal, most parents yell sometimes.

PARENT: Yeah. But I hate it when I yell.

CONSULTANT: I think that's true for most of us.

PARENT: Yeah, probably.

CONSULTANT: May I share a story with you about one thing I learned about yelling?

PARENT: Sure.

CONSULTANT: I used to do lots of therapy with very difficult teenagers who did lots of delinquent stuff. They were very hard on their parents and they almost always did things that ended up getting them in trouble. And one very interesting thing they used to tell me is that they absolutely loved to get their parents angry. I remember a boy telling me: "I love it when my dad's eyebrow starts to twitch or when my mom starts yelling at me and she's spitting and the veins start sticking out of her neck." Why do you suppose these kids love to get their parents angry?

PARENT: I don't know, maybe because they thought they were getting control over their parents.

CONSULTANT: I think that's partly right. I also think that sometimes kids learn, over time, that one thing they really know how to get from their parents is a negative reaction. I mean, most kids know exactly what to do to get their parents angry. And so not only does it give them a sense of control . . . it also turns out that getting their parents angry is one way they can get their parents' attention.

And so the negative attention, the yelling and the anger, turn out to actually be a reward for some kids.

PARENT: Oh, yeah. I get it.

CONSULTANT: And so one thing we want to make sure of is that you don't end up paying more negative attention to your child when she misbehaves than you do positive attention when she behaves well. I'm saying this as though it's simple, but as you probably know, it's very hard to consistently remind ourselves to notice and comment on our children's positive behaviors and it's *very* hard to remember to ignore or only briefly pay attention to our children's negative behaviors.

PARENT: So what can I do, besides stop yelling?

CONSULTANT: Well, it's tremendously hard to stop yelling, although I do have some ideas about that and we can talk about it later. I'll write that down as another possible goal we can come back to. But, before we go there, I'd like to learn more about everything you've tried to do to cope with or deal with your daughter's tantrums.

Find Out Everything the Parent Has Tried Before

In the preceding example, after the consultant told and debriefed a backward behavior modification story, the parent expressed an interest in learning to stop yelling and in other new ideas. In response, the consultant noted the parent's interest, but moved back to gather information about what the parent has tried previously to address the tantrums. Although this might seem like the consultant is stalling or buying time, it's actually a strategy critical to the therapeutic process. Before offering concrete advice, the consultant should gather information about what the parent *has already tried* and what didn't work; otherwise, there's a chance the consultant will offer up an idea that the parent has already tried and that she already concluded is ineffective. If this happens and the parent says, "I tried that and it didn't work," the consultant loses credibility and will have to either back away from the suggestion or figure out a way to get the parent to try a technique she already views as unsuccessful.

It's often impossible to find out everything the parent has tried before, but we recommend being fairly thorough about this.

CONSULTANT: So, I know your daughter is quite capable of melting down in an instant and that her behavior is very frustrating and aggravating. And because her behavior is very frustrating and aggravating, I know you must have tried many things to get her to stop her tantrums. It would be really helpful if you could tell me exactly what you've already tried to get her to stop.

PARENT: Do you mean what I do when she starts to throw a fit or what I do to make it so she won't ever throw a fit again?

CONSULTANT: Actually, I'm interested in both. But let's start with what you've done to make it so she won't ever throw a fit again.

PARENT: I think what I do is I walk around my house on eggshells because I'm always afraid she's going to explode at the drop of a hat.

CONSULTANT: So you find yourself being very careful. What exactly are you careful about doing or not doing?

PARENT: I'm careful not to ask her to do anything unless I really need her to do something. And I'm careful to feed her what she wants. And I'm careful to wake her up very gently. And I'm careful to give her many warnings that bedtime is approaching. I'm careful about a lot of things.

CONSULTANT: *Wow.* That sounds hard. Not much chance to be spontaneous around your daughter. Another thing I'm hearing is that somehow you've developed a warning system for alerting your daughter to when she'll have to go to bed. How has that worked?

PARENT: Actually, it's one thing that has worked a little bit. Bedtime is still tough, but when I give her a one-hour, half-hour, fifteen-minute, and five-minute warning that it's time for bed, it's not so bad.

CONSULTANT: So that's something that has worked a little bit. It's nice you were able to figure that out.

As you explore additional actions or attitudes the parent has tried in the past for dealing with the child's problem behavior, you're likely to ask questions like:

- "What else have you tried?"
- "Have you ever taken your daughter to a counselor or psychologist?"
- "Have you gotten any advice, good or bad, from anyone else (like your pediatrician, mother, father, husband, wife, etc.)?"

When telling you what they've already tried, parents may describe some or many excellent parenting strategies as stupid ideas or miserable failures. Of course, often parents develop negative views of parenting techniques not because the technique is poor, but because they implement it incorrectly. However, immediately confronting parents about failing to use a technique properly is *always* inadvisable. Instead, your main goal is to listen well so you can efficiently gather information to help you formulate something a little new, something a little different, and something a little more effective.

Watching and Listening for Patterns

While obtaining a problem description and information about what strategies and techniques parents have tried previously, you will be simultaneously obtaining information to help develop your case formulation. Although case formulation is discussed in the next chapter, from initial contact to assessment, professionals who work with parents should be observing for patterns to help them develop a case formulation that parents can easily understand. For example, in the preceding situation, it becomes more and more obvious that the mother's 6-year-old *likes control and has emotional difficulties with transitions*. These particular traits may be longstanding in that they may represent manifestations of the child's temperament. Acknowledging these traits will help the parent begin using a common and empathic language for understanding the dynamics occurring between her and her child.

Additionally, when you notice that control and transition are challenging for the child, you may also begin wondering to yourself whether the parent has similar issues. For example, in this case the mother later labeled herself as a "control freak" and acknowledged having difficulties planning for transitions.

The interview process described in this chapter focuses on building the working alliance and on an informal and collaborative assessment procedure. Depending on your particular approach, this process may stand on its own, or may be supplemented with more formal assessment techniques. Additionally, although the procedure we described emphasized gathering behavioral data and observing for backward behavior modification, practitioners also could use this procedure with other theoretical perspectives. For example, the assessment approach could easily emphasize parent–child attachment dynamics or parental cognitive distortions instead of basic behavioral principles (Ainsworth, 1989; Bowlby, 1988).

LOOKING BACK AND LOOKING FORWARD

In this chapter we've discussed a number of tasks or behaviors that parenting consultants might use when working individually with parents. These tasks and behaviors are designed to help you make connections with parents and to gather initial assessment information. Additionally, at the end of this chapter we provide a checklist of these specific strategies and techniques. Despite our inclusion of this checklist, we hope you will remember to nest these strategies in the three core attitudes we discussed in Chapter 1. Sometimes as we eagerly look forward to learning the "techniques" or "nuts and bolts" of a particular approach to counseling, we forget the critical attitudinal components. At the risk of being redundant, we remind you to: (a) be empathic, (b) use radical acceptance, and (c) maintain an attitude of collaboration, especially when using specific techniques.

CONCLUDING COMMENTS

Your initial contact with parents is primarily about relationship connection and development and secondarily about gathering assessment information (Rogers, 1980; J. Sommers-Flanagan & Sommers-Flanagan, 2009). This initial contact establishes the foundation from which you will work. Your goal is to behave as a compassionate expert, trying your best to understand parenting challenges. You will need to provide comfort, empathy, reassurance, and validation, honoring parents as being the best experts on their own family situations. As you collaboratively gather information about the parents' family situation, you can work from several different theoretical orientations, including person-centered, behavioral, cognitive, solution-focused, attachment, and choice theory. Be sure to tend to your countertransference potential as well. The following checklist may help you in remembering and balancing the wide range of strategies and techniques used during this critical therapeutic stage.

Checklist for Initial Contact and Assessment

- ☐ Meet, greet, normalize, and comfort.
- ☐ Discuss confidentiality.
- ☐ Describe the therapy or consultation process (use a collaborative role induction).
- ☐ Honor the parent as expert.
- ☐ Listen for the positive motives and provide sincere compliments and reassurance.
- ☐ Check with the parent or ask permission as you begin a goal list.
- ☐ Avoid getting caught up in criticism, negativity, or hopelessness (watch out for your countertransference).
- ☐ Get a reasonably thorough problem description.
- ☐ Take time out from your problem-description task to join with and empathize with the parent.
- ☐ Ask: "What else happened?" or "How did things get better?"
- ☐ Help the parent identify goals and solutions that are within their control.
- ☐ Make empathic-validating-universalizing statements when possible and appropriate.
- ☐ Watch for backward behavior modification.
- ☐ Find out everything the parent has already tried.
- ☐ Begin watching and listening for child and parent behavior patterns.

CHAPTER FIVE

Collaborative Problem Formulation

Many American parents consider themselves independent individuals who prefer working out personal problems privately on their own rather than seeking professional help. As understandable as this perspective is, problem-solving is usually more effective when two or more people partner to collaboratively identify and work on life's problems and challenges. Lydia Sicher (1991) articulated this general rule in an article titled "A Declaration of Interdependence." Humans are by birth and nature social beings who often solve problems more efficiently in a context that provides social support and psychological stimulation.

This chapter is about collaborative problem formulation with parents. If professionals independently identify family problems in ways that don't fit with parent perceptions, the likelihood of termination or resistance is greatly increased. Parents bring into the room the expertise and understanding of their family situation, which needs to be respected and incorporated into the problem-formulation process. Working collaboratively, we need to get as clear as we can about the nature of the problem as presented and experienced by the parents.

Problem formulation flows from the previous chapter, where we focused on methods, strategies, and techniques for connecting with parents and beginning the problem-exploration or assessment process. Occasionally, as discussed in Chapter 4, it's possible to start a goal list from the very beginning of an initial session. However, as the goal list grows, it's helpful to develop a formulation or model for solving parenting problem(s) and achieving parenting goal(s).

Theoretical and Practical Perspectives on Problem Formulation

As you obtain problem descriptions from parents, you'll naturally begin considering your professional problem formulation. No doubt, you'll draw on what most practitioners draw on: your theoretical and empirically based knowledge and clinical and parenting experience (Skovholt & Starkey, 2010). For example, if you are meeting with the mother we met last chapter, upset by her daughter's tantrums, as you try to understand what's causing and maintaining the child's tantrum problems, your internal dialogue may be guided by any of the following six theoretical-empirical-experiential perspectives:

1. **Behavioral:** This mother is reinforcing her daughter's tantrums and ignoring her positive behaviors. She's probably doing this unintentionally and doesn't understand the ramifications of her parental attention. What I need to do is to build her awareness of behavioral contingencies and provide her with education about the power of positive reinforcement (Kazdin, 2008). Then, we can collaboratively develop an intervention designed to help her use passionate positive reinforcement and boring consequences (see Chapter 9, Parent Homework Assignment 9-1: Backward Behavior Modification) so her daughter isn't getting so much attention and positive reinforcement for tantrum behaviors.

2. **Adlerian:** This child wants power and control. I need to help Mom see this pattern and teach her strategies for avoiding power struggles. Because the purpose of her daughter's behavior is to gain power and control, together we need to find alternative ways for her daughter to experience power and control. I will need to work with Mom to develop logical, natural, and pre-planned consequences for when her daughter becomes too controlling (see Appendix B, Tip Sheet 5: The Goals of Children's Misbehavior).

3. **Family Systems:** This mom is working way too hard to solve her daughter's problems. As a consequence, the daughter has retreated to the other polar extreme and is not at all invested in dealing with her own issues, problems, or challenges. I need to educate Mom about family systems and then, together, we will develop a plan that helps Mom let go of some of her responsibility for the problem so the daughter can begin picking up more responsibility for the problem (see Chapter 9, Parent Homework Assignment 9-6, Problem Polarization).

4. **Constructive or Solution-Focused:** Both mom and daughter are contributing authors to a narrative where this girl is highly inclined toward temper-tantrums and Mom is helpless to do anything about it. In fact, Mom has to tiptoe around the home as if she's walking on eggshells. This parent needs information on how to change her attitude toward tantrums (see Appendix B, Tip Sheet 4: I've Got a *New* Attitude). We also need an intervention that refocuses both the mom and daughter on the daughter's ability to control her emotions and the mom's courage to face potential tantrums or meltdowns (see Appendix B, Tip Sheet 3: Character Feedback).

5. **Choice Theory and Reality Therapy:** This parent has been drawn into a struggle over control. She's trying to control her daughter but probably doesn't want to win at all costs. Instead, the mom needs to learn about and implement choice theory principles, including: (a) The easiest and most logical behavior to try to control is your own, and (b) all you can provide to others is information. Given this understanding, she and her therapist should

work together to develop a new plan, one that deemphasizes parental control and empowers the daughter to make positive choices. This plan should outline exactly how Mom wants to think and act before, during, and after her child's tantrums (see Appendix B, Tip Sheet 2: Choice Theory 101).

6. **Attachment Theory and Therapy:** The child's tantrums are driven and maintained by attachment dynamics. Although the tantrums have dysfunctional qualities, they may constitute a primary way in which the child gets her attachment needs addressed. To deal with this dynamic, the parent can be educated about attachment models and then coached to attend to her child's attachment needs proactively in ways that help modify the dysfunctional way in which the attachment dynamics are being played out (see Appendix B, Tip Sheet 6: Enhancing your Child's Sense of Security through Attachment).

Using "Experience-Near" Language With Parents

The key to using any theoretical perspective with parents is to use examples and illustrations that are experience-near and constructed from the parent's linguistic world (Kohut, 1984; Neimeyer & Mahoney, 1995). Experience-near or linguistically appropriate interventions are more easily comprehended by parents because they're consistent with the parents' recent or vivid life experiences. These interventions rely primarily on parents' language and vocabulary. In contrast, experience-distant or linguistically unfamiliar theoretical explanations or practical suggestions may be so disconnected from the family's life experience that the explanations and suggestions are difficult to understand and nearly impossible to put into practice. Whatever theoretical foundation you choose, both the language and examples you use should be easily and quickly understood by the parent on the street (and in your office).

For example, although it can be tempting for behaviorists to help parents develop a sophisticated *variable ratio reinforcement schedule*, it's much more effective to use language like "surprise rewards" and "boring consequences" to communicate intervention plans to parents. Similarly, summarizing behavioral research by stating, "In general, whatever you pay attention to tends to grow" is a linguistically simplified way for parents to conceptualize a behaviorally based intervention.

Using Scientific-Mindedness

Stanley Sue (1998), a renowned multicultural researcher, has written extensively about a helpful concept he refers to as *scientific-mindedness*. Scientific-mindedness involves forming hypotheses about clients rather than coming to firm or premature conclusions about them. Subsequently, therapists or consultants then test their initial hypotheses about minority clients and act on the basis of the data they obtain rather than their prejudices or prejudgments. Scientific-mindedness is a crucial perspective to maintain whenever providing human services, regardless of theoretical orientation.

Case: Caleb Gets Some Control

Donna, a 28-year-old Native American mother scheduled a parenting consultation to talk about her 9-year-old son, Caleb. On the intake form, she indicated that Caleb would not do his homework. This instantly made us wonder if Mom had unrealistic developmental expectations about her son and his academic behavior. After all, how much homework should 9-year-olds be expected to do? We entered the consultation with an initial hypothesis that perhaps the mother was unrealistically achievement oriented and/or pushing her poor little 9-year-old son far too hard.

Scientific-mindedness can guide all human services professionals to actively formulate hypotheses about specific client behaviors, attitudes, and emotions, as long as these hypotheses are treated as *guesses that need testing* rather than as factual conclusions. As a parenting professional, you'll benefit from using a scientific attitude as you work with both initial and ongoing hypotheses about the problems you hear. Having a scientific attitude means that we collaboratively gather data from the client to test the validity of our hypotheses rather than rushing forward to conclusions.

As is sometimes the case, our initial hypothesis about Donna and her son was incorrect. Donna was a calm and committed parent with very reasonable expectations about her son and his academic performance. After establishing a connection and conducting a problem analysis, it became clear that Caleb's homework problems were directly related to the fact that he was not doing his regular schoolwork during school. Consequently, his teacher and school counselor had developed an ambitious behavioral plan, which partly included him staying in at lunch and recess to complete his schoolwork and partly involved him taking leftover schoolwork home for completion. Donna was having trouble getting her son to sit down and complete his leftover schoolwork in the evenings.

Over the years, we've discovered that our initial hypotheses about parents and the problems they present almost always need tweaking to fit the individual parents we're working with. This discovery has led us to work hard on being aware of our reflexive judgments about parents (e.g., Donna initially sounded to us like she might be pushing her son too hard).

We've also discovered that we need not sit back and formulate theoretically driven hypotheses in isolation when we have an outstanding source for hypothesis generation sitting in the room with us. Parents have many hypotheses about the problems they're experiencing; asking them about their best explanations for their child's problems establishes a collaborative mindset and will provide you with helpful information about how to formulate and articulate the child-family-parent problem.

Asking Parents for Their Best Explanation for Child Misbehavior

After initially honoring parents as the best experts on their child and after eliciting a detailed problem description, it's useful to ask parents about their *best guess* or *best explanation* for why their child is displaying whatever problem that has been discussed. We recommend using words like:

I'm curious. You live with Caleb and you've faced this problem of his not doing his schoolwork for a while. I'm sure you've had ideas rumbling around in your head about why this is happening. What do you think? What's your best guess for why Caleb is having this schoolwork problem?

Interestingly, although parents often respond to this simple question with amazing insight, they usually don't volunteer their insights without first being asked the question. It's as if they've quietly formulated a theory to explain their child's problem and are just waiting to be asked their opinion. Sometimes the disclosure is simple and directly related to exactly what we've been talking about. But, in other cases, we're surprised at how parents take this question as an opportunity to share something new or go deeper; often we hear a previously undisclosed fear or worry about what might *really* be causing their child's problem. For example, in Donna's case, we heard the following response:

I think it's my fault. Caleb lived with his grandparents last year and his school didn't give him what he needed. Now he's joining me here and it's a big adjustment. Caleb hasn't had much stability. His dad isn't involved and never has been. I finally have a stable man in my life and Caleb is just now starting to get used to that. I think that's why he's having trouble adjusting at school. It's just too much change and I feel terrible about this whole thing.

Obtaining this information from Donna is helpful for several reasons. First, if we design a solution that's inconsistent with Donna's best explanation, we're less likely to engage Donna in implementing the solution and less likely to see a successful outcome. If our proposed solution or intervention is opposed to Donna's best guess, she's less likely to understand it and less likely to follow through with our recommendations.

Second, sometimes when working with parents there isn't time to gather details about Caleb's family background and personal history. Instead, because time may be limited and parents are impatient about obtaining guidance, one goal is to focus on the parent's current problem description and offer simple, straightforward solutions or interventions. Donna's disclosure helps us glimpse the child's family history without getting bogged down in details better dealt with in a longer-term therapy model.

Third, as much as we believe we have great insight to lend parents, in all likelihood, Donna's insights and inclinations will serve us better than what might be perceived by Donna as experience-distant insights from an outside consultant who has never spent a single minute in Donna and Caleb's home. By asking about the parent's best explanation for the family problem, we're likely to receive contextual information that will allow us to formulate and frame a standard parent education intervention. In this case we might not have heard about Donna's guilt without asking the best explanation question.

Sometimes when you ask parents for their best explanation, you get a response you'd rather not hear. Such responses might provide you with insight into the

parent's culture, biases, fears, or unusual beliefs about the world, but can be difficult to handle. For example, we asked a young father going through a divorce
about his best explanation for his 12-year-old daughter's distressing choice of
clothing. He replied, "I hate to tell you, but she wants to dress just like her mother
and that woman is a slut. No morals. No sense of right and wrong. I'm afraid my
daughter is drawn to that life." We've also had parents report that their best guess
was that their child was possessed by the devil, genetically flawed, or damaged by
the trauma of a car wreck as an infant. You get the drift. These aren't necessarily
helpful or even testable hypotheses. However, like everything else parents say, it's
best to treat these ideas with respect. In cases where parents have negative or
destructive hypotheses about their child's behavior, it might be helpful to say
something like the following:

- "I can tell you're really worried about this problem. You've thought about it
  long and hard, and you're worried that it might have causes beyond our
  control."
- "Tell me a little more about how you came to this explanation."
- "For you, what's more helpful and less helpful about this explanation?"
- "While keeping your ideas in mind, would you mind if we consider some
  other ideas about why this is happening?"

Unusual, offensive, or startling parental hypotheses about the cause of their
child's troubling behavior are not as outlandish as they seem at first blush. Most of
us have a few such hypotheses about life tucked away somewhere in our belief
systems but don't readily admit them. If you can step back and admire these parents for their candid answers, offer empathy (though not agreement), and make use
of whatever information the explanation gives you, you'll be working in the true
spirit of collaboration, using radical acceptance to help find middle ground.

Brief Empathy Stories: A Pre–Problem Formulation Technique

Homework completion, as articulated in Donna and Caleb's case, chores, and
other seemingly simple problems can actually become quite intractable problems
that cause parents and children substantial misery. As a consequence, before providing a problem formulation for homework completion or other entrenched
behavior patterns, we often tell a brief empathy story.

CONSULTANT: One time I was at a conference with a world-famous family therapist. He was telling stories about working with families with huge, scary problems, like severe eating disorders, alcoholism, drug abuse, and domestic
violence. Then he told a story about a family that came to see him, and during
the goal-setting process, the mom turned to him and said, "My main goal is to
get my son to keep his room clean." He turned to her and replied, "That's a great
idea, but because it's nearly impossible, let's start with something easier." Then
they worked on the family addictions problems.

The reason I'm telling this story is because getting Caleb to do his homework at home is a lot like getting a child to clean his room. It seems very simple, but as you know, it can be very, very difficult and frustrating.

In this situation, an empathy story might be useful for two purposes: (a) It's almost always facilitative to find a way to resonate with and have compassion for the parents' frustration over problems that seem relatively normal or minor; and (b) empathy stories provide an excellent foundation for helping parents see that parenting involves an experimental or problem-solving mindset.

CONSULTANT: Because getting kids to do homework is so hard, we need to look at it as an experiment. All we can do is try out a few ideas and see how they work. If it's okay with you, I'll share a few ideas and you give me feedback on them as we go. I'll write down the top ideas, you can try some of them out, and then come back in about a month and tell me how they worked.

PARENT: That sounds good to me.

CONSULTANT: Remember, all we're doing is trying out different conditions for Caleb to do his homework. Whether he chooses to do it or not will be up to him.

The message to Donna is clear: The consultant or therapist will generate, along with Donna's input, a variety of ideas that could be applied to Donna and Caleb's situation. This message is based on an implicit assumption that Donna is not directly in control of Caleb's behavior—but that by experimenting with her behaviors (over which she *has* control) she may produce positive changes in Caleb's behavior.

An Adlerian-Driven Problem Formulation for Donna and Caleb

Since the prominence of Adlerian child-guidance clinics in the 1930s, psychological approaches based on Alfred Adler's theories have been effectively applied to parent–child problems (Bitter, 2009; McVittie & Best, 2009). Adler's theories continue to form the foundation for many contemporary approaches to parent education and training—including the Systematic Training in Effective Parenting (STEP) system (D. Dinkmeyer & Dinkmeyer, 1979).

The renowned Adlerian therapist, R. Dreikurs (1950), described four main psychological purposes for children's misbehavior:

1. Attention
2. Power and control
3. Revenge
4. Displaying inadequacy

Understanding children's misbehavior from a Dreikurian-Adlerian perspective can be illuminating for parents. Sometimes referred to as the *goals of misbehavior*, this theoretical lens helps parents conduct a simple and relatively straightforward functional behavior assessment (something even behaviorists like). It's also consistent with the catchy phrase we mentioned in Chapter 3, *Get curious, not furious* that helps parents adopt a more reflective and less reactive parenting style.

In Donna and Caleb's case, talking about the goals of misbehavior nicely dovetailed with Donna's best explanation for Caleb's homework problems.

CONSULTANT: I really appreciate the compassion you have for Caleb and all he's been through. Your idea that he's just had too much change and disruption in his life could well be contributing to his homework problems. He's been through a lot. But there's no way to know if that's what's at the root of the homework issue.

PARENT: Right. I know. I just feel guilty about that.

CONSULTANT: Sometimes kids feel like they've had no control over all the change in their lives, so they'll control whatever they can control . . . like homework!

PARENT: *Uh-huh*. But what I am supposed to do?

CONSULTANT: I have several ideas . . . most of them are related to your idea about Caleb having too much change and disruption in his life. We need to help him get a better sense of stability and control and that might help him do better with his homework and in general. Do you mind if I share some ideas with you?

As you can see from this example, we're emphasizing the link between Donna's best explanation and the approaches we're about to offer, the first of which will be special time. The linking of the parents' ideas and the consultants' interventions is a crucial skill.

For the purposes of continuity, we briefly continue with the Donna-and-Caleb case as the consultant begins describing special time. Later, in Chapter 7, we return to the special time intervention and provide a different example of how it might be used with parents of a teenager.

PARENT: I don't mind at all. That's why I'm here. Tell me what I should do.

CONSULTANT: The first idea is for you to do a very structured activity with Caleb that's especially good for kids like him who've been through separation, divorce, or other stressful times. It's called 'special time' and it only takes about fifteen to twenty minutes two or three times a week and it's like a vitamin pill for his emotional health. It might be very helpful for him. [The consultant continues to link the upcoming intervention with problems or issues that Caleb has experienced.]

PARENT: Okay.

CONSULTANT: During special time, you give Caleb one hundred percent of your attention. You also give him most of the control. You should use a timer and start it by saying something like, "Caleb, this next twenty minutes is your time. It's 'Caleb time.' You get to be in charge and we'll play any way you want." Of course, the usual forbidden behaviors are still forbidden. For example, he can't hit or hurt or break toys or insist you spend the twenty minutes eating marshmallows. Most kids don't need you to tell them that in advance, but sometimes it's a good thing to make clear because if any of those behaviors start, special time immediately ends.

The most important thing to remember is that during special time you're just like a mirror. For example, if Caleb begins playing a game with you, you just follow along and even if he cheats, you just notice it—sort of like a mirror. You might say: "Right now you're winning and it looks like you're cheating." Then, if he says, "No, I'm not!" you just say, "It looks like you're cheating, but you're saying you're not cheating." Or, if he says, "I'm your big brother and we're running away from home because our mom is so mean," you might be thinking, "That's crazy. I'm not mean," but you'd say, "We're running away because our mom is so mean."

It might be hard for Caleb when the twenty minutes is up. He might get upset or complain but you just need to end the special time, because although it's okay for him to be in charge and get one hundred percent of your attention for twenty minutes, you should be in charge for the other twenty-three hours and forty minutes. If by chance he's upset and won't help you clean up, just ignore that or reflect it like a mirror ("You're mad our special time is over") and then try to have so much fun while cleaning up that he may even want to jump in and help out.

The coolest things about special time are that you give him a dose of one hundred percent attention and one hundred percent control and then, as he plays, you have a glimpse into the issues that he's emotionally chewing on or trying to master. That's why if he starts acting out a scene where you're in a family that's constantly moving or something like that, all you do is reflect back what he's saying so he can just play out his emotional struggles or challenges right in front of you. It gives him a dose of the predictable stability that you think he's missed out on, and he may show you his emotional issues.

How does this sound to you?

PARENT: It sounds really good. I think Caleb will love it. He loves it when I play with him.

CONSULTANT: And you can keep playing with him normally with normal rules. Special time is just a little something extra. Also, special time shouldn't be taken away as a punishment or consequence (unless he breaks one of the basic rules during the special time). Special time should happen at the times you and Caleb have planned for it.

PARENT: So, should I schedule it for a specific time three days a week?

CONSULTANT: Whatever works best for you and Caleb. But, if you schedule it, you should be sure to do it at that time.

PARENT: Right. I could see him getting very upset if we planned it and then didn't do it.

CONSULTANT: One last thing about special time. There's an old theory about why children misbehave. And although Caleb's not really misbehaving much, this theory makes a lot of sense to a lot of parents. The theory says kids misbehave to get attention, power and control, revenge, or excitement. Because much of what Caleb has experienced, like the divorce and moving, has been outside of his control, he may be trying to recover a little control and power in his life. Special time gives him a dose of power and control and he doesn't need to misbehave to get it. [The consultant continues with more linking of Caleb's experiences and problems and adds a theoretical explanation.]

In Donna's case, it may or may not have been helpful to add a theoretical explanation. Our sense is that Donna would have responded well to the special-time intervention based solely on the idea that it would provide Caleb with a "vitamin pill for his emotional health." Explaining the theory is less important than communicating to parents in ways they'll intrinsically understand and appreciate.

Also, we should note that in Donna and Caleb's case there are many other issues worthy of exploration and intervention. For example, it may be essential to communicate with the school and facilitate a more reasonable or effective schoolwork completion plan because the existing plan is not working. The preceding vignette illustrates one way the consultant can offer a potential solution that fits well with the mom's formulation of the problem and that might also address her guilt.

Multi-Theoretical Problem Formulation

Our approach to working with parents is dogmatically multi-theoretical or eclectic or integrative. As previous researchers and practitioners have emphasized, it's important to shift our theories to fit the client and not expect the client to fit our theory (Lazarus, 1997).

In this next case, we continue with the homework theme, but focus on how collaborative problem formulation might look with an older child.

Case: Understanding Jo Jo's Underachievement

The single mother of a 15-year-old daughter, Jo Jo, contacted us for an appointment. She reported feeling rather perplexed about her daughter's remarkable ability to avoid doing homework. "She's got an IQ in the 120s," she claimed, as she shared several exasperating stories of Jo Jo's chronic underachievement.

The good news about this case was actually very good news. The mom reported having an excellent relationship with her daughter. She noted Jo Jo was not interested in alcohol or drugs, and happily reported that many of her teachers continued to like Jo Jo despite her consistent inability or unwillingness to turn in homework assignments. She shared a story of how Jo Jo had become the "go-to gal" in her math class. "Everybody knew she knew more than anybody else." But Jo Jo's overall grade was only marginally passing because her perfect test scores didn't completely offset her extremely low homework assignment scores.

In developing a problem formulation with Jo Jo's mother, we asked the best-explanation question and she responded with: "I think it all might boil down to her being bored. I remember being bored when I was in school and I had some of the same problems." We also asked her about how she and others around Jo Jo (her school counselor and teachers in particular) responded to her chronic underachievement. It was quite clear from her responses that everyone was very invested in Jo Jo's academic success—everyone, that is, except Jo Jo.

As early as elementary school some of Jo Jo's teachers had her pegged as an intellectual standout. Some of her teachers had even claimed she had the potential to go to Stanford or Harvard. But now Jo Jo's mother sat in our office concerned that she might not having enough credits to graduate from high school.

In the spirit of collaborative case formulation, we discussed the "bored" hypothesis with Jo Jo's mom and developed an intervention related to the possibility that her daughter's underachievement and lack of motivation were related to feelings of boredom. However, we also began tracking alternative (but not mutually exclusive) formulations, including the polarization principle.

The polarization principle is based on family systems theory. Although there are polarization principle variations, its occurrence generally springs from a situation where at least one parent is very motivated and invested in his or her child's success in a particular area of functioning. When this happens within a family, it's not unusual for the parent to provide nearly all the motivation for success, while the child remains nonchalant, displaying absolutely no motivation. In this situation, it was apparent that Jo Jo had very little motivation to complete her homework assignments while, in contrast, her mother and various school personnel were strongly invested in Jo Jo's academic success.

To complicate the situation, Jo Jo had a history of attention-deficit disorder (without hyperactivity). Over the years she had taken a variety of medications but the medications produced undesirable effects and weren't helpful. Additionally, one psychologist suggested that Jo Jo might have an anxiety disorder and she was given a serotonin-selective reuptake inhibitor (an antidepressant medication) — again, to no avail. Over time, Jo Jo had repeatedly garnered the attention of her mother, medical/psychological professionals, and school personnel without many positive results.

Based on our brief contact with Jo Jo's mother (about 30 minutes of rapport building and case formulation) we developed three separate but compatible case formulations and shared them with her. First, we emphasized that when it came to academic performance in general and homework completion in particular, it was likely that the polarization principle was functioning. We came to this conclusion in part because Jo Jo's mother reported trying a wide range of reasonable rewards, punishments, and other motivational tools on her own and in conjunction with Jo Jo's school personnel. Given that so many different external motivational factors had been employed, we hypothesized that some form of polarization (or oppositionality) had taken hold.

Second, we suggested that Jo Jo might have some anxiety or fear associated with failure or success. Certainly, for years she had been intermittently burdened with high expectations, and for many youth, high expectations complicate performance and can result in diminished effort. This is because of a variant on *self-handicapping* — the young person never takes a risk or applies true effort because of a fear of failure to live up to expectations (McCrea, 2008). We further surmised that her fear of failure might be associated with her history of an ADD diagnosis, which may have contributed to Jo Jo's adopting a personal narrative that included beliefs such as, "I'm the sort of girl who doesn't do homework assignments and always does worse than everyone expects."

Third, we adopted Jo Jo's mom's best explanation. Despite the fact that she may have been projecting her personal history and challenges onto Jo Jo, it also made sense that a girl as smart as Jo Jo might be bored by school and especially bored by homework assignments requiring her to regurgitate academic material she had already mastered.

We should emphasize that, as we discussed each of these formulation options, we carefully checked in with Jo Jo's mother, using a strategy derived from Constance Fisher's work in the area of collaborative voice assessment (Fischer, 1979; Fischer & Finn, 2008). Specifically, we frequently asked, "Does this make sense to you?" and "Do you think this idea could fit for Jo Jo?"

In the end, we developed and shared a list of specific recommendations with Jo Jo's mother. As we shared these recommendations we emphasized that it was impossible to tell with certainty and in advance whether any of these ideas would work. In saying this, we further emphasized that parenting often involves experimental behavior—with parents "trying out" various strategies and then observing to see if a desired outcome emerges.

The case of Jo Jo illustrates a problem (and solution) formulation that integrates several theoretical perspectives. First, the polarization principle, based on a family systems model, was discussed. Second, a narrative model where Jo Jo was seen as a girl who had adopted a maladaptive internalized view of herself was articulated. Third, Jo Jo's mom's perspective that Jo Jo was understimulated was also discussed, a perspective consistent with modern Adlerian theory that can also fit a behavioral model.

A Behavioral Approach to Homework Completion

As noted previously, many of our best friends are behaviorists and so we would be remiss (and perhaps put in timeout or not invited to desirable social events) if we didn't consider and articulate a behavioral case formulation to homework completion. We offer this in contrast, but not in opposition, to the approaches described previously.

Consider this excerpt from Kazdin's book, *The Kazdin Method for Parenting the Defiant Child* (2008):

> *A point chart for this activity might be as simple as one point for every ten minutes of uninterrupted sitting and working. So, two points for twenty minutes, three points for thirty, and so on. Put points on the chart and praise along the way—at the beginning you'll be marking the point every ten minutes, if he earns it—and also be sure to praise him at the end of a successful session. (You may come to believe that the promise of points is carrying the main weight of the program, but that's not true. Really, your praise is more important than ever. Points and praise go together and remember that when I say "praise," I mean "effective praise": enthusiastic, specific, unqualified, coming as close on the heels of the child doing the desired behavior as you can, and delivered whenever possible via more than one sense—voice plus touch, for instance.) The homework chart should be visible from the place where he does his homework; remember that its presence will*

act as a setting-up event to encourage the desired behavior. You can set up the usual structure of short-term and long-term rewards. There should be some small things he can earn for a few points. If he can get up to, let's say, four points per day, make the price of the smallest rewards three points. (pp. 90–91)

Kazdin's knowledge and description of this behavioral approach is fabulous. However, parents can be put off by the mechanical and tedious nature of behavioral interventions. Although all interventions should be considered in light of whether they comply or deviate from basic behavior modification principles, less mechanical and less tedious parenting interventions are often preferable.

In addition, many professional parenting experts point out that when parents stick too closely to behavioral psychology for managing children's behavior, their purpose can seem too focused on control and too removed from a warm and loving relationship. Kohn (2005) describes how behavioral psychology can translate into a destructive parenting style that he refers to as *conditional parenting*:

When we use punishments and rewards and other strategies to manipulate children's behavior, they may come to feel they're loved only when they conform to our demands. Conditional parenting can be the consequence of control even if it wasn't the intention, and, conversely, control can help to explain the destructive effects of conditional parenting. (p. 48)

A Kinder and Gentler Behaviorism

The good news is that it is possible to teach parents behavioral principles without being overly mechanical, tedious, or conditional.

Case: Singing the Bedtime Blues

A young couple came in to talk about how to best handle their active and intense 2-year-old daughter. As we discussed their parenting challenges and asked for a problem description, they provided the following nighttime scenario, which we then addressed using a parent-friendly behavioral formulation.

CONSULTANT: Give us an example of a situation where your daughter is especially challenging.
FATHER: We could tell you about last night.
MOTHER: That would be a good one.
CONSULTANT: Okay.
MOTHER: You tell it.
FATHER: We've been having trouble getting our daughter to go to bed and stay in bed. Usually we lay her down with the bottle and she goes to sleep with it. But even that hasn't worked lately. Last night, it was about ten P.M. and I held her with the bottle. She was just pushing the bottle around and trying to play. And then I put her into her bed and she just kept trying to play. At ten-thirty she was back out of her room. She had on a cowboy hat and sunglasses and still wanted to play. She was out for a while and we put her back in bed at eleven and she just got back up and out of her room right away. She didn't seem tired at all. At

midnight we put her back in bed with another bottle and tried holding the door shut but she just kept on yelling, screaming, and crying. By one A.M., she finally fell asleep in my wife's arms on the couch and she took her to bed. I have to be up by six A.M. for work and so I had already given up and gone to bed myself.

CONSULTANT: This was last night?

FATHER: Yep.

CONSULTANT: You two look surprisingly good given what you just went through last night.

MOTHER: [Smiling] Thanks, but we're exhausted.

CONSULTANT: Can I ask a few more questions so we're sure we completely understand the situation?

FATHER: Sure.

CONSULTANT: What's your daughter's usual bedtime?

MOTHER: We try to get her to bed about nine o'clock, but sometimes it's a little later.

CONSULTANT: Does she still nap?

MOTHER: Oh, yeah. Sometimes for two or three hours. Yesterday she'd napped until almost five.

CONSULTANT: So it makes some sense that she wasn't all that tired last night.

MOTHER: Yes.

CONSULTANT: What happens if you have her not take naps?

FATHER: She'll just crash at about eight o'clock and then be up at midnight and we can't take that.

CONSULTANT: Lots of families have bedtime rituals for their children; what do you guys usually do?

FATHER: Mostly we hang out on the couch. We have our six-year-old go to bed first and then about a half-hour later we give our daughter her bottle and put her in bed.

CONSULTANT: Anything else?

MOTHER: We've tried reading, but our daughter just tries to play with the book.

In this particular case, John S-F was doing co-therapy with a graduate student who had substantial experience consulting with parents of young children. To model a collaborative communication style, he turned to the graduate student and said, "Carol, I've got some ideas about what might help with bedtime for these guys, but I know you've got lots of experience with parents and little ones and so as I talk I hope you'll jump in and maybe together we can come up with a new plan for how to help this little girl get on a better sleep routine."

This situation was especially delicate because both John and Carol were very aware of several poor bedtime practices the couple was using. The challenge was to stay as positive as possible, while helping the parents understand why and how they needed to revamp their entire bedtime routine.

JOHN: One thing I can say for sure is that your daughter absolutely loves to be with you guys. Being with you two on the couch is way better than being alone in bed—even with a bottle.

FATHER: Yeah, but she's driving me crazy. I've been way too angry about this. We've got to get her to go to bed and stay in bed.

CAROL: I think we can help, but it will mean developing a whole new bedtime plan, because she's obviously a very determined child. How would you both feel about that?

FATHER: That's fine with me.

MOTHER: Me, too.

JOHN: Okay. Let me know how this sounds to you. Here's what I'm thinking. First, it's really a good thing that she's not going down with the bottle any more because that can be a bad habit and it's not good for her teeth. And so it's good news that she's started giving up that sleep strategy on her own. But let's make a list of the other things we need to try out. First, from what you say, even though I'm almost always against waking up children, it sounds like it's really important not to let her take naps past three or four P.M. in the afternoon. Let's put that on the list.

With lots of checking-in and other collaborative interactions, John and Carol generated the following list for the parents to try out:

1. No naps after 3:30 P.M. If she's sleeping then, gently wake her up and engage her in some playful or comforting activities.
2. Give the bottle at 8:30 P.M., before the nighttime bath.
3. Have a nice warm bath at about 8:45 P.M.
4. Slip her from her bath into her jammies and right to bed (the natural cooling of the human body after a warm bath stimulates drowsiness).
5. If you want to read to her, keep the book away and if she tries to reach out and play with it, just say "no" and leave the room. You can try a story instead of a book, too.
6. If she leaves the room after her official bedtime, in a boring voice, just say "No, it's time for bed," and return her there without any fun or pleasant interactions.
7. Even if she's being as cute as can be, do not smile or laugh at her. Just say, "No, it's time for bed."
8. If she sleeps in too late in the morning and there's no reasonable nap time, skip the nap, but try to keep her awake until at least 8:30 P.M. If she gets up at midnight, again, just be boring and consistent and say, "No, it's time for bed."
9. Do not let her join you on the couch or in any way reward her for *not* going to sleep.

This case formulation was primarily based on behavioral psychology. It seemed obvious to us that the 2-year-old daughter was getting far too much attention (positive reinforcement) from her parents when she got out of bed. The parents were especially able to hear this formulation when it was initiated with: "One thing I can say for sure is that your daughter absolutely loves to be with you guys." This is a good example of how important it is to develop a positive problem formulation or frame that parents can non-defensively embrace. Sometimes to help parents of young children understand behavioral psychology and the power of positive (and negative) attention, we say things like:

- "You probably already know this, but right now, you're the most important person (people) in your child's life."
- "Attention from you is the biggest reward you can give your child—and it doesn't even matter if it's positive or negative attention."
- "Almost everything your child does right now is mostly designed to get your attention."

Behavioral principles are based on decades of solid scientific research. It's critical for parents to understand the basics, such as how they might be inadvertently reinforcing a behavior they would really like to extinguish. However, there's a big difference between developing an awareness of behavioral contingencies versus applying behavioral contingencies in a rigid, systematic, and controlling manner. We support the former and, except under exceptional circumstances, eschew the latter.

We also recognize there are two polar-opposite and fairly popular approaches to helping children sleep through the night. These approaches capture the extremes of *science-individualism* and *attachment-collectivism*.

There are two dominant scientific-individualistic approaches to children's sleep disturbances (Kuhn & Elliott, 2003). These are the *extinction* procedure and the *graduated extinction* procedure. The graduated extinction procedure is sometimes referred to as the "Ferberization" or "cry-it-out" method (Ferber, 2006). These approaches emphasize the establishment of a strict routine for putting the child into his or her own bed and then either cold turkey (extinction) or progressively (graduated extinction) extending the time periods between entering the room to check on the child in bed (but not to remove the child from bed). Eventually, the focus is on letting the child cry it out rather than responding to the child's crying in ways that serve as rewards. Research suggests that this approach significantly improves sleep onset and sleep outcomes (Kuhn & Elliott, 2003).

The alternative approach to helping children sleep is often referred to as *co-sleeping* or the *family bed* (Thevenin, 1987). This approach suggests that the best option for emotional health is to have the child (or children) sleep with the parents. Children and parents from many cultures have employed the family bed and offer great testimonials about how this is the most loving and healthy way to help children develop natural sleeping cycles.

Generally, physicians do not support co-sleeping (too physically dangerous and disruptive to the parents' sleeping), and family bed proponents dislike the Ferber method (too cold and emotionally isolating; Ramos & Youngclarke, 2006). As you can see from the preceding case example, we tend to advocate a kinder and gentler behavioral approach. Interestingly, we've seen parents use behavioral approaches very lovingly and consistently and we've seen parents use the family bed approach in a way that seems to insure child safety. As a consequence, our recommendation is for you to work individually with parents on this issue because many of them will have strong feelings about using approaches associated with either of these two extremes. Ferber himself has moved toward a more moderate perspective on children's sleeping (Ferber, 2006).

Dangers of Strict Behaviorism

As most parents and humans recognize, love and affection is consistently the most powerful positive reinforcement that exists in families (and on the planet). And, unfortunately for those who go too far in implementing strict behavioral management plans, love and affection is not typically the most salient outcome. John Watson, the late great behaviorist, proved this nearly a century ago.

Watson is a great historical example of why parents shouldn't be too extreme in applying to their children behavioral principles that were originally developed for training and managing animals. Watson (1924) was extreme in his conviction that he could shape and control the destiny of humans through behavioral training. He stated:

> Give me a dozen healthy infants, well-formed, and my own specified world to bring them up in and I'll guarantee to take any one at random and train him to become any type of specialist I might select—doctor, lawyer, artist, merchant-chief and yes, even beggar-man and thief, regardless of his talents, penchants, tendencies, abilities, vocations, and race of his ancestors. (p. 104)

Consistent with his theory, Watson published a popular parenting book that instructed parents to avoid rocking, cuddling, and kissing their children (J. B. Watson & Watson, 1928). His views were actually quite popular at the time not only because he was prolific, but also because he was well connected with the American media. For example, he published magazine articles in *Ladies' Home Journal* and *McCall's* instructing mothers to put their infants on strict feeding schedules and not to spoil their infants by being responsive. He also suggested that if parents absolutely must kiss their children they should do so on the forehead, but that shaking the child's hand was a much preferred method of displaying affection.

Watson applied his theories to his own children and the results were tragic. One of Watson's sons committed suicide and the other experienced chronic bouts of depression and suicidal feelings. Ironically, his surviving son attributed the ability to overcome and cope with depressive and suicidal feelings to a very long and positive experience with psychoanalytic psychotherapy—which happened to be the approach that Watson had dedicated his life to opposing.

Overall, parents need to be aware of behavioral principles, and education in this area is important. However, in every case it's essential for behavioral principles to be used within the context of a warm and affectionate relationship. Children need to feel loved by their parents regardless of their specific behaviors.

CONCLUDING COMMENTS

The take-home messages in this chapter are simple. Be aware of a wide variety of theoretical perspectives. Ask parents what they suppose is the best explanation for their child's behavioral or emotional problems. Listen closely to parents' explanations and respect what they say. As you begin to formulate the problem, make sure parents can easily understand your language and theoretical perspective and link it to the parents' experiences. Finally, although you should be knowledgeable of behavioral principles, avoid advocating a cold, mechanical, or tedious approach that communicates to children that their parents' love is conditional.

Checklist for Problem Formulation With Parents

- ❒ Keep a broad range of theoretical perspectives in mind when working with parents.
- ❒ Remember, make the theory fit the parent and not the parent fit the theory.
- ❒ Use "experience-near" language with parents.
- ❒ Use scientific-mindedness to avoid coming to premature conclusions about parents.
- ❒ Ask parents to tell you about their best explanation for their child's misbehavior.
- ❒ Tell brief empathy stories to let parents know you "get" how challenging children's behavior can be, even if it is relatively normal behavior.
- ❒ Find a way to link the parent's best explanation to your primary problem formulation.
- ❒ Think about behavioral contingencies and teach parents to be aware of behavioral contingencies, but avoid mechanistic, tedious, and conditional intervention approaches.

Creating and Providing Guidance, Advice, and Solutions

Not long ago, as one of us was working with a teenager in psychotherapy, the young man began rambling on about smoking cigarettes. He said: "I like it, but I hate it. I know I could run so much faster if I didn't smoke. But I like it."

This boy articulated the human spirit's remarkable ability to experience deep ambivalence. You may recall at some point in life feeling the angst of a love–hate relationship. Perhaps you were attracted to someone or something or some place with a force equal to your revulsion. In the midst of this great ambivalence, you may have longed for guidance. "Ah," you may have thought, "if only someone would tell me what to do and how to do it."

Even though the previous chapters have had case examples that included offering ideas and guidance, this chapter more directly furthers our discussion of the process of offering guidance and advice to parents—parents who are often sitting on the fence of ambivalence when it comes to changing their parenting habits or behaviors. This ambivalence is natural and should be respected. It's up to you as a parenting professional to identify a few good ideas that parents will be willing to try in their private lives and with their precious children. When parents are ready to listen, offering constructive ideas and having them enthusiastically accepted is surprisingly easy. Other times, our excellent advice seems to bounce off an invisible force field.

For most parents and in most educational and therapeutic settings, advice or guidance is the anticipated intervention. Parents want advice and will be disappointed if they don't get any. However, if the advice isn't given in an empathic, sensitive, and respectful manner, parents will typically reject the very advice they have asked for. To address this challenge, this chapter focuses on the advice-giving process, approaches to assigning parent homework, and concluding individual educational or therapeutic sessions. Additional information about specific interventions and advice-giving content is included in Chapters 7 through 9.

HELPING PARENTS LISTEN TO AND ACCEPT USEFUL ADVICE

It's easy for professional helpers to blame parents for resisting advice. After all, we're the educated experts, so parents should recognize our wisdom. Parents who don't eagerly accept our advice might be seen as either stubborn or irrational. In reality, when parents resist our advice the problem is usually ours rather than theirs.

Delivering good advice to parents is similar to getting email delivered, read, and understood by the correct recipient. We need to follow three basic rules:

1. *Get the right address:* Every individual has a unique email address. If we don't type that address correctly, the message will never get there.
2. *Individualize the message:* Although bulk email sometimes gets through, it might get quickly discarded as spam unless the potential recipient believes it's a valuable and personalized message.
3. *Communicate coherently:* If we don't write the message in language understood by the recipient, our communication is unlikely to be effective.

We use this analogy to emphasize that, just as we don't usually blame someone for not receiving an email, we should never hold parents responsible for not receiving or not "getting" our messages. It's our responsibility to get the correct address and to construct a personalized message that has the best possible chance of being received and understood.

Readiness to Change

As a helping professional, you may already be familiar with the *readiness to change* concept. We review this model briefly because it fits well with the process of working with parents.

Based on their *transtheoretical change model*, Prochaska and DiClemente (Prochaska, 1995; Prochaska & DiClemente, 2005) claim that clients who come for assistance will vary with respect to how ready they are to accept advice and make life changes. They identify five stages of change. These include:

1. Precontemplation
2. Contemplation
3. Preparation
4. Action
5. Maintenance

The Precontemplation Stage   Parents in the *precontemplation* stage may experience parenting difficulties, but they don't see themselves as having a problem or skill deficit. Solution-focused therapists refer to precontemplative clients (or parents) as *visitors to treatment* (Murphy, 2008). These parents generally don't seek therapy or consultation on their own. However, if you work with court-mandated parents you may have professional contact with precontemplative parents.

Precontemplative individuals usually resist direct guidance or advice. However, in our experience, parents can move rapidly through the stages of change—entering the room behaving as a precontemplater and leaving (after less than an hour) firmly within the action stage.

Case: A Father in Precontemplation

A married couple with four children jointly attended an initial consultation session that was being offered at reduced cost through a research grant. Within the first two minutes, the mother acknowledged with apparent trepidation that she had "dragged" her husband to the session. In fact, John had already used his keen clinical intuition to sense that the father might be less than optimally motivated (i. e., precontemplative). This was because immediately prior to stepping into the consultation room the father rather aggressively joked that he and John might "get into a shoving match" once they got inside the consultation room.

Given this antagonistic beginning, the ensuing interactions were quite surprising. After his wife "outed" him as a precontemplater, the father quickly found a lens through which he could see himself as a contemplater. He stated: "Well, I didn't know this meeting was part of a research project. If I'd known that, I would have been happy to come from the beginning. I'm glad to help you out."

Of course, being glad to help out with a research project isn't exactly the enthusiastic embrace for learning we hope to attain—but it was an entry point and mood shifter. The father was no longer aggressively resistant. He had transformed himself into a helpful participant.

Following the father's disclosure about being helpful, the mother began describing their parenting challenges. John responded with active listening and empathic comments, by framing the problem as a minor issue and then reframing it as a goal. The father listened, intermittently joined in the conversation, and enthusiastically agreed with John's description of their minor problem and initial goal statement. The goal was *to reduce the yelling that occurred in their home.*

Toward the middle of the session the father shared two very personal stories about his childhood. At one point, his wife exclaimed, "I didn't know that!" A bit later (toward the session's end), the father volunteered to set his watch alarm for the same time each evening so he could remind himself to become more proactively involved in the children's bedtime rituals. In fact, the parents agreed—using concrete and specific language—on exactly how they would modify their bedtime ritual to better involve the father. They left the office as a united front—and without having engaged in a shoving match.

Not all precontemplaters will move quickly to the action stage. However, in our experience, the stages of change are not inflexible positions. We frequently have parents move from precontemplation to action during a single session. Then again, on our bad days we've inspired action-oriented parents to retreat to precontemplation.

The biggest tool for moving parents from precontemplation (resistance) to action (cooperation) is respect. If you show respect to parents using the skills discussed in this book and take great care to never give the parents a reason *not* to change—change is more likely. If you disrespect parents, well, we're fairly certain you know what happens then.

The Contemplative Stage   Clients who are aware of a problem, but haven't yet taken steps toward action, are in the contemplative stage (Prochaska, 1995; Prochaska & DiClemente, 2002). Like the ambivalent young smoker in this chapter's opening paragraph, these parents may attend their sessions with mixed feelings. They may have ambivalence about being in the room with you and they'll usually be undecided about making personal changes.

By definition, all parents who show up for parenting assistance are a little bit contemplative. Helpful phrases to use with these parents include: "You've really been noticing and thinking about this," or "This has been on your mind and you've given it some thought, even before you came here." However, in the stages of change model, contemplaters are usually not considered ready for action-oriented advice or homework assignments. This could be a problem, especially because the whole point of working effectively with parents is to either offer educational information or stimulate insight and behavior change. Generally, the hope is that a parenting consultant will be able to offer practical and concrete advice before the first session ends.

We address this problem by consistently acknowledging that parenting is often experimental and that it's hard to know exactly how children will react to different parenting techniques or strategies. This allows us to gently suggest that parents give something a try as an experiment. Additionally, when parents admit frustration, we like to use empathic irony and note that it appears that their current strategy (although an excellent idea) isn't exactly working the way they were hoping. This understatement often moves parents toward preparation and action.

The Preparation Stage   During the preparation stage individuals become convinced they have a problem. For parents, it might come as something like, "Wow. I'm really getting way too angry way too often. This is serious. I need help." Most commonly, parents have reached this stage in a soft way. They don't believe they have a big problem or that they desperately need professional help. Instead, they've experienced a repeating and slightly disturbing or distressing pattern. For example, their child is consistently not listening or is misbehaving in some way that brings the parent to question her or his (a) parenting competence or parenting efficacy; (b) ability to manage stress related to childrearing; or (c) child's emotional/ behavioral well-being. To connect with parents who present in this stage of change, it's helpful to lightly focus on and resonate with:

- Parental feelings of inadequacy
- Stress associated with wanting to be a good parent or caregiver

- Mild concerns about the child's well-being or emotional health
- How admirable (and cool!) it is that the parent loves his or her child so much that he or she is meeting with a professional to discuss parenting strategies

Overall, it's important to affirm that parents have made a good choice to come in and talk about parenting with an unbiased professional.

The Action Stage   During the action stage clients and parents are taking action designed to change unhealthy or destructive behavior patterns. Given this definition, it's obvious that many parents are on a continual action-oriented course. They go online and read about parenting, they buy parenting books, they talk with friends and relatives, they attend play groups and parenting classes, they talk to their pediatrician, and they come for therapy or consultation. In this sense, every parent whose feet hit the floor of your office is at least partly in the action stage.

As you may recall (from Chapter 4), at the beginning of an individualized consultation session, professionals should share the power with parents by stating something like,

> This is your time. If you want me to listen more, tell me. And if you want me to give you more advice, you can tell me that, too.

This statement, because it honors the parent's need for control and a sense of self-destiny within the educational or therapeutic context, helps parents see themselves as an actor within the action stage.

Parents in the Maintenance Stage   Change often involves two steps forward and one step back. The maintenance stage is happening when parents have made changes and are struggling to succeed, or are succeeding in maintaining those changes. For example, many parents who seek professional help would like to yell less and they often leave their initial meeting with renewed hope for accomplishing that goal. Unfortunately, it's extremely difficult for parents (or anyone) to quickly and successfully stop (or even reduce) their yelling. Consequently, they struggle to succeed, sometimes going several days without yelling and then relapsing into a yelling episode. Yelling episodes are then typically followed by guilt and self-recrimination.

We should note that it's nearly universal for parents who yell at their children to wish they could get what they want without yelling. At the very least, they usually want to decrease their yelling behavior. Very few parents enjoy yelling at their children, and if they do, they have a problem too serious to address within a brief therapeutic or educational model.

Hardly anything in psychology escapes controversy and such is the case with the stages of change model. Although intuitively and logically appealing, some data suggests the stages of change model is not a particularly good predictor of which treatment approaches should be employed at any given time (Sutton, 2005; West, 2005). As discouraging as this may seem, we take solace in the proposition that nearly all parents to some extent have internal motivation to become better parents—at least a little better. Our job is to engage them where they are and to help them move forward toward their ideal parenting self.

A GREAT INTERNAL FORCE FOR POSITIVE CHANGE

As discussed previously, parents often have ambivalence about seeking advice and assistance. They want change, but they may not want certain kinds of advice. They are wary of being criticized, worried they have failed, and sometimes defensive. However, perhaps because we're optimists, we're convinced, for reasons we discuss next, that the desire for help can win out over fear and resistance.

Somewhere inside, most parents recognize in the misty folds of their consciousness a little voice that whispers, "You can do better than that." Of course, in really miserable times, that little voice turns mean, gets louder, and shouts unhelpful messages and inappropriately degrading comments about our personal character. Most parents can relate to this observation. Somewhere inside us is a voice that at least occasionally urges us to do better at parenting—to dig deeper, try harder, and be smarter.

Many theories of personality and psychotherapy describe an internal force that pushes or pulls us toward self-improvement. Although these theories are often incompatible, there is also common ground. At some points, Freud referred to this force as the *ego*. His words, carved in a memorial to him in Vienna, capture some of this continuous movement forward: "The voice of reason is small, but very persistent." Rollo May identified this force as the *daimonic*, claiming "The daimonic is the urge in every being to affirm itself, assert itself, perpetuate and increase itself" (May, 1969; p. 123). Jung believed that by paying attention to interacting with our unconscious, great creative and constructive acts were possible (J. Sommers-Flanagan & Sommers-Flanagan, 2004a). And Rogers' (1942) belief that we move toward an ideal self, Maslow's (1970) self-actualizing tendency, Glasser's (1998) quality world, and Adler's (1927) striving for superiority all represent powerful forces that push and pull us forward toward some improvement, perfection, or complete self.

We discuss the great internal force for positive change here because when working with parents we should always try to identify, align with, and work with that force. As health professionals and agents for individual and social change, we believe we should help parents become their ideal version of complete and excellent parents.

Reading over our statements about this great and powerful internal force, we recognize that we may sound more like Yoda from the *Star Wars* film series than 21st-century psychologists and counselor-educators. Nevertheless, we believe there is substantial theoretical consensus on this point. That is, every parent who steps into your office has a great (or small, but persistent) internal force for positive change. It's our job to recognize, activate, nurture, and capitalize on that force.

Activating the Great Internal Force

If you've read the first five chapters of this book, you already know most of what you need to do to activate the great internal force for positive parental change. In this section we outline strategies for delivering advice in a manner that connects with this positive force and makes it more likely for parents to accept and implement advice.

As you listen to parents and begin formulating interventions in your mind, be ready to jot down these ideas, using careful, legible handwriting. You should do this on a separate sheet of paper from your case notes because you can use this to copy and hand to parents as your parenting prescription. Most parents will absolutely love the fact that you take notes for them and then hand them over at the end of your meeting.

After Listening, Paraphrasing, Expressing Empathy, and Working With the Parent(s) to Develop a Case Formulation, Ask Permission to Offer Advice This strategy represents some of the best and most straightforward guidance you'll ever get for working with parents: Before you offer advice, ask permission. For example:

> I've been listening for a while and I've come up with a few ideas that might be helpful. Is it okay with you if I go ahead and share them now?

We've never had a parent respond to this question with "No." Virtually every parent eagerly and enthusiastically says something like, "Yes, that would be great" or "Of course—that's why I'm here!" When parents explicitly consent to hearing your advice, they're more likely to accept it.

Offer Suggestions Using a Humble and Respectful Attitude For a number of years there was a character on National Public Radio named Dr. Science. Dr. Science came on the radio with a deep and authoritative voice and said, "I know more than you do." This particular approach, although entertaining, is the antithesis of how we recommend working with parents. This is true even though you probably *do* know more than the parent when it comes to identifying and articulating constructive parenting strategies. But of course, when you're really an expert and you're secure about yourself, you don't need to lead with a Dr. Science attitude. Instead, it's best to be humble and to emphasize to parents that all your suggestions are merely suggestions and perhaps worthy of a try or two. For example, you might say:

> As you know very well, parenting is hard and you're facing a big challenge. You know your family much better than anyone else and so I'm taking a risk and hoping these ideas might work for you. I don't know if they will, but I think it's worth giving them a try to see what happens. You might come back next month and tell me what a bunch of bad ideas I gave you or you might come back and say that something we talked about really worked. Or, you might even develop a new idea of your own after you leave here.

A key part of the preceding statement is that it gives parents 100 percent permission to return and criticize you or to flatly reject what you've offered. Paradoxically, once you've given parents that permission, rarely do they find the need to tell you that you're useless. Additionally, this statement includes a suggestion—a technique associated with hypnosis—that the parent might even develop a new idea on her or his own.

Use Tentative and Gentle Language   In truth, it takes a bit of chutzpah to start offering suggestions and advice to parents after having known them for 30 minutes or less. This approach is quite presumptuous. To compensate for what might be experienced as an overly confident and bold strategy, it's good form to offer your advice with great gentleness.

After observing several sessions, one of our trainees commented, "I can see you're using words that are easy for the parent to accept. Like, instead of saying 'Here's some homework,' you said, 'Here's something you might try.' And instead of saying you had advice or solutions, you said, 'I've got a few ideas that might be helpful.' I noticed you were tentative and gave suggestions instead of being bossy or offering formal advice."

Before you next work with parents, try out and try on some gentle and suggestive language. Compare, "You should try . . . " with "You might try . . . " and compare "I've got some advice for you" with "I've got a few ideas I'd like to share. Is it okay with you if I do that now?"

Use Storytelling   Hardly anything captures the challenges and solutions of parenting better than a good story. When working with parents of relentlessly persistent children, John likes to tell the following story.

Case: "How About Now, Mom? Can I Have It Now?"

One time I was at the grocery store and I saw a mom with three boys. The boys were about 8, 10, and 12 years old. Given how hard it is to navigate a grocery store with children, I immediately felt sympathy for her, but she seemed quite poised. The 8-year-old, in particular, had an amazingly intense look. The mom had purchased a specific "treat" for each child. As she stood with her purse open at the check-out line, the 8-year-old hovered over her and repeatedly asked, "Can I have my Milky Way now, Mom? Can I have my Milky Way now, Mom? Mom, can I have my Milky Way now? Can I have it now? How about now?" In response to each question, the mom calmly and patiently said, "No." Finally, when asked for what must have been the 10th time, the mom, trying to focus on paying for her groceries, finally used a powerful limit-setting technique. She said, "The answer is 'no' and if you ask me again, the Milky Way is mine." I was super-impressed.

As the mom paid for her groceries, the 8-year-old was silent. But I could almost see the wheels turning in his brain. Being an exceedingly persistent boy, I guessed he was mentally searching for a loophole to his mother's limit. After she paid, he pounced, using his new strategy. He got up next to her and asked, "How about when we get to the car, Mom? Can I have my Milky Way then? Can I have it in the car? Can I have it then, Mom?" Now, I was super-impressed with the 8-year-old. What an excellent example of relentless persistence.

In the end, my disappointment was that the mom let her 8-year-old have his loophole. She just responded, once again, with "No." And I heard them going back and forth while leaving the store. The boy was asking, "How about half of it, Mom? Can I have half of my Milky Way in the car? And the mom was responding again with "No . . . No . . . No."

The problem within this scenario is that whenever parents don't follow through with a clearly stated appropriate limit and reasonable consequence, the child learns something. In this case, he may have learned that it was acceptable for him to find loopholes around his mother's limits. This is, of course, a minor example and a relatively innocuous incident. But, as parents, we should try to make sure our children are not rewarded for wearing us down. This is no big deal if our goal is to reinforce them for wearing us down. But, if we want our children to actually listen when we set a limit and offer a consequence, then we really need to follow through on the consequence.

This story provides great grist for the parenting mill. If parents see themselves in the story, they may feel renewed motivation to not let their children wear them down. They may also understand the dynamic more clearly when they hear it described as happening to a third party. Either way, hearing stories that represent problems and stories that represent solutions can help activate the great internal force for positive change. If you work with parents and interact socially in the world, you will collect your own stories quite easily. It's important to keep a good collection handy.

We should note that in the preceding story the mother may have followed through on her promised consequence, but did so in the car—rather than in the grocery store where she knew her son might melt down in public. Additionally, the story is a great example of a strong and diligent mother. But in the end the lesson is that persistent children will quickly learn whether they can wear us down, and that's very important for parents of spirited children to understand.

Compliment the Parent and Affirm Previous Problem Resolution Attempts We discussed the importance of complimenting parents earlier, but as one of our friends repeatedly mentions, redundancy works. When it comes to activating the great internal drive for improvement, almost nothing works as well as a sincere and clearly articulated compliment. Unexpected compliments from authority figures are especially powerful; most parents don't expect a compliment from a mental health professional. Frequently we've observed, immediately after giving a compliment, a parent's response of: "Thank you. But I know I could be doing this better."

It's also important to acknowledge, affirm, and show empathy for previous problem resolution efforts. Comments like, "You've been working very hard at this" or "Most parents couldn't come up with as many different ideas for dealing with your daughter as you have" can increase parental interest in your advice and counsel. Of course, as with all compliments, you should never say them if you don't believe them.

Modify Your Recommendations Based on Interactive Feedback With Parents As you finish providing parenting recommendations and your session is moving toward its end, most parents will sit back, listen, and accept your recommendations.

However, in the spirit of Constance Fischer's and Stephen Finn's collaborative assessment model, which we alluded to earlier, rather than simply telling parents your advice, it's important to engage them in an interactive process (Fischer & Finn, 2008). You can use interactive questions like: "How does that sound to you?" or "Do you think this idea is a good fit for your situation?" Typically, parents will affirm that your recommendations sound good to them.

Occasionally, parents will interrupt as you're providing recommendations to clarify what you're saying or to question the usefulness of your recommendations. They may even directly and assertively tell you that your ideas don't sound good. In every case when this happens, you should double-back and revise or eliminate your recommendation. You can do this with a statement similar to the following:

> Good. Thanks. I'm glad you're telling me this strategy doesn't fit for you. How about we just cross it off the list?

Sometimes, deep philosophical differences will cause parents to disagree with your recommendations. This can even happen with what we consider one of the most universally appropriate, healthy, and relatively innocuous procedures of all: special time, described in the previous chapter (see Appendix B, Tip Sheet 7: Special Time). Parents can object to the idea that children will be the "boss." You can modify the instructions:

CONSULTANT: Oh. Okay. My apologies. I didn't mean for her to really be the boss . . . but just for her to take the lead in playing for about fifteen or twenty minutes. It can be a good experience for her to feel like she's in control and then for her to learn what it's like to shift back and forth. How about if you just said, "Salena, for the next twenty minutes I want us to play together and for you to show me what you would like to do."

For many reasons, some parents aren't comfortable giving up control—even if it's only for 15 minutes three times a week. If that's the case, simply back away from the language of the child as "boss" or "in charge" and go with language the parent can more easily tolerate. If you sense there's no language on the planet that could ever make special time an acceptable activity, just cross it off the list and thank the parent for making his or her preferences clear.

Sometimes parents will speak with open derision about positive reinforcement, referring to it as bribery and condemning it as an unacceptable strategy. In general, we advise against pushing back too forcefully against parents who take this stand. This is because parents who make these statements often have considered this issue for a long time and have strong and deep feelings against "rewarding my kid for doing something he should be doing anyway."

On the other hand, depending on your rapport with the parent, you might push back gently, only after accepting and embracing the parent's perspective.

Case: An Old-Fashioned Dad

PARENT: Maybe I'm old-fashioned, but I'm really not into all this bribery baloney. If I acted like kids do these days when I was young I'd have been picking myself back up off the floor. I think we're too easy on kids today. Why should I reward my kid for doing something he should be doing anyway?

JOHN S-F: You're making a great point and I agree with what you're saying about too much praise. In fact, there's a guy who wrote a book on this exact subject and he called it, *Punished by Rewards* [Kohn, 1993], because, as it turns out, giving kids too many rewards or rewards that are too big can actually reduce their internal motivation to do something. [John is using agreement or forced teaming to increase rapport and goal alignment and decrease resistance.]

PARENT: I'm glad I'm not the only one who thinks that.

JOHN S-F: You're not. I agree with you. In many ways we're too easy on our kids. But I guess I'm not a big fan of knocking kids down, either.

PARENT: Yeah, I didn't mean I thought *that* was a good idea. I just don't understand why things are so much different now. We never talked disrespectfully to our parents back then. They wouldn't stand for it.

JOHN S-F: I don't think you should stand for it, either. [Another strong agreement/ alignment.] So, let's focus on fixing two things about these recommendations. Let's come up with a very clear plan for exactly what you should do when your son speaks disrespectfully to you and let's come up with a way for you to be positive with him—without resorting to bribery or too many rewards.

In this example, John initially embraces the parent's position on excessive praise. Instead of arguing about the definition of *bribery* (which was especially tempting because it's one of John's favorite arguments), he finds common ground. Once he does that, the parent becomes more flexible, which is illustrated by the parent's positive response to John's mild confrontation on "knocking kids down."

Remembering that Parents Want to Change

The preceding strategies can activate parents' interest in and motivation to change their parenting behaviors for the better. But just in case your confidence in the great internal force for positive change is not yet established, we offer a quote from Kohn (2005) on human motivation:

> I once heard someone . . . declaring that "human nature is to do as little as necessary." This prejudice is refuted not just by a few studies but by the entire branch of psychology dealing with motivation. Normally, it's hard to stop happy, satisfied people from trying to learn more about themselves and the world, or from trying to do a job of which they can feel proud. The desire to do as little as possible is an aberration, a sign that something is [terribly] wrong. It may suggest that someone feels threatened and therefore has fallen back on a strategy of damage control, or that rewards and punishments have caused that individual to lose interest in what he's doing, or that he perceives a specific task—perhaps incorrectly—as pointless and dull. (p. 90)

One reason many different approaches to working with parents can be effective, including brief parenting intervention models, is because nearly all parents very much want to change for the better.

WRITING A PARENTING PRESCRIPTION AND CLOSING THE SESSION

Although we recommend that you begin formulating a parenting prescription (or list of ideas) early in every session, when you formally review it and physically offer it to parents you're typically signaling the beginning of a session's closing. This section reviews details associated with parenting prescriptions as well as activities linked to closing a session.

Writing the Prescription

Handing the "prescription" to parents is a critical component of our intervention model. In an initial evaluation of a brief parenting consultation model, on an open-ended qualitative measure, over 70 percent of parents reported that receiving "concrete ideas, strategies, and advice about behavior and communication" was a positive part of their experience (J. Sommers-Flanagan, 2007, p. 27). This finding has remained consistent in that parents almost always identify concrete ideas and advice as the most positive part of their educational or therapeutic experience. Recently, upon receiving a handwritten description of what parenting interventions to try during the ensuing week, a physician-parent smiled and said, "So, a written prescription, huh? Just like us. I like that."

Initially, we began writing parenting prescriptions as a memory aid. We noticed some parents came to their sessions with notepad and pen, ready to take notes, while others just sat and listened. As a consequence, we started taking notes and making lists with the idea of giving them, along with various tip sheets, to parents. Eventually, we recognized how much parents appreciated a copy of our in-the-moment recommendations. Also, having a photocopy of the recommendations given to parents provided an excellent guide and springboard for subsequent sessions. We now consider the parenting prescription or *list of ideas* an essential component of working effectively with parents. Although we could easily offer parents printed guidance and recommendations, the personal touch of handwritten advice seems important. After considering the terms *prescription* and *recommendations*, we settled on maintaining consistency in the gentleness of our language and now use the heading *list of ideas* at the top of our "prescription" pad (see the worksheet).

Tip Sheets and Homework Assignments (aka: Home Activities)

Tip sheets and homework assignments are alternative and overlapping strategies. They are extensions of advice-giving and designed to get parents to try or practice new and different parenting behaviors after the session has ended. To be effective, advice must be clear enough for parents to understand exactly what they should do differently. Tip sheets and homework assignments are efforts to clarify advice so it can be taken home and implemented. Although we refer to parent homework

Two Sample Prescriptions

Session-One Recommendations (Prescriptions)
for a Four-Year-Old Boy

Suzanne and Tom attended an initial parenting session to learn how to better cope with their 4-year-old son's "stubbornness and emotional meltdowns." They were both very engaged in the meeting and the following list of ideas was produced.

List of Ideas: Suzanne and Tim

1. Responding to Jimmy's temperament and mood:
   a. Be aware of the physical triggers for bad moods (hungry, tired, sick, or in physical discomfort or pain).
   b. "No" always stays "No" if Jimmy is angry or obnoxious.
   c. Monitor and supervise him and give feedback for positive and/or undesirable behavior.
2. Use mutual problem-solving (see Chapter 8, Parent Homework Assignment 8-3).
3. Use special time (see Appendix B, Tip Sheet 7).
4. Use surprise rewards (catch Jimmy being good and suddenly offer him a reward of attention, time, or something he likes . . . consider this a spontaneous family celebration).
5. Collaboratively identify (together) reasonable rewards and natural consequences. You might do this with Jimmy or just as parents. (The key here is for you two to have some ideas for what you can do before the tantrum or manipulative behavior starts. Keep it small and simple and easy to apply and make it fit for your family.)
6. Consider reading the book, *Raising Your Spirited Child*, by Mary Sheedy Kurcinka (1991).

Session-One Recommendations (Prescriptions)
for an Eight-Year-Old Girl

Molly was an adoptive parent of an 8-year-old girl. Molly immediately reported that her daughter was her "shining star" as well as the source of her deepest angst. At the time of the initial appointment, she indicated that she was feeling like "a complete failure as a parent . . . or at least pretty close to that." Molly was very verbal during the first 30 minutes of her session but as soon as the parenting professional indicated he was ready to offer suggestions, she settled in and listened attentively and enthusiastically. The following list was generated.

List of Ideas: Molly

1. Share control with your daughter whenever possible or reasonable.
2. Mutual problem-solving: Begin with "I hate it when we both get upset and start yelling at each other. Don't you?" (Then follow with Chapter 8's Parent Homework Assignment 8-3.)

(Continued)

3. Giving clear choices:
    a. "Here's your choice. . . . "
    b. "When would you like to clear off your desk—now, or in fifteen minutes?"
4. Acknowledge her control and honor her independence.
5. Character feedback: Try saying (only when you mean it):
    a. I love your spirit.
    b. I love who you are.
    c. You're the kind of girl who knows how to listen.
6. Find new ways to give her power/control and attention:
    • When a fight or conflict begins, try declaring: "I've decided to stop arguing. You can keep arguing if you want to, but I'm stopping." Then, step away from the situation and if she pursues you and tries to keep arguing, stop responding to her.
7. Check out the book, *Kids, Parents, and Power-Struggles*, by Mary Sheedy Kurcinka (2001).
8. Express empathy and set limits at the same time.
9. When she acts in an obnoxious or aggressive way, the answer to what she wants is "No."
10. Next time:
    a. How to respond when adoption questions come up.
    b. What are appropriate behavioral expectations for an 8-year-old?

assignments from here forward, as noted previously, when working directly with parents we tend not to use the words, "homework assignment." Instead, we find using less authoritarian words like "home activities" or "something for you to try out" is often more palatable for parents. However, we recognize that some parents may respond more to an authority-based directive like, "I want you to go home and do this homework and report back to me on how it worked!"

Providing Tip Sheets   The tip sheet process is fairly straightforward. We recommend that you peruse the tip sheets in Appendix B, as well as additional tip sheets and ancillary materials available online. You'll likely find yourself attracted to some tip sheets and use them liberally, while you avoid using others.

We believe in using tip sheets with parents, but recognize their limits. Tip sheets are particularly appropriate for motivated parents who speak English (or whatever language the tip sheets are printed in) as their first language. Even though our tip sheets are written at a 6th-through-8th-grade level, parents with limited educational background may have an aversive reaction to the written word. It's appropriate to offer tip sheets to all parents, but to be sensitive to the parent's reaction to an assignment that involves reading. Make sure you make it clear to the parent that reading the tip sheet is optional, not required. Tip sheets may be provided at the end of a session or electronically via email following the session.

Giving Homework or Home-Based Assignments   Giving parents homework is less straightforward and allows for more creativity. Generally, there are three main ways to give homework.

First, the homework can be directly issued by you, the expert, and follow a standardized format. This option is best if you have limited time or if you have a very direct personality. Some tip sheets double as homework assignments (see Appendix B, Tip Sheet 7, which includes a specific homework assignment). Another example of expert-generated homework is illustrated by John's advice to a parent in Chapter 7, where he tells a father to (a) tell your son, "I love you" every day; (b) hug him every day; and (c) do something fun with him once a week.

Second, parents sometimes generate assignments for themselves. The assignment may emerge from your discussion. For example, a parent might spontaneously say something like,

> I really think my son and I need to spend more time together.

After this comment, you can help the parent develop concrete plans for how to make it happen. You might follow with,

> What you said seems important. How do you suppose you two can make that happen?

These interactions contribute to a process where you and the parent work together to turn the parent's idea into a clear assignment (or prescription). This is an example of parents prescribing their own best medicine.

Third, sometimes you and a parent may collaboratively develop a unique home activity project or experiment. This approach may be the most effective, because it helps parents problem-solve, move beyond what hasn't worked, and feel ownership in the homework.

Although the home activity is formulated collaboratively, initially you may need to lead parents toward a collaborative brainstorming and problem-solving approach. For example, if you want to help parents contribute to generating ideas for how to handle it when their children lie, the following nine questions might stimulate new and potentially helpful strategies:

1. "When is your child most likely to lie to you?"
2. "When is your child most likely to tell you the truth?"
3. "Is there anything you do that seems to help your child be more honest?"
4. "Is there anything you do that seems to make it more likely that your child will lie to you?"
5. "What are some ways that other parents you know handle their children's lies?"
6. "Have you tried any consequences for lying or any rewards for truth-telling?"
7. "In your heart, what worries you most about your child's lying? Have you ever sat down and shared these fears with your child?"

8. "In your heart, what do you hope for most from or for your child? Have you shared that?"
9. "Think hard about yourself. Do you ever tell any lies in front of your child?"

Scheduling Follow-Up Contacts

Whether you're working in an individual or group modality, it may be appropriate—or expected—that there will be follow-up contacts. It's also perfectly acceptable to conduct single, stand-alone parenting therapy or consultation sessions with no expectation of a second appointment. Published data and years of anecdotal reports indicate that many parents feel good about this model (J.Sommers-Flanagan, 2007). However, when faced with complex parenting situations or when you or the parents believe it may be helpful, two or more individual or group sessions can provide greater depth and clarity. Many different multisession therapy and consultation models are discussed in the literature and can be used in conjunction with the principles and strategies described in this book (Bitter, 2004; Bratton, Landreth, Kellam, & Blackard, 2006; Sheridan & Kratochwill, 2008).

At present, our general practice has been to work with parents using a brief, two-session model with additional sessions scheduled as needed. Depending on your setting, you may have time limits or much more freedom. When we follow our two-session format, the second session is usually scheduled at the conclusion of the initial session. Unless factors dictate otherwise, we generally schedule session 2 about three to six weeks following session one. Our rationale is that this gives parents time to implement and evaluate ideas suggested in session 1. Most parents are happy to wait a month for their second appointment—acknowledging that it's useful to have time to try out the suggestions.

When a second session is part of the plan, we typically write the day, date, and time of the second session on the list of ideas given to parents at the end of session 1. The purpose is to increase return rates. This approach can be modified for groups, using preprinted homework or appointment cards. We've also found that reminder calls can be helpful. This may be because parents are especially busy or because our culture now includes routine reminder calls for medical and dental appointments, and so there is a growing expectation that professionals will call clients or patients to remind them of upcoming appointments.

Reflection and Self-Evaluation for Parenting Professionals

After closing an individual or group session, mental health and human services providers should engage in reflective activities. These activities are designed to evaluate our effectiveness or outcomes. Several approaches for evaluating parent therapy or consultation outcomes are available.

Standardized Questionnaires or Inventories   Many parent-focused questionnaires or inventories for evaluating parenting intervention effectiveness exist.

These include the Parenting Stress Index (Loyd & Abidin, 1985); the Parenting Sense of Competence Scale (Ohan, Leung, & Johnston, 2000); and others. Additionally, it may be appropriate to administer questionnaires to parents, teachers, or other caregivers in order to evaluate child behavior within and outside of the home (e.g., the Behavior Assessment System for Children; Merenda, 1996; Reynolds & Kamphaus, 2002; the Achenbach Child Behavior Checklist; Achenbach & Edelbrock, 1978; Greenbaum, Dedrick, & Lipien, 2004).

Satisfaction Ratings   Although satisfaction ratings have been criticized in the scientific literature, they may still provide individual practitioners with useful information (Pekarik & Wolff, 1996; Pekarik & Guidry, 1999). For example, in our research (as well as other satisfaction rating research) the norm is for parents to provide very high satisfaction ratings. Therefore, if you use a 5-point Likert-scale satisfaction measure (see Appendix C), you should always expect average ratings of at least 4 or 5. If you're not consistently obtaining high satisfaction ratings, you should obtain qualitative feedback from parents to determine why they perceive your services as less than highly satisfactory.

The Counselor Reflection Inventory   To help determine how closely your pre-session and in-session behaviors match the general approach described in this book, Appendix C includes a post-consultation-session *Consultant Reflection Inventory (CRI)*. This instrument can be reviewed prior to an initial individual or group session and then completed immediately at the session's conclusion. The CRI is primarily a teaching tool, but is also currently being evaluated as a potential outcomes predictor.

Concluding Comments

Single-session approaches to working with parents can feel jam-packed with tasks and activities, but such is the nature of brief interventions. If you're working from a brief individual model, advice-giving should signal the beginning of the closing of a parenting therapy or consultation session, even though it may begin 20 to 25 minutes or more before the session ends. The primary purpose of advice-giving is to encourage parents to experiment with new (and hopefully better) parenting approaches. To facilitate advice-giving, this chapter describes a number of approaches, including tip sheets and homework assignments (or home activity projects).

If you've educated individual parents on what to expect during their professional contact, they will probably understand that when you (a) ask them for permission to share ideas; (b) begin writing down specific intervention ideas; and (c) begin interactively sharing these ideas, you're heading down the home stretch. Then, because everything you discuss related to the next session is listed on the "prescription" (including the session's date and time), the actual mechanics of ending the session are minimal and you are free to wish parents the very best in their plans to try some new ways of being.

Checklist for Providing Guidance, Advice, and Solutions

- ☐ Remember to never blame the parent for rejecting your advice.
- ☐ Identify and align with the great internal force for positive change.
- ☐ Use principles and strategies from Chapters 3 and 4 to resonate with parents' positive intentions.
- ☐ As you listen, express empathy, and formulate the problem, clearly and legibly begin writing down your intervention ideas.
- ☐ Before offering advice, ask permission.
- ☐ Offer suggestions using an experimental attitude and mindset.
- ☐ Use tentative and gentle language.
- ☐ Use storytelling.
- ☐ Compliment the parent and affirm previous problem-solving efforts.
- ☐ Modify your recommendations based on interactive feedback from parents.
- ☐ If you're planning additional sessions, write the date and time and topics to be discussed during the second or next session on the "prescription."
- ☐ Hand the prescription to the parent.
- ☐ Provide tip sheets or home activity projects as appropriate.
- ☐ Reflect on and evaluate the parent intervention outcomes.

PART THREE

Practical Techniques for Parenting Challenges

So far, this book's primary focus has been on how to develop a therapeutic relationship with parents and how to interact in positive and constructive ways during counseling or consultation sessions. In Part Three, the focus shifts to very specific techniques and strategies that practitioners can teach to parents. The goal of these techniques and strategies is to help parents become sources of positive influence in their children's lives. Part Three includes five chapters focusing on relationship power, indirect and problem-solving power, direct power, ongoing issues and complications in working with parents, and special situations.

CHAPTER SEVEN

Teaching Relationship-Based Interventions to Parents

Barbara Coloroso, a well-known parenting expert, often emphasizes how important it is for parents to have and show empathy for their children's challenges. She makes a case for her perspective in her (1995) parenting book titled, *Kids Are Worth It*:

> *If I wouldn't want to be slapped across the face, why would I slap my son? If I wouldn't want to be screamed at when I made a mistake, why would I scream at my daughter when she dropped the cake I had decorated for my mother-in-law? If I wouldn't want to be ridiculed when I attempted to learn to roller-blade at age 43, why would I ridicule my daughter as she jerked the car out of first gear into second after being shown ten times how to do it smoothly? If I wouldn't want my gardening skills to be compared with my neighbor's, why would I compare my son's math performance with his older sisters'? (p. 14)*

Coloroso is making the case that parent–child relationships work best when parents put themselves in their children's shoes and then treat their children in ways they would want to be treated themselves. In her book she educates parents about the facilitative power of empathy—which brings us back to a central person-centered therapy theme (Rogers, 1961).

Early in this book we emphasized that *an empathic, accepting, and collaborative relationship between human services professionals and parents* facilitates positive parenting attitude and behavior change. Additionally, in Chapter 3 we claimed that *a respectful and high-quality relationship between parent and child* functions as a *foundation for parental influence*.

Empathy is as close as we can get to a universal relationship enhancer. When in distress, empathy is what we look for from our friends, our family, and professionals. Empathy is the foundation for positive practitioner–parent relationships and parent–child relationships.

This chapter focuses on empathic, relationship-based interventions that practitioners can use with individual parents or as content in small or large parent education groups. As we have emphasized throughout: When parents feel understood (empathy), they're more likely to be understanding (empathic) with their children. Secondarily, as Coloroso implies, when children feel understood, they're more likely to experience positive growth and development.

INTERVENTIONS AND SOLUTIONS

The interventions, techniques, and homework assignments in this chapter and online tip sheets linked to this chapter have a common goal: To provide parents with ways to improve the quality of their parent–child relationship. These relationship-facilitating interventions may help parents develop solutions to parenting challenges regardless of whether the parenting problem is very general (e.g., "I have a strong-willed child!") or very specific (e.g., "My child is three and he's not potty-trained and it's driving me crazy").

Teaching Special Time and Non-Directive Play

Due to our emphasis on relationships as a driving force underlying positive change, special time has been mentioned in examples previously, but we cover it again here for two reasons.

First, special time is both an activity and a concept. As an activity, decades of research and clinical practice have shown that children obtain benefits from non-directive play interactions (Landreth, 2002; Webster-Stratton & Reid, 2003, 2010). Consequently, up to this point, we've focused on special time as a non-directive play interaction. However, special time is also conceptual. Even parents who are unable or unwilling to engage in child-directed play usually understand that special time also represents the idea of simply making time and expending effort to be with their child on a regular basis. This is what most people mean when they talk about quality time; virtually all parents understand that their children, no matter what age, can benefit from individualized time with Mom, Dad, or other important caregivers.

Second, previously we focused on special time as a non-directive or child-directed play activity appropriate for children 10 years old or younger. In this section, we focus on special time with older children.

Case: "That Dog Don't Hunt"

John reports the following case example:

Many years ago I worked with a 15-year-old boy (Michael) in therapy. Michael's mother had brought him to therapy. After two sessions, it became clear that Michael had a difficult, conflicted, and hostile relationship with his father (Bert). Unfortunately, Bert was uninterested in therapy and so I continued meeting with Michael alone for a few sessions.

Four weeks into therapy, I was contacted by Michael's mother. Michael was scheduled for an Individualized Education Plan (IEP) meeting at his school and she hoped I could attend. She wanted school personnel to hear a therapeutic perspective. Michael agreed to the plan and so I went to the meeting.

Somewhat surprisingly, Bert was also at the IEP and so I had a chance to introduce myself. Before the meeting, several of us were milling around the hall. I decided to try to connect with him—my underlying motive was to see if I could make the idea of a father–son relationship therapy session more appealing. We chitchatted awkwardly. I made a point of sitting next to him in the meeting.

Twelve people were present (including Michael, his mother, his father, and me). After about 10 minutes discussing Michael's academic performance, I decided to ask Michael a projective question in front of the group. I asked, "Michael, what if you did really well on a big test, whom would you tell first?" Without hesitation Michael said, "My dad, my mom, and Mrs. Finney" (Mrs. Finney was the Special Education teacher).

I was delighted with Michael's answer. It was a perfect chance to encourage Bert to join us in therapy. I turned to Bert (who had been silent to this point) and said, "I noticed Michael said you would be the first person he told about his test. You must be incredibly important to him and so I'd like to invite you to meet with Michael and me for a therapy session."

Bert put his hand on my shoulder and gave me a shove. He then went on a verbal tirade for about three minutes where he rather disjointedly accused school personnel of failing his son. Everyone sat stunned until finally, Bert swiveled back to me and said, "I'll come up there for therapy. I've done it before in my life and I'll do it again!"

At that point, I wished I could turn back to him and say, "Um, nope. Never mind. That offer is officially retracted."

The next week, Michael and Bert arrived at my office, but refused to sit in the same room at the same time because they weren't speaking to each other. I met with them separately. When alone, Michael made it perfectly clear—as adolescents are so capable of doing—that he had no intention of ever speaking to his father again. End of conversation.

I had even less hope for my meeting with Bert. He was initially irritable, but surprised me with his dedication to Michael's well-being. I actively listened for a while, empathizing with his frustration and his hopes and wishes for Michael to be more successful. He also discussed his high expectations and how he forcefully was pushing Michael to work harder and smarter. Michael was flunking every class at his high school. This was my chance to see Michael's father as something other than just an angry guy. He also quickly admitted, "I'm no perfect father," which I appreciated.

Eventually I began using validation and reassurance. I told Bert I thought it was "great" that he had high expectations. I added that I thought Michael was lucky to have a father who cared about him enough to come talk with me. Then I provided Bert with relationship-enhancement advice based on special-time principles. The following is a paraphrased therapy dialogue.

JOHN: I think it's great that you have high expectations for Michael. You should keep those high expectations.

FATHER (BERT): All right.

JOHN: But I think you should also add three new things to the mix.

FATHER: That's okay. That dog don't hunt anyway. [This was taken to mean that the father's high expectations, in and of themselves, weren't working to improve the situation.]

JOHN: Great. Do you love your son?

FATHER: [Nodding] Yes.

JOHN: Then, every day, I want you to say to him, "I love you."

FATHER: Uh, yeah. Usually I leave that to the wife.

JOHN: Okay. But can you do it?

FATHER: Yes, I can.

JOHN: Second, every day, I want you to touch your son in a gentle and loving way.

FATHER: You mean like giving him a hug?

JOHN: That would work.

FATHER: All right. Usually I leave that to the wife, too, but I can do it.

JOHN: And third, at least once a week, I want you to take time to do something with Michael that he really enjoys. Not necessarily something you enjoy, but something he enjoys.

FATHER: That's easy. He likes four-wheeling. We can go four-wheeling together.

JOHN: Okay. Try these three things and keep your high expectations and we'll see what happens.

FATHER: All right. I can do that.

My session with Michael's father ended and he thanked me for meeting with him. Michael grudgingly left the waiting room to ride home with his dad.

The next afternoon I received a telephone call from Michael's mother. She said:

> I don't know what you did or what you said, but it's amazing, they're talking again. And this morning, when they were in the kitchen and I was in the next room, I thought I heard them hug. And then, when Michael walked out to go to school, I saw there were tears streaming down his face.

This case is the best anecdote we have for the effectiveness of special time, tailored for a particular family. John gave Bert three simple tasks—all of which were designed to help communicate love and connection to his son. To his credit, Bert was able to accept the advice and implement it with his very challenging teenage son.

This case also helps us remember that even the most edgy, cranky parents love their children, and often they're trying, without success, to be a positive influence. Sometimes, the most important guidance these parents need is direct information on how to shift from a negative and nagging relationship to a relationship where their love and affection becomes clear and unquestionable. In the end, Michael didn't transform from a straight-F student to a straight-A student. But six months later his father and mother reported significant academic and relationship improvement.

Broadly formulated, special time is a communication of love and interest. Whether taking place through child-centered play (as with younger children), or through quality time with older children, it honors children with intentional positive attention. When parents engage in special time, they're sending the message: "You're important to me and I love you. I love you so much that I'm dropping everything else to be with you. Right now, there is no place I'd rather be than spending this time with you." This is a powerful and healing message. As we stressed earlier, in Covey's (1990) terms, this technique involves parents making deposits in their parent–child relationship bank account.

Special-Time Homework   As in the preceding example, special-time or quality-time homework is often clear, directive, and standardized. The special-time tip sheet includes a home-based assignment and is in Appendix B.

However, a more collaborative approach to creating a special-time assignment is also possible. For example, if you think special or quality time between parent and child might be useful and you're not convinced you want to go with a standardized homework assignment, you might ask some of the following questions:

1. "What do you and your daughter do for fun together?"
2. "When do you and your son find yourselves enjoying each other?"
3. "What would be a fun or interesting activity for you and your child to do together?"
4. "What does your daughter like to do?"
5. "Do you play any family games together?"
6. "Describe for me the last time you and your son had lots of fun together."

As you ask these questions and listen to the answers, you may find information to help you develop an individualized parent–child homework assignment.

Case: "I Want to Spend More Time with You"

In a recent session, a parenting consultant collaboratively developed a relationship-enhancing intervention.

PARENT: I think you're saying that my teenage daughter and I should spend more quality time together. But the problem is that she doesn't want to spend time with me. She ignores me. She only wants to spend time with her friends.

CONSULTANT: That's a good point. Lots of parents say exactly what you're saying. Sometimes it doesn't seem like teenagers want any time at all with their parents. And although that's partly true, it's still important for parents to stay as connected as possible to their teens. Can I share some ideas about this with you?

PARENT: Sure. If you've got ideas about how to get my daughter interested in spending more time with me, I'm all ears.

CONSULTANT: Let's think about this together. One idea that's worked for some parents is to completely let go of your emotional reactions to being rejected. For example, I've had parents decide to offer, every day, to do something fun with their teenager. And, pretty much every day, the teen says "No thanks," or rolls her eyes and says something like, "Mom, that's totally uncool."

PARENT: Yeah, I can relate to that.

CONSULTANT: What I'm suggesting is that the offer is as important as the acceptance. You just make a relationship connection offer a daily routine and you plan on your daughter saying no. The key is to just keep trying, but to not worry when your daughter says no . . . because it's the message that you *want* to spend time with her that will eventually sink in and help improve your relationship.

PARENT: Okay. Maybe I can just ask her to do things, but what should I ask her to do?

CONSULTANT: What sorts of things do you sometimes do together?

PARENT: Once in a while we cook together, but that's about it. It only happens if she's in a really good mood or if I force her to cook with me.

CONSULTANT: That's great. Does she have any favorite foods?

PARENT: Yeah. She likes pizza and she likes to go out for Mexican.

CONSULTANT: How about this? Every day you ask her to do something. Sometimes you just say something like, "Hey, I'm free this afternoon if you want to do something" and other times you say things like, "I'm thinking of trying out a recipe for breakfast burritos, would you like to help?" Or ask her if she wants to try out making homemade pizza . . . or if she wants to go out with you for lunch at a Mexican place on Saturday afternoon.

PARENT: Okay. I like these ideas.

CONSULTANT: Now . . . the key is to never feel hurt or to use guilt or anything if she says no. Just be perky and say, "No problem, I'd love to spend time with you, but I know you're busy" and drop it. On the other hand, if you need her to do something, like help cook a meal, it's different; then you just tell her, "I need your help on this," and build the expectation that she'll participate. It's important not to confuse these options. If you want to require something together, do that. But the rest of the time make sure she knows she has a choice and let her accept or reject your offer and then accept her response.

PARENT: I can try that. How long and how often should I do this?

CONSULTANT: It's reasonable to do it every day for two weeks just to break the idea in. She'll wonder what's up and you can just flatly say, "I decided I want to spend more time with you" and leave it at that. No manipulation. Just say what you're wanting and keep with it. After the first two weeks you can spread it out more, but even if it's never successful, you'll be giving her a message that you value her and she won't be able to miss that message.

In this example, the consultant does nearly all the work, but the parent provides crucial information that gives the homework assignment a greater chance for success. The goal of a collaborative homework development process is to have the parent leave your office thinking, "That's a good idea" or "That's a good fit for me and my family."

Parent Homework Assignment 7-1

Creating Special Family Times

Special time for families can be formal (as described in Tip Sheet 7) or less formal. This homework assignment is for parents who want to work on creating spontaneous special time for family connection.

Idea 1: **Be a keen observer of what your child loves.** This can be as simple as noticing when and why your child smiles. If you watch for these happy or joyful moments, you'll undoubtedly be able to generate ideas for how to help create more happiness and joy.

Idea 2: **Ask yourself some questions to get even more in touch with how you might create more special times.** These questions might include:

1. "What do you and your child naturally do for fun together?"
2. "When do you and your child find yourselves enjoying each other?"
3. "What would be a fun or interesting activity that you and your child could do together?"
4. "What does your child like to do on his or her own or with his or her friends?" "Is it possible for you to be involved in any of these . . . even as a supportive person to create the situation?"
5. "Do you play any family games together with your child?"
6. "What did you do for fun when you were younger?" "Is there any way to smoothly (without big expectations) introduce your child to something you love to do?" (for example, playing cards, fly-fishing, second-hand shopping, arts and crafts, etc.)

Idea 3: **Sometimes when your child seems to need your time and attention, drop everything and focus on your child.** Although it's not healthy for you to "be there" for your child and cater to his or her every desire, it's important to occasionally stop whatever you're doing to give your child your undivided attention. This might involve turning off the television, closing your laptop, putting down the newspaper, or powering down your telephone. The point is that you want to, at least occasionally, give your child the clear message that she or he is your number one priority. This message will help you put a deposit in your child's emotional bank account.

Idea 4: **Speak up about your positive feelings.** It's not unusual to forget to consistently express your love for your child. As a consequence, you should try to say "I love you" to your child on a regular basis. However, perhaps even more important are spontaneous statements about how you "like" your child. Try that out. When you see something you like in your child's personality or behavior, just say, "I like who you are" or "I like it when you do that." Interestingly, saying you like your child can convey even more important meaning to

(Continued)

them than saying "I love you." In addition, be clear about wanting to spend time with your child by saying things like, "I want to spend some time with you," and then scheduling it if you need to.

These are four simple ideas for creating special time in your family. Take a minute to think about these ideas and then improve on them by creating new and better ideas that fit your family and help you intentionally have more fun and more special times together.

HELPING PARENTS DEAL WITH THEIR ANGER

Parental anger, or more accurately, *angry parent behavior*, is a factor that erodes parent–child relationship quality. Angry parent behavior can involve scolding, hitting, insults, and other verbal and physical behaviors.

Angry parent behavior is difficult to modify. Typically, parents need substantial motivation to change anger-generated behavior patterns. Similar to methods for limit-setting with children, we try to help parents create a clear and simple plan for dealing with their anger more effectively.

Often parents express dismay with their repeated negative interactions with their children. Parents report that, despite their best intentions, they can't stop themselves from criticizing, yelling, and sometimes hitting their children. In these situations, parents often feel their anger rising and yet also feel unable to constructively contain it.

Our approach to dealing with this problem is, not surprisingly, to lead with empathy and validation. Anger is a normal reaction to many parenting challenges, and one most of us have experienced. After offering an empathic ear, we help parents build a new plan for dealing with future anger. No doubt, they'll be feeling it again, perhaps very soon. Finally, we encourage parents to take ownership of and practice their new plan. Old habits die hard. New ways of being require practice and determination.

Case: "I Think She Likes Yelling"

In this case, the consultant is working with a couple to address parenting issues, and the mother discloses that she finds herself yelling too often at her two young (ages 6 and 8 years) children.

MOTHER (NAN): I try very hard not to yell, but I can't seem to stop myself.

FATHER (ED): She does yell a lot. I think sometimes she likes to yell.

MOTHER: [Glares at husband]

CONSULTANT: Hang on a second. Ed, I know you're saying what it looks like to you, but I don't think that captures what it feels like to Nan on the inside. Most parents tell me that yelling happens when they feel desperation. My guess is that Nan doesn't enjoy yelling, but that sometimes she wants so badly to get the kids to listen that she yells out of desperation and tries to get them to cooperate. It probably doesn't feel enjoyable. [This is a risky, but necessary, confrontation and reframe.]

MOTHER: That's exactly right.

FATHER: Okay. You're probably right. It just looks that way to me sometimes.

CONSULTANT: And as you've both said, Nan is with the kids more often, and the parent who's with the kids more is often the biggest target for defiance. With all that in mind, I've got some ideas about how Nan might start feeling a little more control over her yelling and get a little more cooperation from the kids.

MOTHER: That would be great.

FATHER: I agree.

CONSULTANT: Another thing that's important to remember is that it's humanly impossible to never feel angry toward our children. Anger is normal and natural. Usually we feel anger when we care deeply about something. Nan, you'll feel angry again and probably soon, so a big part of this involves making a plan for how to deal with it when it comes up, because it will.

In this case, it was obvious that Nan felt out of control and Ed was feeling a bit smug or superior. The glare that Nan directed toward him when he volunteered his theory about her yelling was blistering. However, rather than drifting into marital conflict, the consultant moved through the conflict using empathy, reframing, and universalization, and by giving both parents new words to describe why Nan was yelling. To do this it was pointed out that yelling is a natural behavior that emanates from desperation and anger, and not from personal enjoyment.

The second key part of this intervention involves helping parents make a new plan.

CONSULTANT: It's important to remember that you'll be angry again. You can't stuff your angry feelings and say and do nothing, so you need a new plan for exactly what you'll do next time your children misbehave. You can't just decide to stop yelling. Most of us tried that and it doesn't work very well. You need something else to do instead. Does that make sense?

PARENTS: Yes.

CONSULTANT: Nan, this new and improved plan is all about you and only a little about your children. It should be a plan you feel good about and have a chance of enacting successfully. Your child's misbehavior may or may not continue. You just need to do something different. What possibilities come to mind for you?

The consultant is using a solution-focused "Do something different" task and, while doing so, can engage one or both parents in a problem-solving process. In particular, the consultant is thinking in the back of her mind about ways Ed might be supportive by being available when Nan calls for his help (like tag-team wrestling). Additionally, this is a time when the consultant might share a brief personal story about how he effectively dealt with yelling (as long as the story is compassionate and joining, not condescending, and offers hope for positive change; see online resources at http://www.familiesfirstmontana.org/ for John's favorite yelling story).

The third part of this intervention involves making a plan to practice the new plan.

CONSULTANT: Okay. Now you both came up with ideas about what Nan might do to deal with her anger instead of yelling. Having good ideas is important, but ideas won't magically cause less yelling. It's really hard to stop yelling. Sometimes that's because your kids are so used to it that they'll automatically keep misbehaving until you yell—because that's the established pattern. Because of that, unless you think it through mentally by imagining exactly what you will do and practice the behavior physically (with a friend or with Ed), you may quickly return to yelling because that's what you all know best. Which of these new alternatives to yelling could you two practice together?

In this case it will be critical for Ed to support Nan as she experiments with alternatives to yelling. Like many spouses, he will need to be coached on what to say and do. Most importantly, he'll need to agree to refrain from criticism and to notice and comment on her progress (as long as that's okay with Nan), because his current attitude is likely contributing to Nan's anger and yelling. Getting a commitment from Ed should be conducted in a direct and positive manner.

CONSULTANT: Ed, can I be completely straight with you?
ED: Uh, yeah. Sure.
CONSULTANT: For couples, it's always easier if both people make changes. I know Nan's yelling is completely her responsibility. But, at the same time, you have the power to make this situation better or worse. If you just stand back and let Nan sink or swim, in a way, you'll be contributing to the yelling. If you support her, if you take your share of time with the kids when she needs you, if you tell her you love her and how great she's doing, you'll be contributing to the solution. It's really up to you. Can you step up here?

As with all interventions, the exact wording needs to be your own. Our tone may seem too direct and confrontational. However, if you do brief work with parents, you'll need to find the right words for talking with parents in a way that engages them in the change process. In fact, we've found that parents, especially fathers, appreciate a brief, respectful, and direct approach that acknowledges their power within the family system and challenges them to contribute to a healthier and happier family.

In the end, Ed agreed to take complete responsibility for the kids three times a week so Nan could go to the gym and work out. They also agreed to sharing the bedtime ritual more equally, because being on her own to put the children to bed was annoying Nan. For her part, Nan agreed to develop a monitoring system for her anger and to take a break on her own (if Ed wasn't home) or to ask Ed to step in and take over the parenting responsibilities. Ed agreed to step in when Nan made the request.

Homework for Parents With Angry Behaviors   Similar to clients with substance abuse problems, parents struggling with anger, yelling, or aggressive behaviors may respond defensively when these issues come up. You need to use your therapeutic skills to normalize or universalize parental anger. Saying something like the following can help: "I want to tell you that if you find yourself getting angry with your child, you're not alone. Many parents tell me about being surprised and shocked at the anger they can feel toward their children."

As noted with Nan and Ed, making a new plan for dealing constructively with anger is essential. One method for making this point is to tell a story about yourself or other parents who successfully managed to reduce their destructive angry responses. Several storytelling examples are included online at http://www.families firstmontana.org/.

Anger-related homework for parents can be standardized or developed from your educational or therapeutic session. A sample anger homework assignment is included in Parent Homework Assignment 7-2.

Parent Homework Assignment 7-2

Sample Anger Management Homework

We give the following assignment to parents interested in controlling or managing their anger.

Step 1: ***Before starting, make a clear commitment.*** Think about it. Do you really want to express your anger differently? If so, make a list of the top five or ten reasons why you want to change your anger behaviors. Also, make a list of the benefits you'll experience from changing this behavior.

Step 2: ***Get curious before you get furious.*** Take time to contemplate the "buttons" or "triggers" that, when pushed or pulled, result in an angry reaction. Draw some big buttons on a sheet of paper and label them. Common parent buttons include: (a) child disobedience, (b) children having a "smart mouth," (c) children who lag behind when you're in a hurry. Try to identify a reasonably long list of the main child behaviors that trigger your anger. Remember, when it comes to dealing with anger constructively, knowledge is power.

Step 3: ***Identify the signs and symptoms of your increasing anger.*** Some people say they become angry very quickly and that it's hard to identify the signs. This may be the case for you. If so, study your anger patterns and ask for feedback from someone who knows you well. Your anger signals may include (a) feeling hot; (b) muscular tension; or (c) thinking angry thoughts. The purpose of knowing your anger signs is so you can begin derailing the process as soon as possible.

Step 4: ***Think prevention and self-care.*** We're all more likely to get angry when stressed or when short on sleep. For some parents, prevention will help you move from having anger flareups to anger sparks. Prevention ideas include:
- Regular time to work out at home or at the gym (e.g., yoga, dance, or kickboxing)
- Hot baths or hot-tubbing

(Continued)

- A regular date night for Mom and Dad
- Getting a therapeutic massage
- Regular meditation

Many other self-care strategies are available. Make your own best prevention and self-care list and then incorporate your unique self-care strategies into your life on a regular basis.

Step 5: **Make an excellent plan for what you want to do instead of engaging in negative anger behaviors.** Excellent plans are specific, clear, and easy to immediately implement. For example, you might decide—because music is a natural emotional shifter—that you'll take a three-minute break to listen to one of your favorite calming songs if you feel yourself getting angry. To accomplish this, it will help to have a preplanned statement to make ("Daddy needs a quick break") and a prerecorded playlist on your iPod or other music device to immediately listen to.

Step 6: **Practice your plan.** The best-laid plans aren't likely to happen unless you practice them. Brain research suggests that whatever we practice (even as adults) generates changes in our brains to make us better at whatever we're practicing (Jenkins, Merzenich, Ochs, Allard, & Guic-Robles, 1990). This also makes good common sense. Whether you repeatedly bite your fingernails or repeatedly get very angry and yell, you've developed neural pathways in your brain that make these patterns more likely. The best way to address this neural pattern is to develop a new neural pattern by practicing new anger behaviors. For example, if your plan is to use your spouse as a partner and for one of you to tag the other when you get too stressed and need a break, don't just say, "How about if we tag each other when we're stressed?" Instead, say it and then physically practice it like you're preparing to perform in an upcoming drama production. It will feel silly, but practicing or rehearsing is one of the best ways to change an undesirable repeating behavior pattern.

Step 7: **Reward yourself.** Many people make the mistake of thinking they should be able to change pesky, habitual behavior patterns solely on the basis of willpower. If that were the case, most of us would be practically perfect. Instead of completely relying on willpower, develop a reward system for yourself. For example, if you make it an hour or a day or a week without an undesirable anger explosion, give yourself a reward. Your reward can be as simple as thinking a positive thought ("I'm doing very well at this"), or a much more elaborate system of awarding yourself points for handling life's challenges calmly and taking them away when you blow up. If you have a spouse or romantic partner, the two of you can develop a program for supporting and rewarding each other. Self-behavior management is one of the best uses for behavioral techniques.

Helping Parents Honor Their Children's Emotions

A social worker friend of ours who frequently works with children and families in schools has a wonderful perspective on children's emotions. He explains this perspective to parents (usually slowly and with great deliberation):

> You should remember that the door to your children's emotions locks from the inside. This means your child can lock you completely out of his or her emotional life. If you pound at the door or try to break the door down to get at your child's private inner feelings, you can guess what's likely to happen. You may break down the door, but there will be damage. And next time your child might lock her or his feelings up in a safe . . . and you won't be given the combination. The best you can do if you want to know your child's deep feelings is to consistently and gently knock at his or her emotional door. You can let your child know, "Hey, I'm out here. I'd love to hear what you're feeling." But that's about it. Your best strategy is to be a safe and kind parent who regularly expresses interest in what your child is feeling. Then, once the trust is strong, one day you may notice the door to your child's emotions is opening up a crack now and then. Or, sometimes, you'll notice the door flying open and powerful and hard emotional words come rushing out. When that happens it's especially important to listen respectfully and let your child feel what she or he is feeling. (M. Perry, MSW, May 17, 2001, personal communication)

We like to think that most parents want to listen to and understand their children's thoughts and feelings. However, there are some parents who aren't especially interested in listening and some situations that make it harder to focus on listening to children. One such situation, described next, is the stepfamily situation.

Stepparents are a population that requires special knowledge and training. In this section we use a sample consultation dialogue to accomplish two goals: (a) illustrate an intervention designed to help parents (and stepparents) honor their children's emotions, and (b) review common stepparenting myths and realities.

Case: Addressing Stepparenting Myths

Many informational resources for stepparents are available in bookstores and on the Internet (Pickhardt, 2010; Sommers-Flanagan, Elander, & Sommers-Flanagan, 2000). These resources frequently emphasize step-parenting myths—principally because many stepparents enter into their new role with dysfunctional misconceptions. Educational materials about stepparenting myths can motivate stepparents to acquire new knowledge and expectations as they enter into new family roles. The following consultation scenario illustrates some of these destructive myths (see also Appendix B, Tip Sheet 8: Stepfamily Guidelines).

This excerpt includes Samantha (biological mom) and Rex (stepdad-to-be) talking about adjustments associated with Samantha's biological daughters (Maggie, age 14; Kirsten, age 11).

SAMANTHA: We're getting married soon and my children aren't handling it well.
CONSULTANT: What's been going on?
SAMANTHA: They're totally cold and impolite toward Rex . . . even though I've told them this is the way it's gonna be.

CONSULTANT: So it's clear that you two are in love, but your children aren't so keen on the idea of having a "stepdad" in the house. [The consultant is using empathic reflection and framing the issue.]

REX: Yeah. They're making it pretty obvious that I'm not welcome or wanted. I've been trying not to be defensive about it. The other day, when Maggie (the 14-year-old) sneered and rolled her eyes at the idea of us doing a family outing, I told her it hurt my feelings and she just rolled her eyes again.

SAMANTHA: So I sent her to her room and told her we wouldn't tolerate that.

CONSULTANT: That sounds really hard. I imagine it does hurt your feelings quite a lot to be rejected by these kids, especially because you're trying so hard to be loving and kind and friendly and all that. [Rather than jumping in with educational information, the consultant focuses on empathy—empathy attuned to Rex's efforts, not his behaviors.]

REX: Yeah. That's about right.

CONSULTANT: And then, as their mother, it must be really frustrating to see them so unsupportive of the guy you love and will be marrying. [This is empathy directed to Samantha, because both parents need to feel a connection with the consultant.]

SAMANTHA: It's frustrating. I know in my head why they're doing it. Rex and I have been off and on for years and I've complained to them about him, but now we've been working in our couples counseling and things are going well, but they still don't trust him to stay with us. [Mom spontaneously gives her *best explanation* for her daughters' misbehavior.]

CONSULTANT: Even though you're aware of why they might be slow to warm back up to Rex, it still feels frustrating. [Another reflection.]

SAMANTHA: Yes, very much so.

CONSULTANT: Would you two mind if I share with you some information about stepparenting and new families? [Following the empathic attunement, the consultant asks permission to provide educational information.]

REX: Go for it.

CONSULTANT: You two strike me as very reasonable people and it's obvious you care deeply for each other and for the well-being of Samantha's children and so I feel I can tell you this stuff straight up. Probably the biggest struggle for stepfamilies has to do with expectations. Kids are almost always way behind parents in accepting new family arrangements. That's partly because you're the ones in love and so you're ready to move forward with your marriage, but the kids didn't choose this new arrangement, they're not in love, and they need time to adjust and accept the relationship. [After a clearly supportive statement, the consultant tries out some basic educational information.]

SAMANTHA: Yes. We know that. Like I said, I know in my head some reasons why they would have mixed feelings about Rex. But I don't think we should have to deal with their disrespect. [It's not unusual for parents to indicate they already know about stepparenting guidelines, even though their behavior doesn't show it. As an illustration, biological mom stands her ground and amplifies her position; it's clear she's feeling more concern about her boyfriend than she is about her children.]

CONSULTANT: This is why I like working with you guys. You already know some of what the kids are thinking and feeling. And you're absolutely right that you shouldn't accept disrespectful behavior. The hard part is walking the fine line of requiring respectful behavior, but at the same time allowing your children to express some of their natural reluctance and negative feelings. As I'm sure you know, when kids—especially teens—have strong feelings about something, it almost never works to tell them to keep their mouths shut, because then, like Maggie, they'll roll their eyes. And if you tell them not to roll their eyes, then they might completely stop communicating with you about their feelings and then you won't even know how they feel . . . and I'll bet that shutting down Maggie's feelings isn't your goal. [The consultant responds to the resistance with more support and validation and then pushes Mom to agree that getting her daughter to shut down is not the goal.]

SAMANTHA: No. That's right. I do want to know what they're feeling, but I don't want to deal with their disrespect. [Mom agrees to the crucial position that she wants to (a) know her daughters' feelings, but (b) limit their disrespect.]

CONSULTANT: Exactly. And so we need to come up with a very clear plan about how to honor their feelings and their right to express their feelings about something they're not ready for, and yet the plan needs to limit them to polite and respectful communication. Does that sound about right? [Now that there's agreement, it's time to move forward with a plan.]

SAMANTHA: Yes. It does. What do you think Rex? [Mom continues to show concern for her partner's perspective.]

REX: I agree. It's not exactly how I was raised, but I get the fact that they need to express themselves.

CONSULTANT: Samantha, thanks for checking in with Rex on this because it's important to have both of you on board. And here's the hard part for you Rex. I think it was absolutely terrific that you told Maggie the other day that she hurt your feelings. That was an emotional fact that it's good for her to hear. But, seriously, you really shouldn't expect her to care about that right now. This is the tricky part. You can tell her when she hurts your feelings, but remember that right now she's so consumed with her own reactions to you that she can't really care about hurting your feelings. In fact, she may have some loyalties to her dad that make it so she *wants* to hurt your feelings. She may want to scare you off. To be honest, I'm gonna say this bluntly if I may [Rex nods in assent]: You need to be strong enough to deal with her efforts to reject you. You can tell her it hurts your feelings and you can tell her you don't like it, but don't let her scare you away, and be sure to tune into her feelings. Give her the message: "Yeah, you hurt my feelings, but I can see why you're not excited to have me around and, you know, I'm strong enough to deal with that." Does that make sense? It really means being secure in yourself and your position in the family and being a strong adult. [The consultant, as a male, is especially able to connect with Rex and give him a strength assignment, which Rex accepts.]

Rex: Yeah. I get that. I can do that.

Consultant: Okay, now let's get to work on rules for the girls and how they can respectfully express themselves. [After educational information is shared with Rex, the focus moves back to the family plan for allowing respectful emotional expression.]

In this exchange, the consultant assertively navigated the sometimes-treacherous therapeutic terrain between validation and confrontation. At the same time, he engaged in a parallel process—modeling to the parents how they can be accepting but firm with Samantha's daughters. As he accepts Samantha's and Rex's perspectives, but guides them to a more moderate position, he's illustrating how to be a compassionate listener who can also set firm limits and provide educational guidance.

At the end of the session, the following seven-point plan was developed, photocopied, and given to Samantha and Rex. Additionally, the couple was given a copy of the Stepfamily Guidelines tip sheet (see Appendix B, Tip Sheet 8).

1. As long as they say "yes" to at least one 2-hour family event per week, and as long as they're able to stay home and not get into trouble, they can refuse other family events.

2. Samantha will make a point to schedule alone time with Maggie and Emma. It's important for Maggie and Emma to feel they're not losing Mom to Rex.

3. Rex will work to have a friendly, but not too close, relationship with the girls. The point of this will be for them to begin to get used to him—but not to work at having some emotional breakthrough about what a great guy he is. Remember, Samantha is the one who thinks he's a great guy and wants to marry him. The girls aren't there yet and maybe never will be.

4. Rex will treat the girls with the respect he hopes to earn from them and will defer to Samantha when it comes to specific discipline situations.

5. When you're in a situation that requires it, Rex can set limits with the girls—limits that have been discussed previously with Samantha—but he shouldn't get involved in punishing them.

6. Samantha will offer the girls an opportunity for counseling alone or with her. She will also have a serious talk with them about: (a) how she's sorry that she's complained to them in the past about Rex because that was unfair to them and to Rex; (b) how she's open to hearing their feelings and that she understands they may not be too excited about her marrying Rex, but that she expects them to treat Rex with respect; (c) how she plans to continue spending alone time with them, but hopes to have them eventually spend more family time with her and Rex.

7. Samantha and Rex will recognize and expect that the girls will struggle with this transition and so be matter-of-fact and a little disappointed, but not too angry when they fail to be respectful.

Homework for Parents Who Need to Work on Honoring Their Children's Emotions   A rather substantial body of research suggests that listening to, honoring, and not giving in to children's emotions is important to child self-control and emotional development (Dennis, 2006; Eisenberg et al., 2010; Hutchinson & Pretelt, 2010; Katz, Wilson, & Gottman, 1999; Spinrad, Stifter, Donelan-McCall, & Turner, 2004). Gottman and DeClaire (1997) further emphasize that parents can become "emotion coaches" who view their children's strong emotions as an opportunity for (a) emotional connection or intimacy, and (b) emotional education.

Homework for parents that focuses on listening to and respecting children's emotions can be especially complicated. Similar to discipline issues, the challenge for parents is to stay in the middle—to listen well, but to not become too preoccupied with their children's shifting emotions. This means parents should learn good listening skills, but also sometimes expect their children to tough it out, even when emotionally upset. Parents who come for guidance are often struggling with one extreme (not listening and always expecting their children to buck up and handle their emotions like grownups) or the other (hovering over their children in an effort to make sure they never feel sad, angry, or scared and then over-listening to every minor emotional detail in their children's lives). A sample homework assignment designed to help parents reflect on their listening patterns is included in Parent Homework Assignment 7-3.

Parent Homework Assignment 7-3

Why Is Listening to Children Such a Big Deal?

Listening to children—really listening to what they have to say—can be a major pain. Thus the well-known saying, "Children should be seen and not heard." Sometimes listening to children can seem like too much trouble, too time consuming, and of little value.

On the other hand, when you listen closely to children, you often experience surprisingly nice outcomes. The purpose of this assignment is for you to consider the benefits of listening to your children and reflect on whether you want to work on becoming a better listener for your children's sake.

A big problem with listening to children is that they frequently have a lot to say. We recall with fondness a 10-year-old girl who conversed with such breathless intensity that even a huge mid-sentence belch didn't slow her down. If adults are interested in listening, even just a little, children are often ready to talk. Although sometimes teenagers are more reluctant to talk with adults, given the right place, time, and an interested ear, many teens become open and talkative.

Here are some benefits of listening to your children:

- If you consistently listen to your children, they'll be more likely to listen to you.
- If you listen to your children, they'll behave more cooperatively.

(Continued)

- Children will feel respected if you listen to them; this respect helps build healthy self-esteem.
- Listening can slow you down; if you listen to your child before reacting, it can help you be more calm, thoughtful, and moderate in your discipline.

Can you think of additional benefits of listening to your children? If so, consider making a list in case you need reminders.

It's both impossible and unnecessary for parents to *always* listen to their children. In fact, children don't need total attention (or total perfection) from their parents. Children profit when parents try to listen well; your effort can count as much as your accuracy. The point of this handout is not to convince you to listen perfectly all the time, but instead to convince you to learn to listen well at least some of the time.

Evaluating Your Listening Habits

Read the following questions, take a few minutes to reflect on your answers, and then write down your responses.

1. Do you ever "drop everything" and listen to your child or children? What happens when you do? Would you like to do that more often? Do you do it too often?
2. Do you ever listen to your child as he or she talks about a personal activity in which you have absolutely no interest? For example, do you listen as he talks with you about his video/computer game conquests, even though you really don't like video/computer games?
3. Rate how available you are as a listener for your children on a scale from 0 to 10 (0 = Not at all available; 10 = Always available).
4. Rate how skilled you believe you are at listening to your children (0 = I have absolutely no listening skills; 10 = I am the best listener ever).
5. Think about whether you'd like to become more available for listening and/or more skilled at listening to your children. If you want to become a better listener, what can you do to improve yourself?

CONCLUDING COMMENTS

This chapter focuses on three specific relationship-based or relationship-enhancing interventions practitioners can teach parents to use with their children. Each intervention is described and standard homework assignments are provided. Tip sheets associated with each intervention are in Appendix B, and additional material is available online (go to http://www.familiesfirstmontana.org/). It's important for counselors, therapists, consultants, and other human services professionals who work with parents to modify interventions included in this chapter to fit their therapeutic style and their clients' particular problems and needs.

Checklist for Relationship-Based Approaches and Resources

☐ When children need a regular dose of attention and control, consider teaching parents about special time.

☐ Remember that special time can be both a non-directive play therapy approach and a conceptual approach where high-quality parent–child time is emphasized.

☐ Help parents see that it's normal to feel angry toward their children.

☐ If parent anger is a significant issue, help parents develop a clear and realistic plan for dealing with their anger.

☐ Help parents recognize that it's possible and desirable for them to simultaneously have empathy for their children's emotions while setting limits on their children's behavior.

☐ Help parents learn how to make it clear that they love their children, but that despite their love, some behaviors are inappropriate or unacceptable.

☐ Go to the comprehensive intervention checklist and/or the practitioner support website to gather more ideas about relationship-based interventions parents can use with their children.

CHAPTER EIGHT

Sharing Power to Gain Influence

Indirect and Problem-Solving Interventions

Many people, including parents, believe the shortest distance between two points is a straight line. Although this idea is conceptually true, in life there are often no straight paths available. More often than not there are shortcuts and secret off-ramps and pathways that, if you're not paying attention, lead you to dead ends where you have to double back and find yourself no closer to your destination than when you started. Even when traveling by air, sometimes you're rerouted or run into fog or end up circling the runway, waiting your turn to land. Our point: In life, the direct route is frequently not the most efficient option.

This chapter is about indirect and unexpected solutions to problems that need solving. It includes an array of techniques parents can employ to influence their children. These techniques may be used independently, in combination with each other, or in combination with other techniques in this book. As you look closely at how to teach parents these indirect and problem-solving techniques, you may notice their appeal and recognize how sometimes the less direct path of influence is surprisingly more efficient than the direct power path. We recommend that you tweak these techniques so they fit your personal style and approach for working with parents.

THOUGHTS ON SHARING POWER

The techniques in this chapter are about sharing power to gain influence. Feminists might conceptualize this as a general empowerment strategy. When individuals who have historically felt disempowered suddenly feel empowered, interesting things happen. These interesting things often include an activation of energy, a renewed focus, greater clarity of purpose, and an increased sense of personal responsibility.

For children, the goal of an empowerment strategy is for them to have felt experiences that lead them to conclude: "What I think, feel, and do is important." Consequently, as you consider using these techniques, try to avoid conveying the message that the purpose of these techniques is to obtain compliance or manipulate children into behaving in ways adults view desirable. Instead, these techniques work best if they're used to help children and teenagers feel that their perspective, their personhood, and their personal power are valued and respected.

Give Information — Then Back Off

Most parents, at least initially, feel drawn toward actively and directly teaching life lessons to children. After all, as adults, we have far more accumulated wisdom than children and therefore it makes perfect sense to tell them what decisions they should make and warn them of potential life dangers. Many parents also use direct power strategies of lecturing, criticism, praise, and advice-giving to teach their children important life lessons. Unfortunately, life lessons based on direct power are often ineffective. This is likely true because, as Carl Rogers might say, children are more interested in learning about life based on *their own experiences* rather than learning indirectly from parental lectures.

Praise, punishment, lectures, advice, and criticism are external means of influence (Glasser, 2002). When talking with parents, we usually emphasize that praise and punishment strategies involve "outside-in" or external learning. Punishment is a message from the outside that tells children they've done something wrong; praise is a message from the outside that tells children they've done something right.

All learning is partially outside-in and partially inside-out. Children can learn from what others say (often through praise and punishment) and they can learn from their own judgments of their own direct experiences. Generally, children's developmental issues (e.g., individuation, identity formation) make it desirable for parents to intentionally use inside-out learning strategies with their children, at least some of the time.

Inside-out learning emphasizes personal experience and judgment rather than judgments imposed by others. Most parents agree that, although they want their children to be open and sensitive to others' opinions, they also want their children to have an internal sense of direction and integrity. Unfortunately, using direct power to tell children what to think often backfires. Some children oppose their parents simply for the sake of opposing their parents. In these cases, children seem to gain a sense of identity through opposition or rebellion instead of learning to personally reflect on their experiences and then consciously choosing their own behaviors. (See Parent Homework Assignment 8-1.)

Case: Troy's Three Choices

Troy, a teenage boy, came for counseling. Troy was in conflict with his parents about his relationship with his girlfriend. His parents were concerned and had made it clear that they disapproved of the girlfriend and of his relationship with her. This communication left Troy feeling deprived of his personal choice and so he stubbornly clung to his relationship despite the fact that he also had doubts about whether the relationship was a good fit for him. As we worked in counseling, it became clear that Troy had three general choices: (a) He could comply with his parents' wishes and discontinue the relationship; (b) he could oppose his parents and insist on his right to have this relationship; or (c) he could think about his parents' opinions as information and then step back and critically evaluate the relationship himself and decide what he thought was best. We discussed the most challenging outcome of all: that he might end up agreeing with his parents and terminate the relationship and then they (and he) might think they had "won" the power struggle.

As a result of our discussions, Troy decided he wanted a joint meeting with his parents. During the meeting he effectively communicated to them that they had made their position and their concerns very clear. He then emphatically asked them to back off so he could decide how to proceed with his relationship. In the end, Troy broke off the relationship and thanked his parents for giving him the space and time to make his own decision.

This case illustrates the *give information and then back off technique.* The parents communicated their concerns directly. Although they were initially overbearing about what their son should do, eventually, with encouragement, they backed away and gave their son time to independently consider the issues. In essence, by backing off after expressing their concerns, they also communicated trust in their son's ability to make a reasonable decision. One problem underlying this situation is the fact that after expressing concerns, it's often difficult for parents to keep their mouths shut and let their children make their own decisions on their own timeline rather than the parents' timeline.

Asking Permission   Troy's parents might have been even more influential if they had started the process by asking Troy if they could share their opinion with him. For example, they might have asked: "Would you like to hear our thoughts on how your relationship seems to be going?"

By asking for Troy's permission, a new power dynamic is intentionally established. The new dynamic includes some of the following characteristics:

- The parents give a signal to Troy that they have important information they'd like to share with him, but they're giving this signal *before* they provide the information.
- Asking permission gives Troy a sense of empowerment. He may choose to (a) receive the information, or (b) reject the information. He's less likely to feel as though his parents are shoving the information down his throat.

- Even if Troy initially rejects the information by saying "I don't want to hear what you think" or "I know what you're going to say," he can still change his mind and ask for the information later.
- If the parents approach Troy with an attitude of concern, he may feel cared for, which is always a good thing in a parent–child relationship.
- If the parents can respect Troy's right to reject the information, paradoxically, he may become more open to hearing their opinion later.
- Overall, by asking permission, the parents are at least expressing partial faith or trust in Troy and his problem-solving ability.

Exceptions   There are exceptions to every rule. This particular problem-solving technique provides an excellent foundation for exploring exceptions to all indirect and problem-solving strategies. Because these approaches intentionally and explicitly give away parental power, they should be used only when parents feel at least somewhat comfortable trusting their children with the problem-solving process. For example, if Troy's girlfriend is obviously abusing drugs and pulling Troy toward a destructive lifestyle, it may be necessary for the parents to insist on more extreme and directive steps. These steps might include:

- Family therapy
- A drug/alcohol intervention
- More intensive supervision of Troy's behaviors
- Severe limitations regarding Troy's freedom outside the home contingent upon specific communication and "checking-in" standards
- Involvement with law enforcement (if appropriate and/or warranted)

Although not exhaustive, the preceding list provides a sense of how the nature of the parent–child relationship and the parents' trust in their child's judgment interact with the level of directiveness. More directive, limit-setting, and monitoring parenting approaches may be necessary, depending on the severity of the situation.

Parent Homework Assignment 8-1

Choice Theory Communication Skills Training: How to Provide
Information and Then Back Off, Instead of Trying Too Hard
to Control Your Child's Decision Making

As a loving parent, if you're concerned about your children's behaviors, you'll probably have a strong and nearly irresistible impulse to tell them how to live their lives. After all, you're the adult and they should listen to your excellent advice. You may feel the urge to say:

- You need to clean your room *now* because being disorganized and undisciplined is a bad habit that will make your life miserable.

- Alcohol and drugs are illegal and so if you go out and behave illegally, I'll call the police and have you ticketed.
- You need to start caring about your grades at school and that means scheduling time for homework and studying for tests.
- Swearing is unacceptable in this house and if you do it again, I'll wash your mouth out with soap.

Unfortunately, as you may recall from your own childhood, when parents are bossy and insistent about how things should be, children often become more stubborn and resistant. Then parents begin to nag and lecture and the pattern of advice-giving and advice-rejection deepens. This assignment is designed to help you communicate important information to your children without starting an all-out power struggle or negative nagging pattern. The following suggestions are appropriate only if the situation isn't dangerous and you don't need to jump in and directly and forcefully protect your children:

1. *Ask permission.* If you have a strong opinion that you'd like your child to hear, try asking permission to share it. Say something like, "Can I share my opinion on this with you?" Then, either your child will say "yes" and you can share your opinion or she'll say "no" and then you'll need to accept her boundary (in response to a "no," you might say, "Okay. Thanks for being honest with me. Let me know if you change your mind" and then walk away).

2. *Express your intention not to express your opinion.* You could try telling your child, "I have an opinion on this, but I trust that you can work it out, or that you'll ask me for help if you need it. So I'm going to try to keep my mouth shut for now." This gives your child the message that you're trying to respect his ability to work out his own problems. You can also add humor into this or other power-sharing techniques by adding: "You should really appreciate this, because you know how hard it is for me to keep my mouth shut and not give you advice."

3. *Provide your information or opinion and then back off.* If you can't resist giving your opinion, just do it and then back off and let your child consider your input. The key to this strategy is patience. Undoubtedly, you'll provide excellent advice and then your child will look like she's not considering your advice and so you'll have the urge to repeat your advice over and over until you see action. Instead of falling into this pattern, try saying, "Look. I've got an opinion, which you probably already know. But instead of staying quiet, I'm just going to say it and then let you make your own decision on how to handle your situation. It's your life. You have to make your own decisions. But I love you and can't stop myself from telling you what I think, so here it is."

As you probably already know, if you express your opinion you may get a strong emotional response (e.g., "I'm 15 years old and I can make my own decisions!"). Although this seems weird, if you give lots of advice, your children may see your ideas and opinions as evidence that you don't believe they're competent

(Continued)

> to make their own decisions. This is why you should always express your advice with love and concern; avoid sounding as if your main goal is to control your child's behavior.
>
> Finally, if the situation is dangerous or potentially so, skip the less direct parenting recommendations listed above and instead think strategically about how to deliver direct advice that will be heeded. You'll probably need to use a more direct approach than is described here, and you may need to consult with a professional.

Using Praise, Mirroring, Character Feedback, and Solution-Focused Questions

Despite our reluctance to fully embrace behaviorism, we recognize that parents naturally use praise, punishment, and other external cues to give their children feedback about what behaviors are acceptable and unacceptable. However, many parents overuse direct power or external force with their children. If parents want their children to develop internalized decision-making skills, they should also intentionally employ inside-out parenting techniques, such as character feedback, mirroring (encouragement), and solution-focused questions.

Case: Four Roads to Healthier Self-Esteem

FATHER: I'm a single dad and so I have the job of two parents. It's hard, but it's especially hard because I'm a worrier. My girls don't have a mom around and so I get obsessed about their self-esteem. What can I do to boost their self-esteem?

CONSULTANT: That's a great question . . . and a big question. But before we talk about the answer, tell me, what sorts of things are you doing now to build their self-esteem?

FATHER: I compliment them as much as I can. I praise them. I constantly say "I love you."

CONSULTANT: Can you give me an example of how you compliment them?

FATHER: Like last night. The girls were coloring and they kept showing me their pictures and I would say, "That's beautiful!" and "That's wonderful!" and "You two are great artists." Stuff like that.

CONSULTANT: I should say first that I think it's very nice that you're so positive with your daughters. I wish more parents were positive like you.

FATHER: Thanks, but, uh, what else can I do?

CONSULTANT: You're great at using praise and compliments and that's really important, but I've got other ideas about how to expand your self-esteem-building repertoire. Can I share a few?

FATHER: Go for it.

CONSULTANT: Let's take the coloring and picture-drawing example. You're giving out praise and compliments, which is very important. But praise and compliments are what we call "external" or "outside-in" strategies. They build your daughters' self-esteem from the outside in. You're the outside expert and you tell them they're great. There are three other things you could add to that. I'll describe these three options now, but I have a tip sheet that describes them, too.

First, instead of praising and complimenting, sometimes you could use a technique called "mirroring." Mirroring is more of an "inside-out" technique for building self-esteem. To use mirroring, you should watch your children and mirror their positive feelings back to them. For example, you could say, "You look really happy about your drawing," or you could ask a question: "What do you like best about your drawing?" By using these mirroring responses, you're encouraging your children to judge their own drawings. That's why we call it an inside-out approach, because it draws out your children's internal feelings and judgments.

FATHER: Okay. I think I get that, but what if one of my daughters doesn't like her drawing—or, even worse, what if she says "I hate my drawing"?

CONSULTANT: Good questions. You're so good at praise, your daughters may be depending on you for their compliments. If one of your daughters can't think of anything positive, that's okay. No need to get worried. We all sometimes produce things we don't like. But you might try several things. You could just reflect back her feelings and see what happens by saying, "I guess you don't like this drawing so much." Or you could push her to identify two positives and negatives with a comment like, "Well, I see something about it I like, but I don't want to go first. So, first you tell me what you like and then I'll say what I like." Or, you could help her focus on her next drawing with empathy and encouragement by saying, "*Hmmm*. You don't seem too happy with this drawing. Maybe you'll like your next one better." The thing that's important to remember is that false praise or too much praise doesn't help your children build self-esteem from the inside out. Pretty soon, they'll recognize that you always say something positive and they might start wondering if you really mean it.

FATHER: Okay. I get it.

CONSULTANT: That's mirroring. The key is to draw out or reflect your child's judgments. It's even okay to mirror back if she doesn't like her drawing. This is part of respecting her judgment. If she doesn't like the drawing, that's okay, just reflect that back. You can even move a little bit away from mirroring and if you really like her drawing you can disagree with her and say something like, "I see you don't like your drawing, but here's what I like about it."

FATHER: All right.

CONSULTANT: The next method after praise and mirroring is character feedback. Character feedback is when you say something like, "You're the kind of girl who loves to draw." What you're doing with this method is you're making a positive behavior into a character trait. Try that out. Think of a character trait that one of your daughters has and put it into the sentence, "You're the kind of girl who . . . "

FATHER: My older daughter likes to keep all her school stuff organized. So would I say, "You're a girl who's organized"?

CONSULTANT: Sure. Almost anyway you say it is fine. What you're doing is helping her build positive character traits so she begins seeing herself as an organized person.

FATHER: How about my other daughter? She's very disorganized. Do I tell her, "You're a disorganized girl"? That doesn't seem like a good idea.

CONSULTANT: Exactly. When we use character feedback, we almost always use it for positive character traits. With your less organized daughter, you might wait for a time when she displays even a tiny bit of organizational skill and then say, "I notice you can really get organized when you want to." For character feedback, just think of yourself as a mirror that reflects positive behaviors and forms them into character traits. What's interesting about this is that most parents, including me, tend to watch for our children's weaknesses and negative qualities and comment on them. For example, lots of parents and teachers see children misbehaving and can't resist making comments like, "What's wrong with you? Can't you keep your hands to yourself?" or "You're lying again, aren't you? You need to get over that lying problem." Basically, when we repeatedly comment on our children's negative behaviors we help them construct a more negative character. They end up thinking, "I'm the kind of kid who just keeps getting into trouble." The magic of character feedback is that we can use it to intentionally construct positive character traits. I know it's manipulative, but it's being manipulative in a positive way.

FATHER: That's interesting. I do have trouble not commenting when my daughters misbehave. Should I ignore misbehavior?

CONSULTANT: Not always. We should just focus most of our attention on our children's positive behaviors and only a little of our attention on the negative behaviors. Sometimes our children need corrective feedback or input. But if we focus too much on the negative, the negative will tend to grow, because it's getting so much attention.

FATHER: Okay. I think I get that. You said you have a handout on this, right?

CONSULTANT: Right. And there's one last method. The last method is called solution-focused questioning. Here's an example with your less organized daughter. Let's say she shows a flash of organizational skill. Then, you could ask something like, "Wow. How did you manage to get your school work all organized?" Be careful to be curious and impressed, but not too surprised. You know how some parents will say things like, "Who are you and what have you done with my child?" as a joke. Well, that's a funny joke, but it plays on the fact that the child is acting in an unusual way. What we want to communicate is that it's normal for your daughter to be organized when she wants to and so you're showing curiosity about how she manages to get organized. Solution-focused questions with children almost always ask them to reflect on how they accomplished something positive. For example, you could say: "How did you manage to be honest and tell the truth in that hard situation?" or "How did you figure out how to get that puzzle together?"

FATHER: Okay. This one is about focusing on solutions.

CONSULTANT: Right. Let's try one. What's something one of your daughters did well this past week?

FATHER: My organized daughter had a terrible tantrum and then apologized to me.

CONSULTANT: That's great. What would be a solution-focused question?

FATHER: Um, how about this? "What were you thinking when you decided to apologize?"

CONSULTANT: Yeah. That's pretty good. But that might feel like you're investigating or analyzing her thoughts. I might change it a little and throw in a positive character trait, like, "How did you find the courage to come and apologize to me?" That sends her a message that it takes courage to apologize and as long as you agree with that, it might be a nice way to combine a solution-focused question and a little character feedback.

FATHER: I like that.

CONSULTANT: I should also say that often when we ask solution-focused questions of children they just shrug their shoulders and say, "I don't know," which is perfectly fine. The point is that hopefully we're building into them a tendency to reflect on how they managed to do something that was positive or successful.

FATHER: I can imagine my daughter saying "I don't know."

CONSULTANT: Now, I know we've covered a whole lot of ground in the last few minutes, but parenting can be complicated sometimes.

FATHER: You're telling me? I've got two daughters and pretty soon they'll be attracting boys and that will be even worse.

CONSULTANT: Yeah. I guess I don't need to tell you that parenting is complicated, but what I want to say is that I've got this tip sheet for you on praise, mirroring, character feedback, and solution-focused questions and you can take it and just try out the ideas we talked about today that are in this tip sheet. Just practice away and see what happens and we can talk about it more next week.

In this case we see the consultant squeezing lots of nuanced parenting information into a brief time period. This is a very educational approach and most likely to work after the practitioner has established a positive working relationship with parents who are in the action stage of Prochaska and DiClemente's (2005) transtheoretical model. Even in the action stage, most parents can't absorb all this information at once, which is why tip sheets and homework assignments can be so important.

Although the methods illustrated (praise, mirroring, character feedback, and solution-focused questions) are fairly complex, most parents intuitively understand the differences. These methods are only partly designed to improve parent–child relationships; they're also good behavior management and self-efficacy-building techniques, and so they can be used with parents who are being either too negative or too positive with their children.

Giving Homework Focusing on Praise, Mirroring, Character Feedback, and Solution-Focused Questioning The quality of parent–child relationships is strongly determined by the ratio of positive versus negative parent–child interactions. For example, Gottman (Gottman & DeClaire, 2001) recommends that couples engage in five positive behavioral interactions for every negative interaction in romantic relationships. The purpose of giving parents homework assignments focusing on praise, mirroring, character feedback, and solution-focused questioning is partly to help them shift their parent–child interactions toward a positive ratio. Most parenting books, especially from the behavioral perspective, emphasize the importance of increasing praise and positive interactions (Barkley, Robin, & Benton, 2008; Kazdin, 2008).

In the preceding case example, the father was already providing ample praise but needed to become more nuanced and intentional in the way he was interacting with his daughters. But other scenarios are possible. For example, when parents are struggling in their relationships with their children, they often feel unable or unwilling to provide praise. The nature of the homework you assign to parents will depend on your evaluation of the specific parent–child interactions parents report to you. In Parent Homework Assignment 8-2, we provide a generic parenting assignment for helping parents use praise, mirroring, character feedback, and solution-focused questions. This assignment emphasizes distinctions between these different approaches. Depending on your professional assessment, you can direct parents to work on one or more of these indirect power strategies.

Parent Homework Assignment 8-2

Exploring the Differences Between Praise, Mirroring, Character Feedback, and Solution-Focused Questions

If you've been given this homework assignment, you're probably already using many good parenting techniques with your child. This assignment will help you refine your parenting approach to intentionally include even more ways of being positive with your child.

Imagine that a father is busy taking care of household chores while he's parenting his 5-year-old daughter. She's creating some excellent 5-year-old crayon art and approaches her daddy with a finished product and a beaming smile. Dad looks up and takes a break from his chores to admire his daughter's artwork. He returns her grin and says one of the following:

- "This is beautiful!" (An example of **praise**—a form of direct power)
- "Thanks for showing me your drawing. You look very happy with your picture." (An example of **emotional mirroring or encouragement**—a form of indirect power)
- "You love doing artwork!" (An example of **character feedback**—another form of indirect power)
- "How did you manage to create this beautiful drawing?" (An example of a **solution-focused question**—a form of problem-solving power)

If you can increase your awareness of these different strategies, you'll feel more capable of being intentional and positive when interacting with your children. The result usually includes fewer power struggles and more positive parent–child relationship dynamics.

Using Praise

Using praise is simple. For example, praise includes statements like: "Great work," "I'm proud of you," and "Look at what a good job you've done cleaning the bathroom!" When you use praise, you're clearly communicating your expectations and your approval to your child. Praise is best when it's behaviorally specific.

Think about how much praise you use with your children. Are you being clear enough with them about what you want, and are you letting them know when they've done well? As a part of this homework assignment, consider increasing how much you praise your child and then see how your child reacts.

Using Mirroring

Sometimes children don't have a clear sense of how their behaviors look to others (which can also be true for adults). The purpose of mirroring is to help children see themselves through your eyes. After seeing (or hearing) their reflection, children become more aware of their behavior and may choose to make changes.

For now, we recommend that you practice using mirroring only to reflect your child's positive behaviors. For example, if your daughter has a play date and shares her toys with her friend, you could say, "I noticed you were sharing your toys." Or if your son got home on time instead of breaking his curfew, you might say, "I noticed you were on time last night." The hard part about using mirroring is to stay neutral, but staying neutral is important because mirroring allows your children to judge of their own behaviors. If you want to be the judge, you can use praise.

Using Character Feedback

Character feedback works well for helping your children see themselves as having positive character traits. For example, you might say, "You're very honest with us," or "You can really focus on and get your homework done quickly when you want to," or "You're very smart."

Usually, as parents, instead of using character feedback to focus on our children's positive qualities, we use it in a very negative way. Examples include: "Can't you keep your hands to yourself?" "You're always such a big baby," and "You never do your homework."

For your homework assignment, try using character feedback to comment on your children's positive behaviors, while ignoring the negative. You can even use character feedback to encourage a new behavior—all you have to do is wait for a tiny sign of the new behavior to occur and then make a positive character

(Continued)

feedback statement: "You're really starting to pay attention to keeping your room clean."

Using Solution-Focused Questions

Problem-focused questions include: "What's wrong with you?" and "What were you thinking when you hit that other boy at school?" In contrast, solution-focused questions encourage children to focus on what they're doing well. For example, "How did you manage to get that puzzle together?" "What were you thinking when you decided to share your toy with your friend?" and "What did you do to get yourself home on time?"

Solution-focused questions require us to look for the positive. For practice, try asking your child questions designed to get him or her to think about successes instead of failures. After all, it's the successes that you want to see repeated. Of course, when you ask these questions, don't expect your child to answer them well. Instead, your child will most likely say, "Huh? I don't know." The point is that you're focusing on the positive and *eventually* these questions get your children to focus on the positive as well.

Mutual Problem-Solving

Mutual problem-solving is an intervention we use frequently with parents. Variations of mutual problem-solving have been written about by many different authors and from many different perspectives (Edwards, 1999; Greene et al., 2004; Greene & Ablon, 2006). The central feature of mutual problem solving is parent–child collaboration.

Parents who come to see professionals are often extremely committed to their children's well-being and success. As great as this is, when parents vigorously and ambitiously support their children's success, sometimes children respond by losing internal motivation to succeed. We described this before as problem polarization, and in these situations, mutual problem-solving is an excellent intervention.

The purpose of mutual problem-solving is to get children to begin taking at least partial ownership of a problem and to get them to invest in a problem-solving process. By doing so, children assume greater responsibility for their share of the family's problems.

Case: Just Another Homework Battle

PARENT: I just can't get my 12-year-old daughter to do any homework. And when she does, she usually forgets it and never gets it to school. I've tried everything.
CONSULTANT: Tell me some of what you've tried.
PARENT: I've tried grounding her. I've tried docking her allowance. I've tried making her sit at a desk for two hours after school. I've tried offering her money for grades. Nothing works.

CONSULTANT: Wow. That sounds very hard. In fact, it sounds like you're working way harder than your daughter on the homework thing.

PARENT: I sure am.

CONSULTANT: It's funny how that works sometimes. It's almost like the more interested and invested we get in our children's school performance, the less interested and invested they get. It's like there's only so much responsibility to go around and the more responsibility we take on as parents, the less our children take on.

PARENT: Yeah. If she'd spend half the time with her homework that she does fixing her hair in the mirror, we wouldn't have any worries.

CONSULTANT: May I offer you an idea, a strategy, where we can hopefully get your daughter more interested in her homework and get you more interested in her hair?

A traditional, direct power-based strategy for dealing with this problem might involve the parent restricting his or her child from social activities until homework was completed (e.g., Grandma's Rule: "When you finish your homework, then you can call your friends"). Or it might involve the parent working extremely hard (and with some desperation) to come up with rewards for homework completion or grades. When parents begin this process on their own, without first recruiting their child's involvement, the result can be polarization: The more Mom pushes on homework completion, the more her daughter resists.

It's often difficult for parents to implement mutual problem-solving, even when they've had it described to them and even when they've read Parent Homework Assignment 8-3. Similar to special time, the process of mutual problem-solving can sometimes be more important than the outcome. The important message for parents to give their children (and themselves) is that the family is in this together and that the parents are going to decrease their efforts to push, pull, or bribe their children into engaging in specific behaviors. Back to the case example:

PARENT: Sure, tell me how to do it.

CONSULTANT: Okay. Sometime when you and your daughter are both in a good mood, you say, "Honey, we both know that I've been worried about your homework and your grades. But lately I've realized that's backwards. It's your life, and you need to figure out how to get things done in a way that works for you. Do you have any ideas about what would work best for you?"

PARENT: We've tried that. She'll just say to back off; homework is stupid.

CONSULTANT: You're absolutely right. Your daughter's first idea will always be a bad idea, but you just nod, and write down, #1 Mom should just back off, and say, "Thanks. That's one idea." Then add, "I know it's a pain, and it has to get done. That's just how life is. But the important thing is I think you might have ideas about how to get your own homework done, and I want to hear them." If you acknowledge bad ideas and write them down, it's more likely that she'll keep coming up with ideas and maybe she'll even come up with a good one—eventually. In the meantime, don't worry about the bad ideas because, in the end, you don't have to vote for them.

PARENT: What if she doesn't come up with anything?

CONSULTANT: That's where her hair comes in. You offer a hair product or salon visit as one option for a homework reward and write that down right below her idea of "Mom should just back off."

PARENT: Okay.

CONSULTANT: And just keep on with the list. If she gets disinterested, keep at it anyway. The point is that you're giving her the messages "We can figure this out together" and "I'm backing off a little and trusting you and your input on this." I'll get you a copy of our tip sheet that explains this technique in more detail.

Mutual problem-solving is a recalibration of power. Parents back off in ways that allow their children to step up. It doesn't work for everything, but it's a helpful intervention especially when parents have gotten far too invested in something that should matter more to the child. Mutual problem-solving can be used to jointly generate rewards, consequences, and problem-solving solutions or strategies.

Parent Homework Assignment 8-3

Mutual Problem-Solving

Mutual problem-solving brings family members together to solve problems collaboratively. It works best if your child is at least 4 years old. It also works well with strong-willed children who like to challenge parental authority. It includes five steps.

Step 1: Identify the problem together. Present the situation in a way that your child will agree that something is a problem.

Let's say your 6-year-old is very stubborn and won't share his toys with other children and so they don't want to play with him. Here's how you could proceed: (a) Discuss this behavior with your child when he's in a good mood, like when you're drawing or eating ice cream together; (b) describe the situation in a way that makes it so your child will likely agree that the situation presents a problem for him (e.g., "I noticed that when you play with Matt sometimes he gets mad when you don't share your toys and then he stomps off and goes home, and then you're usually upset, because you like playing with Matt. Don't you hate it when that happens?"). Your child will probably agree and say something like, "Yeah, I don't like him doing that," and then you're free to problem-solve together.

Step 2: Identify potential solutions. Say something like, "Okay, since we both agree that you don't like it when Matt gets mad and leaves, let's come up with some ideas to solve this problem."

When coming up with solutions, let yourself (and your child) be creative. Encourage him to take the lead, but if he doesn't, throw out suggestions to get things rolling. Examples include: "We could send Matt home," or "We could practice how to deal with Matt before he comes," or "I could pay Matt one dollar to stay and play with you," or "I could be toy-keeper and time-keeper and keep track of who gets to play with which toy for what length of time," or "If you guys fight over the toy, the toy goes in timeout."

Track all ideas on paper. Be prepared for your child's first idea to be very bad. Even if he suggests something ridiculous, "He should pay me to share!" just nod your head, repeat what he said, and write it down. Don't criticize his suggestions or he might stop giving them.

As you generate possible solutions, remember that eventually you'll have to agree to try out one of these potential solutions.

Step 3: Rate and rank potential solutions. After you've generated at least three or four options (hopefully more) rank the possible solutions. Together, select one to try out for a while. This procedure is mutual and you should agree to check back on how well the solution is working. That way, you can let him try out a less-than-perfect strategy, knowing you'll get to talk about it and encourage a better solution next time. With a 15-year-old daughter who is violating her curfew, your solution list might look like this:

Angie's Rank	Possible Ideas if Angie Violates Curfew	Mom/Dad Rank
#1	Nothing should happen; Angie's parents are so uncool.	#10
#6	Angie is grounded for two weekend nights.	#1
#5	Angie loses her weekly allowance.	#5
#4	Angie has to help cook dinner and do dishes for a week.	#2
#7	Angie loses her telephone privileges for a week.	#3
#8	Angie is fined $1.00 for every minute she's late.	#9
#3	Angie writes an apology note.	#6
#10	Next time, Angie's mom (dad) goes out with her and her friends.	#8
#9	Angie and mom (dad) go for family counseling.	#7
#2	Angie gets 15 extra minutes out if she gets home on time.	#4

To calculate the most agreeable solution, add the rankings and select the lowest number. In this case, there's a tie between having Angie cook dinner and do dishes for a week (total = 6) and giving Angie 15 extra minutes out for getting home on time (total = 6). If there's a tie, you can try both solutions at once.

Step 4: Try out the most agreeable solution. Do this for a predetermined period of time. After agreeing on a proposed solution, say, "Let's try this out for three weeks and then meet again to talk about how things went."

(Continued)

> **Step 5: Evaluate how well the solution worked.** The solution may work perfectly, or you may have to go back and try this again, but either way, stay positive. It's nice to have your original brainstorming sheet to use as a reference for what you thought of last time.
>
> Mutual problem-solving probably won't produce magical solutions. The process is more important than the outcome. The main goal is to give your child the message: "We work on our problems together as a family." This message models the continuous use of a positive problem-solving family strategy.

General Rules for Chores

If asked, most children and teenagers will readily assure you that "chores suck." To make matters worse, parents don't appreciate having butler, maid, and custodian responsibilities in addition to their regular parenting duties. This combination of factors helps explain why so many parents come to consultations complaining of their children's noncompliance with chore requests.

When chores and chore completion are a concern, we typically teach parents about (a) the three-step approach to learning chores; (b) teaming to complete chores; (c) chore menus; and (d) chore contingencies. This problem-solving intervention is especially important because it illustrates how parents can collaboratively and authoritatively work with their children to accomplish family tasks.

The Three-Step Approach   Most children aren't naturally inclined to do chores and aren't particularly inclined to do them well. All too often, children will fail at their first assignment to clean the bathroom (or whatever project they're assigned).

If parents want chore cooperation from their children, the following three steps may be helpful: (a) Demonstrate (by actively teaching) how to do the chore assignment they wish their child to do; (b) do the chore assignment with their child (while providing positive and encouraging comments); and (c) have their child complete the assignment with parental supervision and support. Also, because doing chores is not naturally pleasurable for most children, parents should model how good it feels to get the job done. Finally, parents need to support their child by making positive statements about the child's performance and staying away from critical comments. Criticizing children when they're engaging in an already aversive task is an excellent way to destroy whatever remnants of motivation may still exist. This doesn't mean parents need to pretend their children have done a fabulous job when they haven't, but it does mean parents need to look for the positive and communicate in an encouraging way even when performance is less than adequate.

PARENT: Getting my 8-year-old to help with chores is sometimes more of a chore than just doing it myself.

CONSULTANT: It sounds like you'd like your daughter's help around the house, if it wasn't such a pain.

PARENT: Right.

CONSULTANT: May I share a few ideas?

PARENT: Go ahead.

CONSULTANT: [After explaining the three-step approach to learning chores, the consultant moves into ideas about keeping chore-related interactions positive.] Since doing chores can be a pain for both you and your daughter, let's talk about how to make it more pleasant. Some of these ideas may work for you and some may not, but here are a few. First, consider doing chores together while you listen to music she likes. Second, try doing chores for a very short time period during which she can be successful, even five minutes might be fine to start. Third, set it up so that right after the successful five minutes you transition to something fun. This is so she'll get the idea that you work first and then play and have fun. Fourth, while you're both working ignore her off-task behavior and pay close and positive attention to her on-task behavior. Fifth, if her performance is disappointing, express that in the most positive way you can. Something like, "Sweetheart, I know you can be better help than you were today," is enough. Be sure to avoid long lectures about non-helpfulness, because that could act as a reward. [The consultant writes out these ideas so the parent will have a reminder.]

Teaming to Complete Chores   More often than parents prefer, chore completion is suboptimal. We like to think of it as an example of the two-steps-forward-one-step-back phenomenon.

Children may need support and assistance to complete chores adequately. Some children will be slower at developing positive chore habits and others will be adversely affected by their attitude or mood. However, parents are better served if they stay positive and encouraging. It's especially important to avoid the temptation toward negative character feedback ("Can't you do anything right?").

Thinking of chores as a family activity or obligation can help. It's more motivating when all family members work to accomplish a goal in a particular time period. A friend of ours taught us the following technique:

> Okay, we need to clean up and de-clutter the house. Tonight at six-thirty P.M., I'll set the timer for thirty minutes and, as a family, we'll all run around cleaning and picking up and putting things away. At the end of our thirty minutes we can order a pizza and a movie and celebrate our clean house.

Many parents will immediately object to the "time-limited family project" technique by stating, "Yeah, we've tried that and the kids just sit around and don't really contribute. Then we end up doing all the work and we're angry at the kids for loafing." Of course, consultants should pay attention to this complaint and then try to help the parents reformulate chore activities to promote family success. Part of this reformulation will undoubtedly involve having the parents lower their chore performance expectations and praising or supporting their children for small contributions. It also might involve the natural and logical consequence of the parents eating pizza and watching a movie while the kids eat yesterday's leftovers and go to bed early.

In situations where children have already learned specific chores but occasionally regress because of a bad mood or a bad day, additional teaming techniques may be useful. For example, a parent might be coached to offer something like the following:

> How about I help you out tonight? We're a family and we should help each other. I can see you're not in the best of moods and I can relate to that because some days I hate to do chores, too. So, how about for tonight we work together and get this done in half the time?

Or, with teenagers who are high achievers and who maintain an exceptionally busy schedule, rather than completely dispensing with chore assignments, it might be more helpful to frame breaks from regular chore routines as a part of family support. For example,

> I know you're crazy-busy with homework and volleyball this weekend. How about if I take care of your kitchen-cleaning duties tonight and you can help me out sometime when I'm too busy and you've got free time?

The purpose of these family-teaming strategies is to help children understand the underlying message: In this family we all contribute to maintaining the household and because we're on the same team we help each other and share the load when we can.

Chore Menus   It's generally more effective for parents to give their children choices over which chores they're assigned. For example, if Miguel perpetually is assigned the chore of scooping the dog poop in the backyard, he may eventually feel there's no opportunity for career advancement (or personal choice) and so he may begin resisting his assignment. Now, if it's Miguel's designated dog and he agreed to scoop the poop for 12 years, more complex negotiation strategies may be needed. However, in most cases children experience greater freedom (which they desire) when they at least get to pick their poison (chore). Consequently, we advocate chore menus for children. These menus can be as simple as: "Would you like to empty the dishwasher or collect and take out the garbage?" Or parents may make a master list and let each child sign up for several chores a week.

Chore Contingencies   Some parents vehemently argue that completing chores is part and parcel of being in a family and, therefore, children should do chores without compensation. In contrast, other parents believe chores should be linked to a weekly allowance or some other form of financial remuneration. If you've been paying attention to this point, you should anticipate our response to these polar perspectives: We believe both positions are reasonable and recommend a combination approach.

For many families, it works best if some designated chores are expected contributions to family life. These could be chores that are required as a part of daily living (e.g., washing dishes, de-cluttering, dusting, vacuuming, feeding the dog, etc). Other, less frequent chores could be reserved for when children want to make money. Obviously, consultants should work with parents to develop a system that best fits the individual family's needs and the parents' values.

Using direct power strategies may be necessary and appropriate when it comes to chore completion. For example, we recommend that parents use Grandma's Rule (see Chapter 3) to clearly and concisely articulate their expectations that chore completion precedes recreation. A classic example of using Grandma's Rule is:

> When you finish unloading the dishwasher and wiping down the kitchen counters, then you can turn on the computer and play some games.

Overall, as we think of chores, we're reminded of a wise statement a colleague uses when working with mandated client groups. At the beginning of group he announces: "Well, I know we're all required to be here, but we're not required to have a bad time. So I hope we can make the best of it." When parents lead with a good attitude and positive mood in the face of a required task, often children will begin to follow their leaders. This is the essence of role modeling. (See Parent Homework Assignment 8-4.)

Parent Homework Assignment 8-4

Brightening up the Chore List

As a parent, when it comes to getting your child to do chores, your response may range from "*Ugh*" to "It's easier and simpler if I just do them myself." Whatever your response, this homework assignment is designed to help you develop new strategies and a positive attitude toward assigning and doing chores.

The first step toward joyful chore completion (we're joking about the joyful part) is to adopt a positive attitude. If you hate chores and you expect your children to hate chores and you approach them with dread, the outcome will likely be negative. In contrast, if you pair chore activities with something pleasant, you may inspire a more positive attitude in your children. Try some of the following strategies:

1. Play fun music while doing chores.
2. Schedule the chores about 30 minutes before your children's favorite television show and tell them if they get the chores done, they can watch the television.
3. Do chores together (and act happy).
4. Give your children frequent compliments for their involvement in chores (even if their efficiency or outcome isn't perfect).

(Continued)

5. Have a family meeting where the children get to select two or three chores from a menu and a small reward for completing their chores from a menu of rewards.

6. Schedule pizza and a movie for a family reward after completing chores and then be supportive of and realistic about your children's efforts; but if they fail to complete their chores, let them experience the natural consequence of left-overs (instead of pizza) and an early bedtime (while the chore completers watch the movie).

Concluding Comments

This chapter focuses on four specific indirect and/or problem-solving interventions practitioners can teach parents to use with their children. Each intervention is described and standard homework assignments are provided. Additional tip sheets associated with these interventions (and more) are available online. It's important for therapists, consultants, and other human services professionals who work with parents to modify the interventions included in this chapter to fit their therapeutic style and their clients' particular problems and needs.

Checklist for Indirect and Problem-Solving Interventions and Resources

☐ To help parents communicate directly while not activating their child's or teen's opposition or resistance, discuss and suggest the possibility of *giving information and then backing off*.

☐ Depending on the parent's level of sophistication and understanding of parenting nuances, it may be helpful to teach the differences between praise, mirroring, character feedback, and solution-focused questions.

☐ Mutual problem-solving is often a useful recommendation, especially when parents are taking more responsibility for their child's behavior than is ideal.

☐ Help parents develop plans for handling chores and any other issues where an emphasis on teamwork and communication and simple strategies can make onerous tasks more palatable.

☐ Remember to recommend Grandma's Rule as a direct communication technique for assigning and completing less pleasant tasks first before engaging in more pleasant tasks.

☐ Go to the comprehensive Master List of Attitudes, Strategies, and Interventions in Appendix D and/or the practitioner-support website to gather more ideas about indirect power and problem-solving interventions parents can use with their children.

CHAPTER NINE

A New-and-Improved Behaviorism

Child-Friendly but Direct Approaches to Discipline

"Opposite Day" is a creative, albeit odd, game played by children around the world (http://en.wikipedia.org/wiki/Opposite_Day). Interestingly, this game is often advocated by adults as a means through which children can learn about paradox and inverse relationships. When someone declares, "It's Opposite Day!" it means that everything stated thereafter holds a meaning directly opposite of the statement's content. For example, "It's a beautiful day!" means, "It's an ugly day!" and "I'm so happy to see you" means "I'm so *not* happy to see you." Declaring Opposite Day is complicated, because if it's already Opposite Day, the declaration is false, which has led some to conclude that declarations of Opposite Day should always begin the day before or just prior to the moment the day begins.

If you're confused about this, you're in good company. Although we're tempted to declare it's Not Opposite Day, doing so could really mean it is and then we'd have to start emphasizing how much we hope you're hating this book and how much we hate working with parents and children, and . . .

More seriously, we bring up Opposite Day primarily because it creatively captures the strong natural tendency for parents to use basic behavior modification principles in ways that are directly opposite to how they should be used. This chapter is designed to help you help parents straighten out—or reverse—their backward behavioral strategies in a child-friendly and parent-friendly manner.

Backward Behavior Modification: Using Boring, Natural, and Logical Consequences and Passionate and Surprise Rewards

As we alluded to in Chapter 4, *backward behavior modification* is endemic. Not only do parents tend to pay more attention to negative and undesirable behaviors than they do to positive and desirable behaviors, they also tend to do so with greater force or affect—which further complicates the situation. As noted previously, we learned about this complicated problem directly from teenagers who were in trouble for delinquent behaviors (see Chapter 4).

If parents engage in too much anger, yelling, or passion when their children misbehave, several problems can emerge: (a) The child will experience her parent's passion as reinforcement for misbehavior; (b) the child will feel powerful and in control of her parent (which is quite strong positive reinforcement); or (c) the parent will feel controlled by the child, or out-of-control, both of which further escalate the parent's emotional behavior.

To address backward behavior modification problems, we teach parents how to use "Boring Consequences and Passionate Rewards." The opening case in Chapter 1 is an example of the power of boring consequences. If you recall, the parents of Emma, a very oppositional nine-year-old, reported their "family was about to disintegrate" because of continuous power struggles. However, when they returned for their second consultation session, their family situation had transformed largely as a function of boring consequences. In Chapter 1, we quoted the father's report on how he found boring consequences to be tremendously helpful. Emma's mother was similarly positive:

> Thinking about and then giving boring consequences helped us see that it was about us and not about our daughter. Before, she would misbehave and we would know she was going to misbehave and so we would go ballistic. Giving boring consequences suddenly gave us back our control over how we reacted to her. Instead of planning to go ballistic, it helped us see that going ballistic wasn't helping her and wasn't helping us. It felt good to plan to be boring instead. And the best thing about it was how it made the whole process of giving out consequences much shorter.

The inverse alternative to boring consequences is the practice of passionate rewards. Parents can be encouraged to intentionally pay positive and enthusiastic attention to their children's positive, desirable, and prosocial behaviors. Passionate rewards include parental responses such as:

- Applause or positive hoots and hollers
- Verbal praise ("I am so impressed with your dedication to learning Spanish.")
- Pats on the back, shoulder massages, and hugs
- Family gatherings where everyone dishes out compliments

Passionate rewards are especially important for preadolescent children. As you may suspect, because of increased self-consciousness accompanying adolescence, passionate hugs and excessive compliments for a 14-year-old may function as a punishment rather than a reinforcement—especially if the hugging and hooting occurs in front of the 14-year-old's peers.

Surprise rewards, presuming they're provided in a socially tactful manner, are extremely powerful reinforcers for children of all ages. For example, with teenagers it can be very rewarding if parents suddenly and without advance notice say something like, "You know, you've been working hard and you've been so darn helpful that this weekend we'd like to give you a complete vacation from all your household chores or this $20 bill to go out to the movie of your choice with your buddies; which would you prefer?"

Surprise rewards are, in technical behavioral lingo, *variable-ratio reinforcements*. Across species, this reinforcement schedule has been shown to be the most powerful reinforcement schedule of all. Everyday examples of variable-ratio reinforcement schedules include gambling, golf, fishing, and other highly addictive behaviors where individuals can never be certain when their next response might result in the "jackpot."

When coaching parents to use surprise rewards (variable-ratio reinforcement schedules), we emphasize that the surprise reward should be viewed as a spontaneous celebration of desirable behavior. Overall, we prefer this informal reinforcement plan over more mechanized sticker charts and reward systems (although we don't mean to say that these more mechanized systems should never be used; in fact, when children are put in charge of their own reinforcement systems, these systems can be especially effective).

PERSISTENCE COACHING

A part of the "Incredible Years" parent training curriculum includes a unit on what Webster-Stratton (2007) refers to as *persistence coaching*. Persistence coaching is especially designed for children with attention difficulties and provides an excellent example of intense and passionate social reinforcement. Webster-Stratton (2007) describes the procedure:

> *During* persistence coaching, *the parent is commenting on the child's attention to the task. A parent might say to his child who is working with blocks,* "You are really concentrating on building that tower; you are really staying patient; you are trying again and are really focusing on getting it as high as you can; you are staying so calm; you are focused; there, you did it all by yourself." *With this persistence coaching, the child begins to be aware of his internal state when he or she is calm, focused, and persisting with an activity.* (pp. 317–318; italics in original)

This example by Webster-Stratton not only illustrates focused and passionate attention as a behavioral reinforcer, it also includes components of mirroring, solution-focused strategies, and character feedback. After getting intensive attention and specific feedback for persisting on a tower-building task, children are more likely to overcome negative beliefs about themselves and to begin seeing themselves as persistent and capable.

Some parents will say their child hates positive comments and prematurely conclude that these approaches are destined to backfire and be ineffective, perhaps even detrimental. This will be most likely when children display oppositional tendencies and/or have very negative internal beliefs about themselves. As if it were constantly Opposite Day, it will seem to parents as if praise is punishment and punishment is praise when they're trying to work with their children. Webster-Stratton (2007) comments on this phenomenon:

> *Children with conduct problems usually get less praise and encouragement from adults than other children. When they do get praise, they are likely to reject it because of their oppositional responses. For some children, this oppositional response to praise and encouragement is actually a bid to get more attention and to keep the adult focusing on them longer. Parents can help these children by giving the praise frequently and then ignoring the protests that follow. Over time with consistent encouragement, the children will become more comfortable with this positive view of themselves. (p. 312)*

Our general policy is to closely watch for backward behavior modification and to counter it by teaching parents how to pay attention to positive behavior, ignore negative behavior, and administer passionate and surprise rewards and boring consequences. We're sometimes surprised (and rewarded) by how quickly parents see that they're inadvertently and destructively celebrating Opposite Day, when a regular day would suffice. (See Parent Homework Assignment 9-1.)

Parent Homework Assignment 9-1

Backward Behavior Modification

One amazing thing about parenting is how easy and natural it is to do things backward. For example, imagine your 7th-grader comes home with a report card that has five A's, one B, and one C. If you're like most parents, you'll take a quick look and say something like, "Why'd you get that C?" or, "How can you raise that B up to an A?"

Even though these questions make excellent sense, they're in direct violation of a very basic principle of human behavior. That principle is: *Whatever you pay the most attention to will tend to grow and whatever you ignore will tend to shrink.* Despite this powerful principle, our human and parental tendency is almost always to pay close attention to the F's and C's in life, while only offering a passing glance at the A's.

Another version of the same problem happens with parents who have two or more children. Your children may coexist very nicely together 60% of the day and fight like cats and dogs for the other 40%. Unfortunately, in that situation the natural tendency is to give *almost all* your attention to your children when they fight and *very little* attention to them when they're playing nicely.

The consequence of violating this basic principle is:

- Your 7th-grader feels his efforts are underappreciated and becomes less motivated.
- Your children, sensing that they can get more of your attention by fighting than from playing together nicely, may begin fighting *even more.*

Our *first* point with this homework assignment is to reassure you that it's perfectly natural to pay more attention to "bad" behavior than "good" behavior. But, it's equally true that even though paying too much attention to bad behavior is natural—it's *not* helpful because it can become a reward for bad behavior.

Our *second* point is that you should work very hard to:

Pay more attention to your children when you like what they're doing than you do when you don't like what they're doing.

Or, better yet, try this:

When giving out consequences, be boring, but when giving out rewards, be passionate.

I had this lesson driven home to me many years ago. While doing therapy with teenagers who were in trouble for delinquent behavior, they started telling me how much satisfaction they got from making their parents angry. When I asked about this, they said things like, "I love it when my dad's veins start sticking out of his neck" or "It's cool when I can get my mom so mad that she spits when she talks."

Keep these images in mind the next time your child does something that gets under your skin. Then, instead of a long lecture complete with bulging veins and spitting, be short and boring. Use a monotone to say something like: "I don't like it when you do that."

Then, when your child comes home on time, or gets an A, or plays nice with her brother, or makes an intelligent comment about virtually anything—that's when you should launch into a passionate and positive lecture—complete with bulging veins and spittle.*

---

*These rules may not hold perfectly for your unique child. Some teens may not like much positive attention. That's why you're the best judge of whether a particular parenting strategy will work with your child. We're also kidding about the spittle; that's hardly ever a good thing to see.

POSITIVE AND DIRECTIVE ROLE MODELING (BEHAVIOR SIMULATIONS)

Getting children to stop engaging in negative behaviors is a common goal for parents who come to see professionals. These negative behaviors include whining, biting, hitting, impulsive grabbing, back talk, and more.

Case: "We'd Like to Not Spank Travis"

PARENT: My three-year-old is really an active little boy. He gets into everything. I'm trying to teach him that it's not okay to take things off the counter and that he can't play with our cell phones, but when I tell him to stop he just ignores me or laughs at me. He thinks it's a game.

CONSULTANT: What's your reaction to that?

PARENT: Oh, I feel helpless and frustrated. I don't know what else to do. Some friends recommended we start slapping his hand, but we want to avoid that. We both got spanked growing up and we'd like to not spank Travis.

CONSULTANT: I respect your wish to parent without hitting. Sometimes it seems easier to use spanking, but often it backfires. I know many parents who started with hand-slapping and quickly stopped when their child started slapping back.

PARENT: Yes. I wouldn't want that and that's just the kind of thing my son might do.

CONSULTANT: I have some ideas for how you might be able to teach your son a little more about what you and your husband believe is okay and not okay. Do you mind if I share them with you?

PARENT: Not at all. That's why I'm here.

CONSULTANT: First, as you know, scolding by saying "No!" or "Stop!" only goes so far. And, if you do scold or say "No!" you need to only give one warning and then take action, otherwise your son will learn to ignore you. Your action should be to remove him, or the object, from the situation because it's bad news if he learns that what you want isn't important.

PARENT: So you're saying I can warn him once and then I need to act.

CONSULTANT: Right. And you could try very brief timeouts of about one minute. I'll give you a handout on exactly how to do that. [See Parent Homework Assignment 9-4.]

PARENT: Okay.

CONSULTANT: But what I really want to focus on for you and your son is a positive teaching technique. Sometime, when you're both calm and in a good mood, engage him in a practice session where you set out the cell phone and have him practice leaving it alone. You should be very clear that it's not okay for him to pick it up and that if he sees it lying around, he should just find you and tell you. First, you could play both parts of Mom and Travis. Then, you could have him play you and you play him. Be sure to emphasize words like "No" and "Please stop" and tell him and yourself, "Good job" or "Nice work" many times during the interaction. Finally, you can go through the situation with him as himself and you as Mom and, again, guide him through how he's supposed to act.

PARENT: Okay. I get it.

CONSULTANT: And then afterward, be sure to quiz him by asking him things like, "What will happen if you pick up the cell phone?" and "What will Mommy or Daddy say if you just leave it alone and tell us where it is?" This is because if he can tell you what will happen, he's got a better chance of cooperating with the lesson.

PARENT: What if he does the wrong thing and picks up the phone?

CONSULTANT: Just do exactly what you would do if he really did pick it up. Say "No. That's not okay." And then remove the phone and have him be in timeout for a minute. If he laughs, turn your back and say, "I don't like it when you laugh at me."

PARENT: Okay. I can do that.

CONSULTANT: And later, when your husband is home, you can go through the sequence again and your husband can play all the roles. This way Travis will get a chance to practice, he'll get a chance to get some praise from you when he handles the situation well, and he'll get a chance to know you're completely serious about this specific limit on his behavior.

This positive role-modeling or simulation procedure can be used effectively with a variety of negative behaviors, even biting. The main purpose is to practice and then review the correct behavior, complete with positively reinforcing praise. All the scolding or punishment in the world won't provide the help and guidance children need to learn positive behaviors. (See Parent Homework Assignment 9-2.)

One other caveat with this approach is needed. If parents have too much fun doing a cell-phone skit and less fun doing other things, the child may begin initiating a cell phone consequence just to get attention. This means parents need to be skilled at having fun in other domains to pull off this technique.

Parent Homework Assignment 9-2

Intentional Role Modeling

In this handout, we outline a strategy for intentionally, but indirectly, teaching children positive behaviors through role modeling. This strategy works best if you have at least one other adult available to help. Even for single parents—it helps if you can recruit an aunt or uncle or good friend to help with indirectly delivering educational messages.

Most children don't have skills for dealing with conflict. This may be partly because they just haven't had a chance to see two adults or two children resolving their differences politely. Your goal with this homework assignment is to actively demonstrate to your child or children how to politely disagree and how to respectfully manage or resolve conflict. If you'd like to help your children learn this important skill, you'll need to enact a scenario or conflict situation.

Get your spouse, partner, sibling, or friend to help you with a minor conflict scenario. Be sure to plan it in advance. One of the following situations might help you demonstrate polite conflict and successful resolutions:

- You and your partner disagree on what to have for dinner, on what movie to watch, or on what to do for a recreational outing.

- You and your partner disagree during a political discussion.
- You and your partner discuss a fair balancing of chores in the home.

During your intentional role-modeling, you and your partner should express a disagreement. For example:

You: "I want to go to the lake on Saturday."
Partner: "I'd rather stay home and watch football."
You: "How are we gonna figure this out?"

At this point, you and your partner can choose to illustrate your preferred conflict negotiation and management approaches. What you choose will depend on what you want to role-model or teach. You can teach domination–submission—where one person pushes hard for her or his position and possibly dismisses the other person's perspective. In this situation, the weaker party gives in and a lesson (perhaps not an ideal one) is learned. Or you could teach conflict avoidance where both of you consistently avoid talking about anything you might disagree about.

You can also teach communication and conflict negotiation, where each person makes his or her case and the other party uses active listening (e.g., "Jodie, I hear you saying this particular football game is very important and that's why you'd rather not go to the lake this particular Saturday"). You might choose this approach if your goal is to teach your children how to engage in respectful communication—even during disagreements.

However, you might also decide to demonstrate to your children that couples, partners, or families can also apply a variety of problem-solving strategies to conflict situations. For example, you might decide to illustrate "turn-taking." If so, one of you could offer something like, "How about we do football this weekend and go to the lake next weekend?"

In addition to turn-taking, you could model "compromise." With compromise, each party gets "part" of what she or he wants. For example, the final decision (after modeling a respectful communication process) might be: "Okay, we'll go to the lake and bring the television."

The most important point in this intentional role-modeling activity is for you, as a parent, to become more aware of the fact that your children are almost always watching and listening and learning from you. As a consequence, rather than spontaneously erupting into conflict (and perhaps modeling less-than-positive communication), you can intentionally show your children how two people can communicate constructively and respectfully even when minor disagreements arise.

One complaint parents sometimes offer about this assignment is that it feels fake or manipulative. Our response is to ask you to reflect on your parenting goals and to decide whether you want to intentionally and actively teach your children positive social behaviors or whether you want to unintentionally and passively teach negative social behaviors. What you decide to teach your children is really up to you—we just recommend that you do it intentionally.

A New Attitude and a New Plan for Limit-Setting

Children are powerful beings who strongly influence their parents' lives. Because of this, parents can be reluctant, or even scared, to set limits or give consequences. This is partly why many parents talk as if their two-year-old is in charge of their home.

Sometimes when parents try to be in control of household decisions, children respond with one of their greatest and most powerful weapons — a dramatic and compelling tantrum or emotional meltdown. In some cases, children's meltdown-tantrums can be so overwhelming or humiliating to parents that they back down and avoid setting limits or requiring polite and reasonable behaviors because they're afraid of the next emotional explosion. The following case example illustrates both the new attitude and new limit-setting plan interventions (see Appendix B, Tip Sheet 4 and Parent Homework Assignment 9-3). As you read, think about how you would help parents reformulate their attitude toward tantrums, meltdowns, insulting behaviors, and other extreme power moves children make. Also consider how you could help parents come up with a calm set of responses, with enforceable limits they can feel good about.

Case: A Visit to the Mall

Here's what a parent of a 5-year-old and a 2-year-old explained when she came in for a consultation:

PARENT: My friend invited me and my two kids to meet her and her two-year-old at Bellevue Square for dinner and shopping. I knew better. This friend makes me feel insecure. We met for dinner at this nice café and there's nothing there my kids will eat. After a while, they start running around the café. I settle them down and we walk around to shop and my five-year-old son is running way ahead and I keep trying to get him to get back with us and he won't listen. We eventually get to a pet store and my two-year-old is climbing on stuff and my five-year-old is knocking on the pet-cage glass right where it says "Don't knock on the glass" and he won't stop. Finally, I drag them both to a bench and make them sit there and I yell at them and they start crying and I'm humiliated and have to carry them both outside to the car and yell at them some more. I was one of those parents you see who has out-of-control children and then goes berserk.

CONSULTANT: So, eventually your kids started listening to you? [Focusing on how the negative behavior sequence finally stops can be revealing.]

PARENT: Yes. Because they knew it was over.

CONSULTANT: When you tell that story it reminds me of how kids can sometimes almost read our minds and know when something is really important to us and know when they can take advantage of us by not listening. But then when we somehow make it clear that the fun and games are over, suddenly they get it and cooperate.

PARENT: I felt so uncomfortable with my friend and her potty-trained little girl and I couldn't even come close to controlling my kids. And later that night, when I was talking about it to my five-year-old, I apologized for yelling and losing my mind and I asked him why he didn't listen to me and he said, "I listened, I just didn't do what you said." I couldn't believe it!

CONSULTANT: That's amazing. So, he really did know what was going on.

PARENT: He did and he still didn't cooperate.

CONSULTANT: Can I share some ideas with you?

PARENT: Yes. I'd love some ideas!

CONSULTANT: We used to have a parent educator here who taught a class called, "They only listen when I yell . . . and other parenting myths." The point of the class was exactly what you've been talking about. It's not that our kids only pay attention when we yell, it's that they only comply when *they know* we're completely serious. Tell me, how many times did you have to ask your five-year-old to cooperate before he finally did?

PARENT: It had to be twenty times. I was trying to get him to sit down at the café, to come back to us when we were shopping, to stop knocking on the glass at the pet shop, and he would sometimes partly respond and sometimes not at all, until the end, when he sat on the bench and started crying.

CONSULTANT: Here's what I'm thinking. You already said you set yourself up with this dinner with this friend and her practically perfect two-year-old. I'll bet somewhere inside you were really wanting to avoid a confrontation with your kids and the embarrassment that goes with it. And they sensed you were afraid to confront them and afraid to give out firm consequences and so they just chose not to listen or cooperate.

PARENT: I know. I know. I don't even take my two-year-old grocery shopping anymore because it's too much. And obviously they knew I didn't really want to follow through with any consequences. But what can I do?

CONSULTANT: I have two ideas and the first one will sound really weird.

PARENT: Just tell me.

CONSULTANT: This is crazy, but you need to start looking forward to when your children have tantrums or misbehave.

PARENT: That *is* weird.

CONSULTANT: I know, but unless you look forward to it, with confidence that you can handle whatever they do, they'll sense your dread and fear and they'll be the ones who are confident they can do whatever they want—like run ahead in the mall and knock on the pet store glass cages—because they sense you're afraid to stop them.

PARENT: Okay. I get it. But I don't know how I can look forward to a meltdown in the mall.

CONSULTANT: And that's exactly why we need to develop a nice and clear and practical plan for the next time this sort of thing happens. You need a very simple plan for limit-setting with your children. Because if you have to ask them to cooperate twenty times, they know they don't have to pay any attention or respect to you—until the twentieth time when you're yelling and screaming. The plan should have one or two warnings and then a small consequence. For example, in the mall situation, it might have been embarrassing, but the first time your kids didn't respond to your requests to sit down or walk with you, you could have given a clear warning, something like, "Okay, if you don't walk with me, then we'll go outside and spend some time on the bench until you're ready to come back in." Then, the second time one of them didn't cooperate, you'd calmly collect them and take a brief timeout on the bench or in your car. Then, if it happened a third time, you could turn to your friend and say, "I'm sorry, but it looks like my kids aren't cooperating right now and so I need to take them home." I know that might have felt embarrassing and awkward, but it would communicate very clearly to your children that you are a serious mom who's confident in her limits and decisions.

PARENT: It wouldn't have been half as embarrassing as the way things turned out.

In this case, we developed a very simple limit-setting system. It involved three steps:

1. The first time the children misbehave, give a clear warning.
2. The second time the children misbehave, take them into a brief and boring timeout from the fun.
3. The third time the children misbehave, the fun activity ends.

In addition to these three steps, we discussed managing the children's physical needs by checking if they were hungry, tired, sick, or hurting and planning in advance for outings. We also discussed how she could review with her children, in advance of the outing, exactly what she expected and exactly what would happen (brief public timeout, followed by a disappointing trip back home) if misbehavior occurred. Finally, we suggested that she set up some practice outings where she could quickly and effectively implement the consequences without the pressure of a friend looking on. The purpose of these outings was to practice the plan and demonstrate to her children exactly what would happen if and when public misbehavior occurred.

Overall, this procedure is consistent with what we know from the science of behavioral psychology. As Kazdin (2008) states: "Here's a rough rule of thumb to go by: if you say it twice (the initial instruction plus one reminder), that's reminding; if you say it three or more times, you're nagging and nagging can undermine [your credibility and power]" (p. 172). In addition to Kazdin's good advice, we like to emphasize to parents that most children are amazingly intuitive—like dogs, they can sense their parents' fear.

Parent Homework Assignment 9-3

A Practical Guide to Setting Limits

Unfortunately, children are not born knowing how to deal with frustration, anger, and disappointment. This means it's our job to teach them how to deal with these difficult and sometimes unpleasant emotions.

(Continued)

One way to teach your child about how to handle frustration and other difficult emotions is through limit-setting. If you let your child do whatever she wants anytime she wants to, she'll have trouble learning to cope with frustration. This can happen if you always give your children whatever they want.

Many parents mistakenly think that when they set limits, they need to be mean or especially tough. Don't make that mistake. Good limit-setters are firm, but kind and compassionate. Try to be the kind of boss you'd like to have yourself.

An effective limit-setting strategy includes the following:

1. Set a clear limit or clear expectation.
2. If your child appears upset or resistant, show empathy for your child's frustration, disappointment, or anger.
3. Repeat the limit in clear language (you could also have your child repeat the limit or plan back to you).
4. Give your child a reasonable choice or timeline (this is especially important with strong-willed children; see the following for examples).
5. Show more empathy by joining in with your child's unhappiness (this might include telling a story, if there's time).
6. Enforce the limit on time and with a logical consequence.
7. Stay positive and encouraging.

A Limit-Setting Example

1. *Set a clear limit:* "Dinner will be ready in five minutes, so it's time to turn off your computer game."
2. *Show empathy* by using feeling words: "I know it's hard to stop doing something fun and you're feeling very upset."
3. *Repeat the limit:* "But you know it's time to stop playing computer games."
4. *Give a choice and a timeline:* "Either you can stop playing in the next two minutes, or I'll unplug the computer."
5. *Show more empathy* by joining in with your child's unhappiness: "I hate it when I have to stop doing something I love."
6. *Enforce the limit* on time and with a logical consequence. (Say what you'll do and then do what you said: If you said it will be two minutes, wait two minutes and enforce the limit; don't wait three minutes or one minute).
7. *Stay positive and encouraging:* "Even though I had to turn off your computer in the middle of your game tonight, I'm sure you'll be able to plan for this and turn it off yourself tomorrow."

Remember, although it's your job to teach your child how to become more responsible and how to cope with life frustrations, you won't be able to do this perfectly; no one does this perfectly. Just keep the principles in this homework assignment in mind and practice them when you can.

A New-and-Improved Timeout From Reinforcement

Timeout from reinforcement is an immensely popular behavioral response cost procedure. Unfortunately, most parents use it like corporal punishment; when children misbehave, parents put them in timeout. The problem with traditional timeout as practiced in most households is that parents wield it like a stick when, technically, it's supposed to be the taking away of a carrot.

It's possible that problems with *timeout* arise because the term is so deceptively simple that most people believe they automatically understand what timeout is and how to use it. In reality, there are a number of do's and don'ts that most parents need to learn about timeout; these are detailed in Parent Homework Assignment 9-4.

Timeout from reinforcement is a very brief time period during which children are not exposed to the normally rich, exciting, and rewarding stimulation of everyday life. Timeout is not "thinking time" and it should never be more than 10 minutes. Timeout is simply a break from all potential forms of positive reinforcement (including yelling, lecturing, and glaring).

Timeout Problems and Timeout Solutions

As Kazdin (2008) suggests, if brief and humane timeouts are not working, parents should not escalate their consequences. Instead, they should make *time-in* more enjoyable and work with their child on positive behavior simulations (described earlier in this chapter). Escalating punishment is a bad idea.

Typical complaints parents make about timeout are: (1) My child won't go to timeout; and (2) my child won't stay in timeout. Kazdin (2008) describes, from a behavioral perspective, how to handle children who don't go to timeout:

> *If you declare a time-out and your child folds his arms and says,* No, I'm not going, *and you [shouldn't] drag him, what do you do? First, give him an extra minute penalty. You can do this twice: Up the time-out from two minutes to three, then to four. Then, if that doesn't work, take away a privilege—something significant but brief, like no TV today. Then turn and walk away. Don't give in if he then says,* Okay okay okay, I'll do it, *because then you'd be reinforcing an unwanted sequence. . . . Let the consequence do the work. Resist the temptation to add little zingers. . . . (pp. 142–143; italics in original)*

Kazdin is making several excellent points in this description of how to handle timeout noncompliance. One part bears highlighting: When children refuse to do something physical, parents should not force them into the act. Forcing a physical act is beyond reasonable parent power and control and can result in ugly and undesirable outcomes. Instead, as Kazdin suggests, the parent should shift to a consequence over which the parent has complete control and authority (and the child's physical movements is not one of these things).

Emotions and Emotional Timeouts

Timeouts will often elicit strong emotions and strong emotions will often elicit timeouts. This highlights the question of how to deal with children's emotions before, during, and after timeouts.

Parents are the best experts on their own children's emotional states and so the helping professional's job is to help parents balance a reasonable response to misbehavior (a brief timeout) with their children's need for empathy, emotional soothing, and emotion coaching.

Case: An Emotionally Soothing Timeout

PARENT: When I try to put my child into timeout, he becomes an emotional basket case. He screams and cries and it's really terrible.

CONSULTANT: That sounds very hard. It really reminds me of how important it is for parents to set limits on misbehavior and provide empathy and comfort for difficult emotions at the same time. It's possible to do both.

PARENT: How do I do that?

CONSULTANT: You need to stand firm on not giving in to whatever your child wanted before the timeout was called. So, if your child hit another boy and grabbed a toy, you would never give back the toy or put your child back with the other boy before the timeout was served. You stay firm because whenever your child is aggressive or obnoxious you cannot give in to him and give him what he wants. That's a huge parenting rule.

PARENT: Okay, I understand that.

CONSULTANT: Then, you need to decide how much emotional support your child needs. If he's heading toward inconsolable sobbing, you may need to make it a brief thirty-second to one-minute timeout. Right at the end, you swoop in and comfort and console and help him understand what he did wrong and what he could do next time to avoid the timeout. This is because if your child is sobbing, he's already experienced the punishment and so there's no need to prolong it.

PARENT: But I've always heard you should keep your child in timeout until he behaves, or at least until he's served one minute for each year of his age.

CONSULTANT: There's crazy information out there about timeout. The truth is: The first minute is the most important. Waiting for him to behave or calm down on his own could be too traumatic for both of you. And the one-minute-for-each-year is a general guideline that should be adjusted for individual children.

PARENT: Okay.

CONSULTANT: The only reason you might wait longer would be if you believed your child was pretending to be upset to get your attention. Even then, you shouldn't wait long before offering emotional comfort, maybe two minutes.

PARENT: Yeah, well, I'm pretty sure he's not faking it.

CONSULTANT: Another thing to keep in mind is that some children, and your son may be an example, need help with emotional soothing. He may need a calming timeout more than he needs a bad-behavior timeout. If that's the case, find a big pillow or comfortable spot and have him do his timeout there. And if he's really a wreck, spend the timeout with him and help him recover.

This dialogue illustrates some of the complexities and misconceptions of timeout. For example, when the consultant suggests using a big pillow for a timeout spot instead of the classic chair or corner, she's illustrating that she understands that timeout is a response-cost procedure and not a punishment procedure. The purpose is not to inflict pain or discomfort, but to take away the "fun" of time-in. This is an important distinction for parents to understand and it can be much more productive and effective for children to serve their brief timeout in a comfortable spot (without toys or books). In fact, to promote emotional de-escalation it may even be appropriate for parents to take their child to his or her room and engage in gently playful activities while expressing empathy for the child's emotional state and hope for emotional recovery.

Overall, when choosing to use timeouts as a reasonable consequence for specific behaviors (e.g., hitting a sibling or parent), parents should anticipate their children's potential emotional reactions. These reactions can range from rage and anger to sadness, tears, and inconsolable sobbing. Parents should also consider emotional-recovery timeouts, during which emotional soothing takes place. Finally, parents can role-model timeout behavior by taking one themselves—especially when they're emotionally upset and need to do a little deep breathing.

Parent Homework Assignment 9-4

Following the Rules for a New-and-Improved Timeout from Reinforcement

Most parents use timeout like punishment, but punishment and timeout are really two different parenting techniques. Timeout is a less-aversive and more compassionate alternative to punishment.

- Punishment is the application of something aversive or painful (spanking or scolding).
- Timeout is the taking away of something positive (children are removed from opportunities to have fun or receive positive reinforcement).

The differences between punishment and timeout are subtle but important. When using timeout from reinforcement properly, children should be calmly taken from their usually rich and rewarding environment, but they should not be punished through pinching, squeezing, slapping, scolding, or yelling.

There are two main types of timeout: behavioral timeouts and emotional timeouts. *Behavioral* timeouts are used in response to inappropriate misbehavior. *Emotional* timeouts are used to help with emotional de-escalation or calming.

Tips for Behavioral Timeouts

- Timeout effectiveness is based on how much fun and good stuff is happening during time-in. If your child has lots of fun during time-in, timeout will be powerful

(Continued)

- Timeout should be used in a boring and matter-of-fact manner. Avoid yelling and lecturing.
- The first minute (or two) of timeout is the most important. Don't extend time-out beyond 10 minutes.
- There should be no pushing, holding down, or aggressive touch during timeout. Timeout is not a physical intervention.
- Don't use timeout as "thinking time" or demand an apology from your child at the end.
- Don't do more than about two timeouts a day or continually threaten timeout.
- Teach your child about timeout through practice or rehearsals.
- Praise your child for going to timeout.
- Practice, simulate, discuss, and educate your child about what behaviors cause a timeout.
- Praise your child for completing his or her timeout.
- Stay quiet during your child's timeout.

A behavioral timeout is used immediately after your child has misbehaved. When misbehavior happens, consider saying: "Uh-oh. That's not okay. You need to go to timeout." The timeout location should be a chair or pillow or other location where your child can be separated from the social or family activity. Maintain silence (other than praising your child for going to timeout). Set a timer for between 1 and 10 minutes. Two minutes is appropriate for most children. If your child refuses to go to timeout, don't get physical; simply shift the consequence to something you can control (e.g., turn off the television or computer, send the friend home, end the family outing, assign a "when you/then you" chore, etc.). If you've rehearsed your timeout procedure, it should go smoothly. When timeout is finished, praise your child for completing the timeout and verbally release him or her. Explain the reason for timeout as needed.

Your child shouldn't be required to stay silent during timeout. Many parents incorrectly assume that timeout should continue until children calm down. Calming down and completing a timeout are two different issues. If your child is angry or crying, a consequence has *already been delivered* and so there's no need to continue the scene until he or she is quiet. If your goal is a quiet child, timeout may not be the appropriate consequence. Instead, you may need to implement a quiet time in the child's room or remove him or her from a social or public situation.

Tips for Emotional Timeouts

If your child has trouble calming down after 1 or 2 minutes, you may need to approach and comfort him or her. This is okay. After 1 or 2 minutes you can release your child from timeout. At that point, the behavioral timeout has ended and an emotional timeout may begin.

During an emotional timeout children need soothing and comforting. They still may be angry or upset about not getting what they wanted and you shouldn't give in and give them their desired outcome. Instead, give empathy, comfort, and support. Life is hard and most adults don't like not getting what they want, either. Help them know this. Help them breathe deeply and think about happier times. Help them move past their distress and into a calmer and more comfortable place. This can be a powerful and positive experience for both parent and child. Behavioral timeouts are about limit-setting. Emotional timeouts are about parent–child bonding and emotional regulation.

Letting Natural Consequences Stimulate Life Learning

Generally, parents are wired to protect their children from harm. Hardly any parent will idly stand by and let a child reach out and touch a hot stove. Even fewer will let their children run into the street so they can experience the natural consequence of being hit by an automobile.

As the *love-and-logic* gurus articulate so well (Cline & Fay, 1992), as children grow older we need to let them begin taking responsibility for their behaviors and we need to stop protecting them from the inevitable and sometimes painful natural consequences of their behaviors.

Case: Terribly Tardy Tabitha

The following dialogue illustrates a combination of choice theory and love and logic.

CONSULTANT: It would be great if you had total control over whether Tabitha was all ready for school on time every day. But, she's 12 years old and quite capable of making herself late. Unfortunately, our kids sometimes dig in and exercise control over their own behaviors, despite our best efforts to be a positive influence. And sometimes, they make pretty bad decisions. What I'm getting at is that we shouldn't try to directly control Tabitha, because as she's shown you in the past, she's likely to resist. But we could have you make a few changes yourself and then see if her behavior changes or improves.

PARENT: I know that. I don't really want to control her. I just want her to see how important it is to get to school on time. Despite all my reminders and trying to rescue her from being late, she's piling up the tardy slips at an alarming rate.

CONSULTANT: Exactly. I know being on time is important. You know being on time is important. Tabitha's teachers know being on time is important. But, for some reason, Tabitha is resisting our great ideas. She's proving to us that, in fact, she's the one in charge of whether she's late or not.

PARENT: But, what she's doing isn't even good for herself. She's the one suffering and she's the one who will suffer in the future.

CONSULTANT: And it's very important that we make sure that Tabitha feels the suffering more than you feel the suffering.

PARENT: What do you mean?

CONSULTANT: I mean, you're the one who's here. You're the one who's in distress about Tabitha's tardiness. And she's off whistling in the park. She needs to feel the pain of the consequences of her behavior more than you feel the pain of the consequences of her behavior. It's okay if you feel bad on the inside, but we really need to have you try not to show it to Tabitha—because as long as you're in more distress than she is, as long as you protect her from the consequences of her own behavior, the less likely she is to develop internal motivation to get to school on time.

The preceding dialogue emphasizes three points: (a) Children should suffer more from their destructive or maladaptive behaviors than their parents; (b) parents should not completely protect older children from natural behavioral consequences; and (c) children should be held responsible for their behaviors. Also, as parents retreat from protecting children from their problem behavior consequences, they should do so with empathy and compassion. (See Parent Homework Assignment 9-5.)

In the end, after much work, Tabitha's mom adopted a new perspective on dealing with Tabitha's tardiness. She practiced making the following statement:

Tabitha, I love you and I've decided to stop fighting with you about being late to school and to start enjoying you more. You're a smart girl . . . a young woman, and whether you get to school on time is really up to you. If you want, I'll get you a new clock radio and I'll remind you once each morning about what time it is, but the rest is up to you. I know you're smart enough to figure out how to get to school on time without my help.

Additionally, Tabitha's mom made a firm commitment to regularly make deposits into her emotional bank account with Tabitha. About a month later, she reported that she was amazed at how responsible Tabitha could be on her own. We responded by noting that Tabitha had a good role model and good genes for eventually displaying a high level of personal responsibility.

Parent Homework Assignment 9-5

The Beauty and Power of Natural and Logical Consequences

Life is not easy and children (and adults) learn through struggles, failures, and disappointments. Your goal, as a parent, is to create a reasonable, consistent, and loving home and then let your child struggle with the demands of life. These demands include very basic things like:

- Not getting to watch television after a certain time
- Participating in housecleaning

- Not getting attention 100% of the day
- Having to get ready and get to school on time
- Having to wait your turn to get served dessert or to play with an especially fun toy
- Not getting to eat your favorite food for every meal
- Having to tie your own shoes

As you might gather from the preceding list, even little things in life can be hard for a growing child; but to learn, children need to directly experience frustration and disappointment.

Natural or logical consequences are a necessary part of learning. They help your child get better at surviving disappointments in the world and in your family home. Natural and logical consequences are always related in some way to the misbehavior and are not given out with anger or as "punishment."

Here are some examples:

1. Your children leave toys in a public area of the house, even though they've been told to put toys away when done playing. **Logical consequence:** Use a "Saturday box" or put the toys in timeout. This involves picking up the toys and putting them in a box and storing them away until the next Saturday (or whatever day), when they're given back. This logical consequence avoids the overreaction ("If you don't put your toys away, then I'll give them away to someone else") and the attention-giving lecture ("Let me tell you about when I was a child and what would happen if I left my toys out . . . ") and instead provides children with a clear, consistent, and reasonable consequence.

2. Your children argue with you about a consequence or about you being unfair. **Logical consequence:** You let your children know, "I don't feel like arguing about this" and leave the area. You may want to go to the bathroom to take time away to further develop your planned response. While remaining friendly, another important message to give is, "I know you'd like things your way, but we have rules and consequences for everyone in our family." Of course this may trigger another argument and you can walk away again and tell your children, "I know you can figure this out and not have this consequence next time."

3. You cook dinner, but your children don't show up on time. **Reasonable rules and logical consequences:** If you cook dinner, everyone needs to show up on time and be respectful about the dinner-eating process. That doesn't mean everyone has to eat every bite or provide you with lavish praise for your most excellent meal, but respectful attendance is a reasonable expectation. If your child is late for dinner, one reminder is enough. No drama or excess attention is needed. Just sit down and start eating and enjoying the mealtime process. Possible logical and natural consequences include: (a) Your child prepares the next meal; (b) you put away foods after you dish yourself up and so the child

(Continued)

has to get them out and serve himself; (c) you got there early and prepared the food and so your child gets to stay afterward and clean up; (d) no special rewards (e.g., eating dinner in front of the television); instead, your child eats alone at the table.

To do logical and natural consequences, it's helpful to work on the following:

1. **Take the "punishing" quality out of your voice and the interactions.** This is not about punishment; it's about what's logical, reasonable, and natural. You can even be friendly and positive.
2. **Prepare in advance.** Because you'll be emotional when your children are non-compliant, it's critical that you have a list of logical and reasonable and natural consequence ideas in your head. Otherwise, you will overreact. Going to parenting classes or talking with other parents can help you identify a wider range of reasonable consequences.
3. **Use small consequences.** Your purpose is to teach your child. Your purpose is not to hurt or humiliate. Learning occurs best if children are not emotionally overwhelmed by large consequences. Small consequences provide plenty of feedback.
4. **Use mirroring and encouragement.** Reflect back to your children what they're feeling ("It's very upsetting that you can't play with your toys for the rest of the week"). Let your child know that you think things will go better the next time around ("I know, if you want to, you'll be able to remember to put your toys away next time").
5. **Don't lecture or shame.** Let the small consequence do its work.

BACKING OUT OF POWER STRUGGLES

Some parents who come for a consultation need to step up and exercise more thoughtful, skilled control in the lives of their children. They need to work on setting limits, implementing reasonable consequences, and other more authoritative parenting behaviors.

Other parents have the opposite problem. These parents have taken too much responsibility, offered too many ultimatums, and ended up in destructive power struggles they cannot win. By continuing to insist on their rights to control, these parents are driving their children underground and away. (See Parent Homework Assignment 9-6.)

The Seven Magic Words

Children become adults by practicing. Some of this practicing involves having the right to make choices, even bad and painful choices. For parents who have not learned to back down, we offer the seven magic words. These are words derived from our study of choice theory (Glasser, 1998, 2002). The good news is that by using these words parents can share their thoughts, feelings, and wishes with their children in a way that might help a rebellious child hear their viewpoint. The bad news is that after carefully expressing themselves, parents then acknowledge that ultimately, compliance is not mandatory. And there's even more bad news: These words aren't really magic and parents will need more than seven of them to make them work at all.

The seven magic words are a frame for direct, powerful, and noncontrolling communication. They are: "I want you/but it's your choice." These framing words allow parents to express whatever they want (we encourage positive words) while at the same time acknowledging their child's power and right to self-determination. By explicitly acknowledging their children's right to self-determination, parents may reduce their children's need to prove their independence. Examples of the seven magic words in action include:

- I want you to stay clean and sober at the party tonight because I love you, and I know if you get caught, you might end up kicked off the basketball team; and also, your dad and I can't trust you with the car if we know you drink, but of course I know I can't control you, so it's your choice.
- I want you to graduate from high school, go to college, have a great job, and get rich, but whether or not that happens is really up to you.
- You know I want you to be healthy, eat well, and exercise, but whether you do that is your business. I'll help you any way I can, but it's your choice.

As you can see, the magic words are a frame for parents to express their own beliefs and convictions. This technique allows parents to directly express heartfelt feelings, and even describe the consequences they fear, but to then turn the choice back over to the child.

Some parents will be disappointed with the seven magic words. They wish for true magic and true control. Instead, this frame merely offers an opportunity to briefly and succinctly communicate personal and family values directly to children. In many families, one of these values is to acknowledge and honor the children's individual freedom and ultimate rights to choose how to live their lives. Most parents want their children to learn how to make responsible, life-enhancing choices.

Modifying a Consequence

Sometimes, in the heat of a conflict, parents will threaten or deliver a consequence that, once the conflict has passed, they recognize as unreasonable or ridiculous. If this happens, the parent should modify the consequence. The parent shouldn't let the child argue, debate, or overrule the consequence. Instead, the parent can take a break and return and state something like,

> When we were arguing about you being late last night I said you'd be grounded for a month. I've thought about that and I'm changing my mind because I was angry and upset. You haven't been responsible about getting home on time and so you'll be

grounded for the weekend. I think that's reasonable and that's my decision. I apologize for getting too upset and saying you'd be grounded for a month.

Although many parents wish it weren't so, parenting mistakes will be made. One of the most common mistakes is when parents go too far with a punishment or consequence. When this happens, parents and children are better served if parents can acknowledge their mistake, apologize, and modify the consequence. This process can be a good role-modeling opportunity for parents as it demonstrates that it's possible and desirable to apologize and rectify harsh comments made during an intense emotional moment.

Parenting Homework Assignment 9-6

Problem Polarization: Backing out of a Power Struggle

Families often show peculiar dynamics, especially when it comes to motivation. For example, if your daughter loves computer games and plays them all day, sooner or later you may begin hating computer games. Your daughter probably has enough love for computer games in her little pinky to accommodate the whole family. Similarly, if your son shows no motivation to do homework, you may suddenly find you've got all the motivation for his homework while he has none. This particular family dynamic is called *problem polarization*.

Problem polarization is a tough nut to crack. This is because it's perfectly natural for parents to become obsessed with the very responsibilities that their children avoid. For example, when your child stops showering, you will undoubtedly become more committed to his personal hygiene. The same is true when children neglect virtually any basic responsibility (think about keeping rooms clean, writing thank-you notes, etc.).

The solution to this problem always involves getting your children to take more responsibility for their basic family and personal responsibilities. Of course, you've probably already tried twisting yourself into pretzel shapes trying to get your child motivated to perform these basic tasks. And if you're reading this information, you may be semi-permanently pretzel-shaped and yet your children are still unconcerned about their personal hygiene, homework, chores, and grades.

Although you probably want to deliver one more lecture to get your message across, the truth is you need to let go of your motivation to get your child to behave appropriately. Your best new approach is to get more carefree about your child's personal responsibilities than your child. This is, of course, easier said than done. After all, you're a wise and conscientious adult and you know all too well the dangers of irresponsibility.

The answer to your dilemma is wrapped up in the following question: How can you (without using lectures or punishments) get your child to experience greater distress over his or her personal irresponsibility?

A direct approach might include saying something like this:

You're a perfectly intelligent young person and so I'm going to stop nagging you about your homework. My new policy is to remind you one time every evening and then I'll go off and have some fun myself. Then, if you flunk, it's all you. If you want help, I'm there for you, but I'm not getting hung up on this anymore. I'm a new-and-improved parent who knows you'll do better with your homework if you take more responsibility for it yourself.

After making your "I'm backing off" speech, you should sit down, relax, and see what happens. Even better, you might need to distract yourself with something fun and interesting because, no doubt, your child will have a greater tolerance for a few failures than you.

CONCLUDING COMMENTS

This chapter focuses on six specific directive interventions practitioners can teach parents to use with their children. Each intervention is described and standard homework assignments are provided. The emphasis is on child-friendly directive approaches that are delivered from a place of empathy and respect. Additional tip sheets associated with these interventions (and more) are available online. It's important for consultants, counselors, therapists, and other human services professionals who work with parents to modify the interventions included in this chapter to fit their therapeutic style and their clients' particular problems and needs.

Checklist for Direct Approaches to Power and Influence

☐ Watch for parent examples of backward behavior modification and then gently help parents understand how easy and natural it is to use basic behavioral principles (e.g., such as how paying too much attention to negative behavior can serve as a positive reinforcement) in a way that's contrary to their own goals.

☐ Help parents set up situations where they can actively teach positive behaviors to their children using active role-modeling and behavioral simulations.

☐ Help parents develop a new attitude toward misbehavior—an attitude characterized by confidence in their ability to handle whatever misbehavior happens.

☐ Help parents develop a plan for setting limits and handling misbehavior—so that their new attitude of confidence is bolstered by an actual plan.

☐ Describe and identify how parents can understand and implement new-and-improved approaches to timeout from reinforcement.

☐ Remember to remind parents that natural and logical consequences provide their children with better and more realistic learning experiences than large and illogical consequences (this is also a good justification for why parents should plan ahead

(Continued)

for how they want to respond to misbehavior, rather than responding spontaneously when angered).

☐ Help parents discover and apply the art of backing out of counterproductive power struggles.

☐ Go to the comprehensive Master List of Attitudes, Strategies, and Interventions in Appendix D and/or the practitioner-support website to gather more ideas about direct power and influence interventions parents can use with their children.

CHAPTER TEN

Ongoing Contact, Complications, and Referrals

An extremely time-limited educational or therapeutic model fits well with the needs and interests of many parents. For a variety of reasons, parents will develop an urge to schedule an appointment with a professional. This urge may be sudden or formed slowly over years. Parents often will want to come for an appointment within days of their urge to get help, and so it's ideal to have services readily available. Similarly, parents frequently want to quickly "fix" their parenting or family problem, rather than engaging in longer or more depth-oriented therapy. Due to these factors, when we offer parents choices for longer-term counseling, multisession educational classes, or very brief (one- or two-session) consultations—parents often choose the consultation option.

Similar to brief psychotherapy, when parents understand their consultation or counseling time is limited, they often become more focused in their communication and work especially hard to maximize their benefits within a minimum time period (Levenson, 2004). We've seen this efficiency and focus in the parents whom we've worked with over the years (J. Sommers-Flanagan, 2007; J. Sommers-Flanagan & Sommers-Flanagan, 2001, 2004a, 2007b). From a practical perspective, the brevity and simplicity of a one- or two-session consultation model has been very convenient for collecting research data on consultation effectiveness and for enabling contact, albeit brief, with more parents (J. Sommers-Flanagan, 2007)

However, many parents tell us they don't particularly like the constraints associated with a rigid one- or two-session model. This may be because parents tend to want more of whatever they find helpful. Generally, within our research and practice protocols, we've found that nearly half the parents we see ask for additional sessions. When possible and reasonable, we accommodate these requests.

To this point, we've primarily focused on initial contact with parents and on specific interventions that can be applied within the context of a variety of educational and therapeutic models. In this chapter we discuss ongoing contact with parents, complications, and referral strategies.

ONGOING CONTACT

Models are just models—not rules or laws. They help us because they make processes and outcomes slightly more predictable. For example, if parents are informed in advance that they have only two individual sessions available, they frequently come to the first session ready to work. They know their time is limited and so they may even unload their biggest issues within the first five minutes. Then, during the second session they may take an emotional step back and examine or analyze their new parenting strategies from an intellectual distance. This more analytic stance could be an outcome of our two-session model. It also may make it easier for parents to exit the help-seeking process and return to their independent parenting mode.

Despite the fact that models make life more predictable, different parents will handle time limits differently. Some parents return for additional individual sessions with completely different issues each time. Other parents will obsessively check in with you about each intervention they've tried, soliciting either reassurance or additional guidance. Still other parents, even when they report having had a very successful first session, won't return for additional therapy, guidance, or support; it's as if, because they made progress and see the end coming anyway, they preemptively end the helping process.

In our practice, we've used three different approaches or models for working individually with parents:

1. *Single-session consultations*: In this model, parents know from the beginning that they have one session to meet with an expert and will be on their own from there.
2. *Two-session consultations*: In this model, parents have two sessions, generally scheduled about a month apart.
3. *Family practice model*: In this model, parents are allowed to return for additional sessions as issues arise in their family. Similar to how a pediatrician or family practice physician operates, parents are free to schedule appointments on an *as-needed* basis.

Whichever model you follow will influence session process, content, and relationship development. When fewer, less frequent sessions are used, a more educational and less therapy-like process will generally emerge. More sessions offered more frequently will produce a more therapy-like process. At this point in our work with parents, our preference has been to emphasize time-limited, educational approaches. Within our community we've wanted our work with parents to be a distinct alternative to intensive parent training and longer-term parent counseling. However, no matter which model you choose, consideration of how to manage ongoing or future contacts is necessary.

SECOND-SESSION CONTACTS

In our two-session and family practice models, the second session includes three primary and overlapping components. First, the service provider invites parents to freely recall what they found more and less helpful from the initial session. Second, the provider discusses with parents (a) specific recommendations that were more and less helpful, (b) how initial suggestions might be modified, and (c) potential new recommendations. Third, referrals are offered as needed.

Parent Recall of What Was More or Less Helpful

To standardize the second session opening while honoring each parent's individual style, we recommend the following three questions for beginning the second session:

1. "What do you remember from our last session?'"
2. "What was helpful?"
3. "What wasn't so helpful?"

These questions (a) focus the session, (b) help consultants stay parent-centered, and (c) give parents freedom regarding where to start and where to go.

One problem that can arise during a second session is that you may have a very specific memory of what you thought was most important during session one. However, to remain parent centered, your great ideas and excellent memory should nearly always take a backseat to what the parent thought was important. Also, at the outset of the second session we generally don't know whether the initial session was a grand success, miserable failure, or something in between. This *not knowing* is a good foundation to keep us from making assumptions. The three opening questions give parents freedom to speak from their perspective and experience. They also facilitate continued collaboration.

Dealing With Parents Who Don't Remember Much From the First Session
Starting the second session with the three recall questions will look somewhat like this:

CONSULTANT: Welcome back. It's good to see you again. I have our list of suggestions from last time, but before we go over it, I'd love to hear what you remember from our last visit and what's been helpful and what's been less helpful.
PARENT: Well, it was just good to be able to talk with someone about my daughter. To be honest, I'm not sure if I tried anything from the list, because I lost it the day after our last meeting.
CONSULTANT: That's no problem. I've got the list and we can go over it, but before we do that, I hear you saying, maybe more than anything, it felt good to meet and talk with someone outside your family.
PARENT: Absolutely.
CONSULTANT: That's great. Is there anything else that pops into your mind from our first meeting?

The preceding example is a good illustration of how some parents will seem to have little memory of what was discussed during session one (at least initially). Depending on the time period between first and second consultation sessions, it can be more or less natural for parents to have difficulty recalling specific recommendations from the initial session.

When parents don't remember much from session one, you should relax and give them time to reflect—but not too much time. As in the preceding example, asking "Is there anything else that pops into your mind?" can be useful. But if the parent doesn't remember anything, you can just go to your list and begin a more systematic check-in on the recommendations while watching and listening for the parent's reactions.

Reviewing, Analyzing, and Tweaking Initial Suggestions

Most parents don't bring their list of recommendations to their second session. Consequently, after generating a memory or two in response to the free-recall task, they'll run out of steam. They may stop talking or they may directly admit they can't recall any other first-session recommendations. Depending on the parents' enthusiasm and talkativeness, the transition from free recall to a systematic review of recommendation outcomes may be more or less clear. With very talkative parents reviewing the list may be a challenge. However, in most cases, this transition happens fairly naturally:

PARENT: Really, I can't remember anything else.
CONSULTANT: That's fine. I probably wouldn't remember much either, but I have our list here. The first thing I've got on the list is character feedback; do you remember that idea?
PARENT: Oh, yeah. That's when I'm supposed to tell my son that he's the kind of boy who knows how to stay calm.
CONSULTANT: Right. Were you able to try that one out and, if so, how did it work?

As you review ideas or recommendations from session one, parents usually will display positive, negative, or mixed reactions. Parents also may report using a recommendation incorrectly, but obtaining a positive outcome. It's your job to track parent reactions and outcomes and eventually lead parents toward improving their parenting solutions.

Dealing With Positive Reports   Parents often begin discussing a specific suggestion (e.g., behavioral simulations, boring consequences and passionate rewards) and speak articulately about how nice it was to have that extra tool in their parenting toolbox. This is probably the most common response because parents who show up for second sessions may feel obliged to identify at least one recommendation that was helpful. For example,

CONSULTANT: Welcome back. It's good to see you again. I have our list of suggestions that I copied for you from our last meeting, but before we go over it, I'd love to hear from you about what you remember was helpful and what was less helpful, from our last visit.

PARENT: We thought a lot about what you said about timeout and that it's the first minute that counts. And so we changed our timeout routine. Now, we're using a pillow in the hall for a minute or two. And instead of a full timeout with our three-year-old, we're also using the brief "I don't like it when you hit me" and turn-away-for-thirty-seconds idea. When we were trying to do six-minute time-outs and have him be quiet for a minute before he could get out, it was always a terrible meltdown. Now our son cries a little and then we pat him on the shoulder or on his belly and let him know we love him and it's over. We haven't had any of those traumatic 30-minute timeout struggles. And what you said about him getting the message with a less severe consequence is totally true because the number of times he's been hitting has really decreased.

CONSULTANT: You thought about this quite a lot and decided to go with the shorter and more comforting timeout plan. And somehow, you were able to do it in a way that's working pretty well. It sounds like over the last couple weeks your timeouts have been briefer and less painful for everyone. As you talk about this new plan you look happier and more relaxed right now.

When parents lead with something positive, it's easy to listen empathically and provide support for their self-discipline and follow-through. Sometimes as we do this reflective listening process, we imagine using a bright-orange highlighter to help parents vividly see the words they're using to represent their successes. In the preceding example, the consultant is highlighting that the parents " . . . thought about this quite a lot . . . " and " . . . decided . . . " and " . . . were able to do it in a way that's been working pretty well . . . " and "look happier and more relaxed . . . ." These reflections intentionally direct parents to look at and *own* their positive efforts, insights, abilities, and outcomes. As parenting consultants or therapists, we want to be a source of information and guidance, but *we want the parents to take credit* and attribute positive parenting changes to their own efforts and behaviors. After all, if anything positive happens, the parents make it happen; we just sit in our offices and hope positive changes occur.

Dealing With Negative Reports   Less often, but not infrequently, parents will lead with a critique or negative reaction to a parenting recommendation. Or they'll mention something that was discussed and recommended, but that they chose (either due to lack of time or lack of interest) not to try out. For example, parents may say, with an almost confession-like attitude, "I didn't even try the special-time activity we talked about." Or they may criticize a recommendation as ineffective:

PARENT: I tried that mutual problem-solving and it was a disaster. I bought pizza and got out the markers and my son never came up with anything positive. Finally, I got frustrated because he wasn't even trying and I sent him to his room.

In these situations, rather than reacting with judgment to the parent's words, you should listen with empathy. This can be difficult because you may find yourself having a strong impulse to accuse the parent of misapplication of a parenting suggestion. In this case, we wanted to respond with:

> *No!* You're not supposed to get all hung up on the *outcome*. Mutual problem-solving is a *process*. If your son doesn't contribute, you're just supposed to say, "Well, that's okay, maybe we'll be able to figure out something next time." You're not supposed to get all frustrated and resentful for having bought pizza and then send him to his room.

Fortunately, in the preceding case we restrained our critical impulses. Instead, we returned to an empathic-validating-universalizing statement (described in Chapter 3):

> That sounds very frustrating and disappointing. You made a big effort to set up mutual problem-solving and it tanked. This is one of the reasons parenting is so hard. Sometimes we try something new—something that's supposed to be helpful and effective—but it's like somebody forgot to tell our kids to cooperate and it's just miserable. I'm sorry about that.

You may find it difficult to provide an empathic-validating-universalizing statement if you're feeling stung by parental negativity or criticism. We've sometimes mistakenly focused too much on our own disappointment and defensiveness and not enough on the parents' disappointment and efforts. After hearing parents aim their disappointment and criticism toward our suggestions it's perfectly natural (albeit unhelpful) to feel disappointed and defensive ourselves and then to try to get the parent back with a cross-complaint or retributive criticism (Gottman, Notarius, Gonso, & Markman, 1976). It's also not unusual for our parenting recommendations to seem crystal clear (to ourselves), which makes it even more difficult to understand how parents could leave our office and so completely mess up our excellent advice. But since we recommend that parents practice humility, apologize, and avoid blaming their children when they make parenting mistakes, we should model the same.

Blaming parents for getting it wrong can be direct and obvious or more subtle and passive-aggressive. Either way, it doesn't do much for facilitating positive change. For example, you might think you're doing your best, avoiding big reactions and judgments by saying something like, "I think you misunderstood what we talked about last time." But no matter how true this statement may feel to you and no matter how gently you say it, you'll likely be perceived as blaming because you're focusing on the parents' misunderstanding and not your mis-communicating. Instead, as parenting professionals and role models, accepting responsibility for anything that may have contributed to parental disappointment and frustration is crucial.

Beyond the standard empathic-validating-universalizing statement illustrated above, there are two constructive options for dealing with parental disappointment with parenting recommendations: (a) You can just forget about whatever particular technique you were trying to use with this particular parent and say, "So that idea really didn't fit for you and your family. I appreciate your honesty," and move on; or (b) if you think the parenting technique is worth salvaging, you might take the blame yourself by saying, "I'm sorry; I didn't do a very good job describing that technique last time. If we both decide it has potential, later today, I can try describing it more clearly and you could take another try with it. But let's explore other options first." Not surprisingly, sometimes when consultants go out of their way to take responsibility (e.g., "I'm sorry I did such a bad job explaining that") parents will become less critical and begin sharing the blame ("Well, I didn't really listen very well last time, either").

Whether working individually or with groups, it's almost always useful to hear about what parents recall as helpful or not helpful from earlier sessions. In many cases, they tell us exactly what we expect to hear. Since we were both in the same room, this makes good sense. However, in other cases, by following the parents' recollections (rather than our own), we've heard important and valid perspectives that we might never have discovered. Because parents are unique observers and experiencers, it's crucial to ask them about *their* memories of what was helpful and not helpful before revealing our own perspectives.

When Parents Get It Wrong, But Get It Right   Sometimes parents will enthusiastically, but incorrectly, implement a particular parenting recommendation:

PARENT: I know there were lots of other things we talked about and that I tried, but I can't remember them right now.
CONSULTANT: And that's perfectly okay, because, I've got our handy little list right here. Is it okay if we go through these for a few minutes before we focus on new ideas?
PARENT: Sure. I'd love to hear what I've forgotten.
CONSULTANT: Okay. At the top of our list I have the special time. Did you try that one?

As you undoubtedly recall, the purpose of the special-time assignment is to help parents learn to use non-directive play with their child or children. Unfortunately, although non-directive play is a very positive and healthy experience for parents and children, it's also a very difficult skill to teach and learn. Child therapy or parent training models spend many hours in the teaching and learning of this particular skill set (Axline, 1964). Similarly, graduate programs in psychology, counseling, and social work may include semester-long courses on non-directive play therapy (Bratton, Ray, Rhine, & Jones, 2005; Bratton et al., 2006; Guerney, 2001).

Given how challenging it is to learn non-directive play, it's unrealistic to expect parents to understand and implement this procedure after hearing a 5-minute explanation and reading a one-page tip sheet. Nevertheless, we've been surprised at how many parents return and tell us how well the special-time assignment went, and occasionally it appears they even implemented it correctly. Here's an example of a valiant attempt that may have missed a bit of the point:

PARENT: Oh, yeah, I should have remembered that one! That was a great idea! We did it about twice a week since our last meeting and my son absolutely loved it. He started asking, "Can we do special time?"

CONSULTANT: Then what happened?

PARENT: The first few times I just got out some blocks and we stacked them and then knocked them over together. Then, I decided we should do something more interesting and so one day I had him help me when I was baking a cake. He was great and he really loved it. I think it's been good for both of us.

CONSULTANT: That's wonderful. It sounds like the two of you had some great times together.

As you can see from this example, the parent didn't understand and implement the special-time procedure correctly. She engaged in something other than non-directive play. Nevertheless, she reported a positive result and both parent and child experienced high-quality interactions and these interactions were good for them. When this happens you may find yourself in a dilemma. Should you seize the moment and do more teaching, hoping the parent will understand how to implement the procedure correctly? Or, should you just leave it be and let the parent have her success? In this situation, our usual preference is to just drop the idea of teaching true non-directive play within the context of a brief consultation model and instead support the parent for her success. In essence, here is our reasoning:

- Rather than risk spoiling things by trying additional teaching, we follow a general philosophy of leaving positive outcomes alone.
- Our rigid adherence to a particular technique is less important than the parental sense of felt success.
- We can always revisit this process and provide additional teaching of the non-directive play concept later if there's adequate time and adequate rationale.

To summarize, in most cases parents will report they either (a) implemented a specific procedure and had a positive outcome; (b) implemented a specific procedure and had a negative outcome; (c) implemented a specific procedure in an incorrect or imperfect manner and report a negative outcome; (d) implemented a specific procedure incorrectly but report a positive outcome; (e) implemented a specific procedure and had a mixed outcome; or (f) chose not to implement a specific procedure for one reason or another.

As described to this point, these first four scenarios are relatively easy to manage. If there was a positive outcome, you should review and summarize the outcome using the highlighting and parent-attribution procedure discussed previously. If there was a negative outcome, you can use an empathic-validating-universalizing statement and then apologize for anything you may have done to contribute to the negative outcome. There are always exceptions to these general responses and you can use your best clinical judgment to guide your responses.

Analyzing and Dealing With Mixed Outcomes   Mixed outcomes occur when parents report some benefits from implementing a suggestion or recommendation as well as continuing problems.

PARENT: I tried the things you said about how to handle it when my three-year-old hits me. I told him that he hurts my feelings when he hits me, but he just laughed. I also tried immediately turning away from him, telling him "No," and then walking away for one minute when he hits and he hates that and it seems to make a difference, but then he'll chase me around the house.

CONSULTANT: I'm impressed. It sounds like you took the ideas we talked about and tried them out with your three-year-old. And you discovered some important things. You discovered that not everything we talk about in here will work. But more importantly, you discovered that your son responded better to your actions than he did to your words.

PARENT: Yes. I guess that's true.

In this case example, the consultant uses reflection, but also quickly identifies a key difference between the strategy that was more successful and the strategy that didn't work. This is a nice clarification for the parent and leads to additional recommendations (see Chapter 9, Parent Homework Assignment 9-2: Intentional Role Modeling).

CONSULTANT: Often very young children respond much more quickly to actions than words. Of course your son loves you and doesn't want to see you hurt, but he's not getting the words. He does seem to understand your actions. Some people call this *action-discipline*, because you take a quick action in response to misbehavior rather than expecting your words to work. It can be especially good to use words and actions together. For example, if he hits you, you might turn away and, at the same time, say, "No! Mommy doesn't like it when you hit her."

PARENT: Okay. I can do that.

CONSULTANT: And the fact that your son responds more to action than words makes me think we can develop some additional strategies to help him learn the "No Hitting Mom" rule more quickly. It might be nice to set up a role play with your husband where each of you gets mad and then you ask each other, "Should I hit you?" and then both of you say, "No! No hitting in our house!" and then hug each other and make up instead. You could help him see that you and your husband are in agreement about not hitting each other and that when you touch each other, you do it in a loving and gentle way and that you both like that very much. You'll be modeling verbal communication and a positive outcome.

PARENT: Okay. But what should I do when I walk away and my son chases me?

CONSULTANT: How about if you try just turning away, rather than walking away. And it doesn't need to be long. You can make an unhappy face, fold your arms, and turn away without saying anything other than "No!" and "That's not okay!" And then don't respond for thirty to sixty seconds.

In this example, an additional intervention is quickly formulated. The intervention flows from the intervention that's already partially working. Often, discussions of mixed outcomes won't be quite so smooth. Whenever you're not certain how to formulate new or additional interventions, you should return to questioning and listening to gather information and focus on empathy and validation until you can identify another potential intervention idea and share it with the parent. If, like us, you sometimes can't think of all the potential interventions available to you, it might be useful to keep an intervention list with you during consultation meetings (see the Master List of Attitudes, Strategies, and Interventions in Appendix D).

In this example the parent also needed clarification about what to do when her son chases her around the house. Although some clarification was provided, more work could have been done on generating positive consequences for appropriate "non-hitting" behaviors.

Analyzing and Dealing With Non-Chosen Recommendations   As you review your list of ideas and recommendations with parents from previous sessions, several may have been completely ignored, avoided, or forgotten. This may or may not be an issue. Parents have particular and sometimes peculiar preferences; it may be because you offered many intervention options, and they just selected the strategies that seemed simplest or the strategies they remembered or the strategies they liked best. The guideline to keep in mind is that you should always observe for differences between recommendations parents found helpful, those they found less helpful, and those they ignored. If you believe it would be beneficial, you may return to an ignored or forgotten recommendation, using a collaborative approach.

Offering New Recommendations

During session two and beyond, parents may bring up completely new issues or they may review issues discussed during your first contact. In some cases, parents will come back to unfinished business, and sometimes you will have written a note on the recommendations about an issue that was brought up during session one, but was relegated to a later session because of time limits.

Case: "Bully for You!"

In the following case, a parent dropped a hint about her daughter being bullied right at the end of session one and then returned to this issue with greater intensity at the start of session two.

PARENT: My daughter is still getting bullied and I'm still really not sure what to do.
CONSULTANT: Right. I recall you mentioned bullying right at the end of our last meeting. And the idea at the bottom of our list was for you to do some brainstorming and consequential thinking with her about how to handle the bullying, but we didn't have much time to talk about how to do that. Did you try it out?
PARENT: I wasn't sure what to do. This middle school parenting really has me confused. I don't know what I should do. I started to talk with her and she told me, "I don't want to talk about it" and so I let it drop. But it's still bugging her.

CONSULTANT: Well, let's talk more about brainstorming and consequential thinking. I've got a tip sheet with some basic rules about how parents can handle bullying. I'll get that for you at the end of our meeting. Does that sound okay? [See Appendix B, Tip Sheet 9: Anti-Bullying Tips for Parents.]

PARENT: Yes. I really need help on this.

CONSULTANT: Let me tell you some basic rules about bullying. Bullying is really difficult and humiliating to talk about. Somehow kids feel that talking about being bullied will make it worse and so they just hope it will go away. It turns out it doesn't go away easily. It's a nasty problem. To solve it often requires participation from teachers, school counselors, parents of victims, parents of bullies, bullies, victims, and bystanders. I know that's a long list and I know most kids want absolutely nothing to do with involving all those people. Being bullied can be so humiliating that kids would rather suffer in isolation than ask for help.

PARENT: I think that's exactly what's going on. Sienna is so embarrassed that she'll hardly talk with me about it. There's no way she'd let me talk with anyone else about it.

CONSULTANT: And maybe you won't have to. That all depends on how severe the bullying is and how Sienna's doing. But, one thing for sure: You need a way to tell her that you want her to talk with you and that it's unhealthy for her to suffer all by herself. You also need to reassure her in advance by promising not to tell anyone else about what's going on unless it's dangerous or unless she agrees to let you. Really, the choice is for you to counsel her or for her to go to a professional for counseling—or both.

PARENT: I'm pretty sure Sienna won't go talk with a counselor.

CONSULTANT: And right now there's no need to force that. Give her a choice: Talk with me or talk with a counselor—because it's not right to be bullied and have no one to talk with about it. If you can express that to her with compassion, I think she'll get it.

PARENT: Okay. I can do that. I think she'll choose to talk with me.

In this situation, the consultant is encouraging the mom to directly work with her daughter on how to deal with bullying. This may be a risky step, but it's better than the alternatives (letting her daughter suffer in isolation or initiating a conversation with the school or the bully's parents behind the daughter's back). Coaching the parent on opening up direct communication is a first small and reasonable step.

It's not unusual for second- or future-session content to focus more squarely on issues that cause parents (and their children) significant emotional distress. This mom dropped a hint in session one and it may be that either she's more comfortable in session two or the bullying has escalated. Either way, the mom is zeroing in on a distressing and challenging issue. (For specific information on brainstorming, consequential thinking, and dealing with bullies, see Appendix B, Tip Sheet 9: Anti-Bullying Tips for Parents.)

In this case the nature of the issue and the age of the child make a new recommendation possible: The mother was coached to engage her daughter in an active problem-solving process. Whether this process works—having the mother offer to provide counsel to her daughter—depends on the quality of the existing relationship between mother and daughter.

Some human services professionals will be reluctant to offer parents ideas about how to directly counsel their children. We also feel this reluctance. However, as we've gained exposure to parents and children in the real world, we've found that in some situations the parent is not just *the best possible counselor* for her child, but also *the only possible counselor* for her child (because the child or parent won't agree to anything else). On the other hand, professional referrals should be provided when appropriate or necessary.

During many parenting contacts you'll develop new recommendations during the second session or beyond, recommendations that are completely new and emerge from the additional session rather than the first session. For example, in the preceding situation with 11-year-old Sienna, the practitioner starts with recommendations that were barely mentioned at the end of the initial session. The discussion of bullying and associated recommendations become the major focus of the entire second session. In this situation, you may need to add new recommendations that were not a part of the first session (e.g., call the school counselor and have a confidential discussion about bullying).

Case: "Can We Talk About Big Brother?"

As you might guess, sometimes new recommendations will look and sound very much like the recommendations covered in Chapters 7 through 9. For example, recently a couple scheduled an appointment to discuss their youngest (three-year-old) son's tantrums. We worked on developing strategies for managing tantrums, but when they returned for their second session, they indicated the following:

PARENT: Things are going great with our youngest. The stuff you told us has been helpful and the tantrums have almost disappeared. But now that we have a handle on his behavior we've started noticing problems with our five-year-old that we'd like to talk about. Would that be okay?
CONSULTANT: Of course. What's been going on with your older son?
PARENT: We think it has a lot to do with jealousy. . . .

It's not unusual for parents, after a successful initial consultation session, to shift their primary focus from one child to another or from one problem to another. These parents came ready to work. They knew what they wanted to talk about and immediately launched into their best explanation for their older son's misbehavior. After a discussion about the specifics of their five-year-old, we generated a list of recommendations at the conclusion of the second session (see the worksheet, Sharona and Roberto: Session-Two Recommendations [Prescriptions]). These recommendations looked much like recommendations that might be given after an initial contact.

Sharona and Roberto: Session-Two Recommendations (Prescriptions)

1. Give emotional support while setting limits on behavior: "I can see you're upset because you can't have another piece of candy. But you know no matter how much you yell, you still won't get another piece of candy."
2. Notice the progress and use character feedback (see Appendix B, Tip Sheet 3).
3. Also try using indirect strategies and encouragement:
   a. *Encouragement:* "I notice you're being nice to your brother."
   b. *Character feedback:* "You're the kind of boy who treats his brother very nicely, even when it's hard."
   c. *Praise:* "Good job!"
4. Emotional education and emotional reflection:
   a. Look forward to tantrums because they offer an opportunity for emotional education and emotional reflection.
   b. Keep clear on your plans for dealing with tantrums:
      • Set limits with empathy.
      • Describe small and immediately forthcoming consequences.
      • Describe choices.
5. Never give in to angry behavior or be manipulated.

As you become more familiar with specific parents, it's natural for standard interventions to become less scripted and more personally tailored to fit the parents.

Case: Bedtime Is a Bad Time

Generally, more individual sessions will translate into richer and more nuanced parenting discussions; you will be better able to integrate their knowledge of particular parental quirks and characteristics into the interventions.

PARENT: We've talked before about my struggles with my four-year-old staying in her bed. There just doesn't seem to be anything that will work and I'm not willing to just abandon her. That cry-it-out thing just won't work for me. If I let her cry it out, then I'll be in my bed crucifying myself for being the worst mother on the planet.

CONSULTANT: Right. I remember our discussion of that cry-it-out strategy and I want to emphasize that it really doesn't work for all parents or all kids. You want to be there for your daughter and the thoughts and feelings that you get when she's in her room alone and crying are just too painful.

PARENT: But when I stay in the room with her I'm filled with resentment and anxiety about what I should be doing instead of lying there in the dark.

CONSULTANT: Either way, you find yourself unhappy and dissatisfied. Inside your head it just starts buzzing with criticism and second thoughts.

PARENT: I have no time to myself. No time to wind down at the end of the day. No time to read. No time to relax in the tub. Most nights I'm miserable.

CONSULTANT: So if we could find a way for you to be mentally at peace and to relax when your daughter's in bed, but not yet asleep, that would feel much better.

PARENT: That would feel great.

CONSULTANT: I remember one parent in a situation like yours telling me that she put a little reading lamp in the corner of her child's room. She would sit in a comfortable chair and read in the corner of her daughter's room. The reading lamp served a dual purpose — it was both a nightlight and a reading lamp.

PARENT: Wow. I can see that working. My daughter just wants me in the room. I don't think she'd care if I was reading quietly in the corner.

CONSULTANT: And the key for you is that, if you're reading something you find meaningful, you can let your mind be at peace about what's happening in the moment, rather than being in turmoil or beating yourself up all the time over what you should be doing.

PARENT: I think that could work.

CONSULTANT: How about if you try it out and then come back next month and we check on how it worked?

The solution in the preceding scenario might be difficult to pull off during an initial session. However, as the consultant becomes more familiar with the internal turmoil the mother is experiencing, a tailored intervention is developed that addresses the mother's unique personal issues. The mother senses the "good fit" of the intervention and instantly loves the idea. As you might suspect, the mother was so happy about this minor bedtime routine modification that when she arrived for her next session she was ready to work on additional — and much needed — self-care strategies.

We should note that if we were following a medical model in this case, it would have been easy to mistake this mother's nighttime misery and unhappiness for clinical depression. Instead, after three individual sessions she made several minor parenting and self-care adjustments and vastly improved her personal happiness.

Making Referrals

Making referrals may seem like a simple and straightforward task requiring little discussion. Although this is sometimes true, there are a few issues to address and avoid.

Find Out What (and Whom) the Parent Already Tried   In the past, as naïve professionals, we sometimes provided enthusiastic endorsement of specific parenting or counseling resources without first asking about what the parents had tried. The scenario would look like this:

CONSULTANT: Because you have twins, you really should check out the "Mothers with Multiples" group in our community. It's really an excellent resource.

PARENT: I've been there and really didn't like it.

Or:

CONSULTANT: Dr. Smith is the person you want to see for your daughter's eating problems. She's probably the best psychologist in the state when it comes to eating issues.

PARENT: We saw her and our daughter hated her . . . and we hated her, too.

If you're thinking about offering specific referral or resource information to parents, it's important to find out what referral or resource information the parents have pursued previously. Otherwise, if you offer a professional referral or mention a community resource group that the parents have already tried and discarded, you'll lose credibility and your next suggestion may not be welcomed with the optimism you're hoping for.

If you accidentally offer a referral that the parents have tried and discarded, it's helpful to do two things: (a) Thank the parents for letting you know about their experience; and (b) emphasize the importance of finding a resource that fits for them—because one size (or one therapist or one community resource) doesn't fit everyone.

Provide Parents with Positive and Optimistic Choices When receiving referral information, many parents will pressure you in one way or another to make a choice for them. For example:

CONSULTANT: Since you haven't taken your daughter to a counselor before, I can give you a list of several excellent possibilities. There's Lindsay Morales, Thomas McGill, and Kameron Blackbird. I'll get you their numbers.

PARENT: Which one do you think is best?

CONSULTANT: What's really important is to have a good fit. I'd recommend calling them and speaking with each one and then making your decision.

PARENT: But really, who would you take your own daughter to see?

In this situation we usually respond in one of two ways: (a) If we're clear on who we'd take our own daughter to see, we tell the parent, but note that everyone is unique; or (b) we tell the parent we're not sure and then offer to describe the strengths of each practitioner to see if that additional information helps the parent decide. Whenever possible, making referrals to professionals and resources you can personally endorse is recommended.

Clarify Your Intervention Model With the Parents

Individual intervention approaches can range from single-session consultations, to short-term time-limited counseling, to longer-term ongoing counseling, to longer-term intermittent counseling. Group intervention approaches with parents range from single-session educational classes, to multisession classes, to intensive parent training, to open-ended parent support groups. Whatever model you choose to use, you should be sure to clarify upfront with parents the nature, frequency, and duration of how you'll be working together.

For example, when offering single-session consultations, we provide the following information before the first session and, as illustrated below, toward the end of the first session:

CONSULTANT: Our policy is to do single-session consultations and then leave it to you to reschedule if you want. We recommend that you go home and try out some of the ideas we've discussed, and then, if you want to come back in for a second meeting, you call and schedule an appointment.

In some cases, if you're using a single-session model, parents will be clear that they want additional meetings even before the first session ends. For example, parents may say something like the following, in which case we recommend flexibility, if possible:

PARENT: Well, I already know I want a second appointment.
CONSULTANT: If you're sure about that, then we can schedule one now. But we usually recommend that you wait about a month between your first and second appointment. That will give you time to experiment and see if some of the techniques we talked about today will work for you.

This example emphasizes flexibility from a single-session model, but recommends appointments spaced about a month apart. Obviously, whether you recommend spaced appointments or weekly appointments will depend on your preference, setting, and approach.

When Parents Cancel or Fail to Show

Even highly motivated parents sometimes cancel or fail to show up. How you handle this will depend on your professional setting; it will also depend on your personal preferences.

Parents are independent actors and they'll usually be more than willing to take the steps they need to get the help they want. However, many parents are extremely busy and stressed and so it's not unusual for them to miss appointments (especially if it's scheduled four to six weeks after the initial appointment).

When parents miss an appointment, the core question is: How much responsibility should you take for rescheduling a missed appointment? Our guidelines for this include:

- If parents miss their initial appointment, there's usually very little relationship established and so we feel no obligation to contact them to reschedule.
- If parents schedule a second or future appointment and then call and cancel, we leave rescheduling to them. In that situation parents have taken an active step to cancel the appointment and, if desired, they can take an active step to reschedule it.

- If parents schedule a second or future appointment and then don't show up, we may leave them a telephone message or send them a quick email (if that form of communication has been established). This communication is designed to remind parents that an appointment had been scheduled and that they may reschedule if they like. The rationale for making contact is: We don't want parents to realize they've missed their second appointment (after the fact) and then feel too embarrassed to reschedule. We recognize that this involves a little handholding or enabling, but we feel it's in the best interests of parents and their children to take this extra step.

Deciding on Shorter- or Longer-Term Interventions

Based on our research and practice experiences with parents, we operate on the following three major assumptions:

1. With mildly to moderately distressed parents, a single-session or two-session model with sessions about four to six weeks apart will usually be adequate to significantly reduce parental stress, increase parental confidence, and improve (at least temporarily) parent–child relationships. If parents find these initial appointments helpful, we're happy to work with them longer (and they're generally very happy to obtain more educational and therapeutic services).

2. If parents are more significantly distressed, at-risk for child abuse, or generally functioning at a low level, briefer educational or therapeutic models may not be the most appropriate intervention. However, brief models can be a great way to provide a positive initial experience for distressed, at-risk parents, which can make them more open to more extensive interventions. Nevertheless, our standard recommendation for distressed, at-risk parents is a more extensive parent training or longer-term parent counseling model. Child or family therapy is also more appropriate than a brief model.

3. Given the fact that most parents are deeply involved in parenting activities for at least 18 years, a one- or two-session consultation model may not adequately address their needs. Consequently, we often recommend the "family practice" model where parents return for parent counseling or consultation on an intermittent basis—much as they return for appointments with their pediatrician on an as-needed basis.

There are many advantages of the longer-term family practice parent education and support model. The most obvious is the positive, supportive, and confiding relationship that gets built and maintained between parents and human services providers. Parents appreciate having a "go-to" person to help them with their intermittent parenting challenges. Additionally, if the practitioner uses a positive approach and offers reasonable parenting feedback and guidance, chances are there will be at least small positive benefits and no negative side effects. Also, if parents get their needs met through educational and therapeutic services, they will likely reduce their pediatric or medical utilization.

CONCLUDING COMMENTS

Although brief educational and therapeutic models have advantages, many parents prefer longer-term or ongoing contact with human services professionals. As with longer-term counseling, more contact with parents will allow for greater connection and the work may become deeper and more therapeutic. Nevertheless, because of the urgent and immediate nature of parents' needs, it's crucial for professionals who work with parents to continue to offer concrete suggestions that parents can try out in their family lives. Additionally, it's crucial for practitioners to know how to gently and empathically guide parents who are negative or critical about the techniques that were provided to them in earlier sessions.

This chapter explored the details and dynamics associated with the second session and beyond. The following checklist may help you be more effective as you work with parents on an ongoing basis.

Checklist for Ongoing Contact

☐ Be clear with parents about your time limits and consultation model.

☐ Bring your recommendation list from session to session.

☐ Keep the comprehensive intervention master list (provided in Appendix D) with you in case you need it.

☐ After the initial session, ask the three recall questions and one follow-up.

☐ Reflect and highlight positive parental efforts, insights, abilities, and outcomes.

☐ If parents are negative and critical, avoid being negative, critical, and defensive in return.

☐ When parents are disappointed or critical, use empathic-validating-universalizing statements.

☐ Apologize, take responsibility, and move on if your recommendations didn't work.

☐ If recommendations are implemented incorrectly, but there's a positive outcome, support the positive outcome.

☐ In complex or confusing situations, use your best clinical judgment to guide your response.

☐ Listen for differences between the recommendations that worked and those that didn't.

☐ Offer new recommendations as needed and tailor them to fit parental quirks and strengths.

☐ Before making referrals, find out what (and whom) the parents already tried.

☐ Consider whether, when, and how you want to contact parents if they miss an appointment.

CHAPTER ELEVEN

Dealing With Special Situations and Issues

Throughout this book, we've emphasized that every parenting situation is unique and therefore all parents deserve to be respected and treated as undisputed experts in their personal and family worlds. Despite this uniqueness, there are many standardized procedures and techniques that can be used to help parents find more effective and satisfying ways of interacting with their children.

In this chapter, we address a few specific parenting-related areas that can be challenging at a more profound level than the more common parenting concerns. First, we offer reflections and guidelines that might help when you're working with culturally diverse parents. We also discuss thorny dilemmas you may face when consulting with parents who are separated or divorced, how to handle potential child abuse situations, and take a quick look at post-partum depression and parental guilt. If you work regularly with parents, you'll undoubtedly grapple with all these special situations and dynamics.

PRACTICING CULTURAL HUMILITY

Alfred Adler (1958) claimed that *every child is born into a new and different family*. He believed that with every additional member, family dynamics automatically shift and therefore a new family is born (J. Sommers-Flanagan & Sommers-Flanagan, 2004a). If we extend Adler's thinking into the cultural domain, it might be appropriate to conclude: "Every family is born into a new and different culture."

To be sure, culture is not a static condition; it's a malleable and powerfully influential force in the lives of parents and children. Vargas (2004) stated,

Culture is not about outcome. Culture is an ever-changing process. One cannot get a firm grip of it just as one cannot get a good grasp of water. As an educator, what I try to do is to teach about the process of culture—how we will never obtain enough cultural content, how important it is to understand the cultural context in which we are working, and how crucial it is to understand our role in the interactions with the people with whom we want to work or the communities in which we seek to intervene. . . . I do not want to enter the intervention arena (whether in family therapy or in implementing a community-based intervention) as an "expert" who has the answers and knows what needs to be done. I am not a conquistador, intent on supplanting my culture on others. I have a certain expertise that, when connected with the knowledge and experience of my clients, can be helpful and meaningful to my clients. (p. 429)

In part, Vargas was making the point that it's more important for professionals to practice cultural humility than it is to view ourselves as culturally competent.

A Cultural Dialectic

All professionals should strive to be culturally sensitive and humble, seeking to respect and prize human diversity for the richness, variety, and surprises it brings to life. But while embracing culture, it's important to acknowledge that there's no perfect culture, and sometimes cultural practices need to change or evolve for the sake of a given child, parent, or family. Therefore, although we value divergent cultural perspectives, it's also reasonable to question whether specific cultural beliefs and rituals are useful or healthy to individuals, families, and communities. This is a cultural dialectic—similar to the radical acceptance dialectic discussed in Chapter 1.

When working with parents, it's the professional's job to do the cultural accepting and the parents' job to do the cultural questioning. You should accept the parents' cultural background, heritage, and parenting practices. However, if in the process of examining cultural influences on parenting, parents take the lead in questioning their culturally influenced parenting practices, you can and should remain open to helping parents push against cultural forces to make positive changes. For example, parents may want to discuss any of the following topics with you:

- Whether or not to have their infant son circumcised
- Their daughter's body-image issues as they relate to American cultural values toward thinness
- Whether it's acceptable for their Muslim daughter to attend school or pursue higher education
- Traditional Native American values and their children's potential tobacco use

Helping parents determine whether their own cultural values clash with individual and/or family well-being is a delicate and potentially explosive process. The challenge is to remain relatively neutral while helping parents evaluate cultural practices using their own parent-child-family health and well-being standards.

Case: Tobacco, Culture, and Addiction

PARENT: I'm worried about my son and whether he's started smoking. I use tobacco, in traditional Indian ceremonies, but I usually end up smoking more than I want to, and I see it as a bad habit, too. I'm not sure how to approach this with him because I don't want to be a hypocrite.

CONSULTANT: Tell me some ideas you've had, from your cultural perspective, about how to get the message you want to get to your son.

PARENT: I want him to know that tobacco use should be ceremonial or sacred, even though I use it more often than that. I know regular smoking is very unhealthy and so I don't want him to have it as a habit, but I don't know how to tell him that.

CONSULTANT: If you think about someone from your tribe whom you really respect, how do you think that person would handle it?

PARENT: In my tribe it's really important to respect your elders. I'm my son's mother and he should respect me, but you know how that goes. Maybe if I asked someone else, someone older and with even more respect than me, maybe that would help.

CONSULTANT: Whom would you pick to help you talk with your son about this?

PARENT: My older brother, his uncle, is pretty high up in the Tribal Government and maybe I could ask him to tell my son it would be better not to smoke, even though lots of Indian people smoke.

CONSULTANT: Do you think your brother would be willing to give your son that message?

PARENT: Yes. He's traditional in some ways, but he's very much against smoking and drinking.

CONSULTANT: You and your brother are both right about the dangers of regular tobacco use. As I imagine this discussion, I can see the two of you having a big impact on your son. But I guess there's also the issue of your smoking and your son's knowledge of that. Can you have your brother talk about that with your son, too? Or maybe both of you should do this together. How do you think this might work best?

In this case example, for the most part, the consultant is remaining neutral and respectful of the parent's cultural traditions and yet, at the same time, helping her explore how to get her son a strong and clear message about not smoking tobacco.

Following the Parents' Lead in Cultural Identity and Cultural Understanding

For most of us, culture is so deeply woven into our lives that it travels below awareness. From time to time we may glimpse it and wonder how it came to be that we choose to engage in specific cultural behaviors, such as:

- Sitting on the couch with our children watching *The Simpsons*
- Getting eggs from the store rather than directly from backyard chickens
- Going to church on Palm Sunday where a processional, complete with a donkey, waits quietly in the sanctuary
- Deferring to one's husband
- Expecting our oldest son to take care of us
- Gathering with friends to overeat and watch the Super Bowl
- Wearing a yarmulke, burkha, or garments or pieces of cloth to cover our bodies or heads

Culture carries with it many questions, answers, and mysteries. As you can see from the preceding list, culture is ubiquitous; it's impossible to escape its influence. It's also impossible to accurately judge someone else's cultural identity on the basis of physical appearance or initial impressions (Hays, 2008).

When working with parents, you shouldn't assume parents' cultural attitudes and experiences in advance. This is true no matter how similar or dissimilar to you the parents appear. It's best to begin with a clearly stated attitude of openness and then follow the parents' lead.

CONSULTANT: So, you grew up in Malawi?

PARENT: Yes. I came to the United States when I was twenty-four.

CONSULTANT: I don't know how much of your Malawi tradition influences your parenting and so I hope it will be okay with you if, on occasion, I ask you about that.

PARENT: That's no problem at all.

CONSULTANT: And, as we talk, I hope you'll feel free to tell me about anything that comes up or seems important about your particular cultural approach to parenting.

PARENT: Yes. I'm comfortable with that.

Whether the parent is Laotian, Belizean, Argentine, French Canadian, or from any other cultural tradition, you should remain open to his or her particular and potentially diverse parenting approaches. However, you should also be open to helping parents question whether their own approaches to parenting are bringing them the results they desire. This is your professional duty. Again, the basic principle is to follow the parents' lead in questioning cultural parenting practices and not become a cultural conquistador who tells all parents the one right way to be a parent.

WORKING WITH DIVORCED, DIVORCING, AND NEVER-MARRIED PARENTS

Divorce will probably always be a controversial and conflict-laden issue within our society. In part, this is due to moral issues associated with divorce, but it is also due to the many knotty practical issues divorced parents frequently face.

Divorce Polemics

Because divorce and single-parenting choices still carry stigma, parents will be monitoring for any judgments you might have about them. You may have very strong opinions about divorce or about people choosing to adopt or bear children while single. If this is something you cannot put aside and be nonjudgmental about, it's best to put your views in your informed consent so parents know this explicitly about your practice. In most cases, professionals have values and beliefs they can keep in check while working directly with people who make choices far different than the professional might have made. For instance, you might firmly believe that all children should be born into a two-parent family with parents who are married and committed to the family, but you might still be able to be very helpful to a single gay parent who adopted a 10-year-old disabled foster child.

Because they've sometimes faced moral and religious judgments, divorced, divorcing, and never-married parents have substantial needs for support and education. Consequently, you should prepare yourself to provide that education and support. Their parenting challenges can be particularly acute and confusing.

The issue for practitioners working with parents is to avoid laying blame and guilt on parents for divorcing (generally, they already feel guilty about how their divorce might be affecting their children). Instead, your role is to help divorced, divorcing, or never-married parents manage their difficult parenting situations more effectively. What we need to offer is (a) emotional support for divorce- and post-divorce-related stress and conflict; and (b) clear information on specific behaviors parents can engage in or avoid to help their children adjust to divorce.

Providing Support and Educational Information

Most divorcing and recently divorced parents are in a great deal of distress as parents and need comfort, support, and information. Consequently, we recommend talking with parents about divorce in a manner that's empathic and educational. In the following case, a father with three children has come for help in planning to tell the children. His children are 4, 6, and 8 years old.

Case: Talking About Divorce

PARENT: I'm really worried about how to talk with my kids about the divorce. I can't get the right words around it. I know I'm supposed to say something reassuring like, "Your mom and I love each other, but it just hasn't worked out and so that's why I'm moving out because it will be best for us to live separately." But then I worry that maybe my kids will think even though I love them *now*, it might not "work out" either and then I'll end up leaving them, too.

CONSULTANT: This is tough. I respect how much thought you've given this. Even though the differences between you and your wife make it too hard to live together, it's extremely hard to leave the home and torturous to talk with your kids about it.

PARENT: That's for sure.

CONSULTANT: I can see you love your children very much and it feels really important to talk with them about the upcoming divorce using words that won't scare them too much and that will help them know you and your wife tried, but you have now decided the divorce is for the best. But before we do that, I have a different piece of advice.

PARENT: What's that?

CONSULTANT: You should plan to have more than one divorce talk with your kids. I know you want to do this right and that's great. But the good news and the bad news is that you'll need to have this conversation many times. As your children grow older, they'll have different questions. It's your job to tell them you love them and to explain things in words they'll understand, but not to tell them too much. There's no guarantee they'll understand this perfectly and so it may relieve pressure for you to know you'll get other chances. Some people like to think of it like having a sex-talk. Kids will have different questions about sex at different ages and so parents shouldn't have just one sex-talk. You need to be ready to have a sex-talk at any time as your child is growing up. The same is true for talks about divorce. You need to be ready to talk about it now and whenever your kids or you need to talk in the future. I've got a great tip sheet for parents going through divorce and I'd like to go over that with you, too. [See Appendix B, Tip Sheet 10: Ten Tips for Parenting through Divorce.]

In this situation, the family's educational needs are substantial, so the practitioner will probably offer the father a tip sheet, additional reading materials, and a recommendation to attend a group class on divorce and shared parenting.

It can be difficult for divorcing parents to talk with their children without blaming the other parent. This can be either blatant or subtle. We recall one parent who insisted he had the right to call his former spouse "The Whore" in front of the children "because it was the truth." In these extreme cases, we've used radical acceptance to listen empathically to the emotional pain underlying this extreme perspective and then slowly and gently help the parent to understand that "telling the truth" to the children should focus on telling your personal truth and not on the other parent's behavior. Although it can be difficult for divorced or divorcing parents to hear educational messages over the din of their emotional pain and revenge impulses, it's the practitioner's job to empathically and patiently deliver the message. Usually divorced and divorcing parents eventually see that criticizing or blaming the other parent can be damaging to their children.

Separation, Divorce, and Triangulation

In addition to blaming each other for marital problems, parents in the midst of divorce are more likely than other parents to push professional boundaries. They may:

- Pressure you to provide mediation services (even if you have no mediation training).
- Unexpectedly show up with or without the other parent.
- Haphazardly schedule and cancel appointments.
- Ask you to meet with and evaluate their children.
- Subtly or blatantly pursue you as an expert witness who will take their side and potentially testify for them in court.
- Show up with their children and with the other parent and expect you to talk with them about divorce in front of the children.

When divorcing or separated parents present you with these difficult situations, there can be a natural temptation to grow impatient and judgmental. To counter that temptation, we offer the following advice:

Remember that divorce is nearly always an incredibly emotionally painful, disappointing, and sometimes traumatic experience. Divorce involves the violation of a deeply personal bond. Everyone who divorces has either been rejected by—or has rejected—someone with whom they previously had a loving relationship. This is the worst kind of rejection possible and can stimulate deep and powerful insecurity feelings—even when parents don't show insecurity on the surface. Consequently, we need to lead with compassion for the emotional wounds divorced and divorcing parents inevitably carry with them.

Maintaining a Clear Role

One way divorcing parents push boundaries is by showing up when stressed, without an appointment, and sometimes with the other (estranged) parent. If this occurs, you should be sure to clarify your role, function, and the nature of confidentiality at the outset of your meeting—or possibly choose not to hold a scheduled meeting. Your decision to meet or not to meet should be aligned with your initial informed consent policy.

Another way divorcing parents are likely to push boundaries is by trying to get you to perform functions outside your role and/or expertise. For example, you may be asked to provide mediation, child custody assessments, or therapy for the children.

Mediation　If you're meeting as a consultant with an individual parent, it's important to help the parent know that shifting to mediation may not be appropriate. In such cases you can: (a) Empathize with the need for mediation; (b) firmly clarify that mediation services are different from individual work with parents and therefore require working with a different professional (even if the parents beg you and tell you that, despite your lack of training, you're better than any mediator they've ever met); (c) offer a mediation referral.

Child Custody Assessment　If you're working individually with a parent, or even acting as the family divorce consultant, counselor, or therapist, you should not shift your role to child custody or parenting plan assessment. Divorcing parents may make this request to get you to side with them or testify on their behalf in court. Although testifying in and of itself is not a bad thing, it's inappropriate to do so unless you're officially conducting a neutral, systematic, and objective child custody evaluation, parenting plan assessment, or forensic evaluation—which is not something that can or should emerge from your individual work with a parent. The American Psychological Association has guidelines for child custody assessment procedures (see http://www.apa.org/practice/guidelines/child-custody.pdf). Again, your best strategy is to gently and empathically let the parent know that because you didn't initiate a formal evaluation, you can provide a referral, but cannot do the work yourself.

Child Therapy　In both divorce and non-divorce situations, there are child therapy models that include movement back and forth between parenting meetings or consultations and child therapy sessions (Bratton et al., 2006; L. Guerney,

2001; L. Guerney & Guerney, 1989). If you're following such a model and your role is clear despite your shifting tasks, and you've taken care of potential ethical issues, then it may be appropriate for you to provide both child therapy and parent education. The issues are clarity of role and function, which can be addressed via a carefully and clearly written informed consent process.

CHILD ABUSE REPORTING

Child abuse reporting is always stressful. If you're working with parents and children you should develop reliable and trustworthy professional colleagues with whom you can talk about these issues before and after they arise.

The best foundation for child abuse reporting is detailed knowledge of your specific state reporting statutes (Bryant, 2009). In most states, human services providers are required to report child abuse if they come into contact with direct evidence that leads the provider to suspect abuse has occurred and that it has not been reported. With that general assumption in place, keep the following guidelines in mind:

1. Inform parents of confidentiality limits both in writing and orally at the outset of your initial session. Make this confidentiality limit very clear.
2. Remember that many parents use physical punishment (usually spanking) and that spanking is not generally considered physical abuse.
3. Be aware that there may be cases where parents inform you of a single incident or several incidents that approach the threshold of physical or sexual abuse. For example, parents may report losing it and spanking their child harder than intended or locking their young child in a room for an hour or physically restraining their child while washing out his mouth with soap. If you're not completely clear as to whether these behaviors constitute abuse, we recommend that whenever possible or reasonable you consult with a fellow professional or child protection services official. Bottom line: When uncertain about reporting obligations, consult a colleague and/or a child protection specialist in your state.
4. Whenever you've obtained information that leads you to suspect abuse has occurred, document the steps you've taken. Similarly, if you've obtained information that is relevant to potential child abuse, but you decided not to make a report, documentation is essential. Your professional documentation should include a description of the information you obtained from the parent and of your contact with child protective services (if it occurred) and your reason for reporting or not reporting. For example, you would document: (a) abuse-related information you obtained from the parent; (b) any consultation contact you had with colleagues or child protection services (you should consult, because making these decisions in isolation is unwise) and their respective opinions about reporting; (c) the steps you took to inform the parent (if doing so was reasonable); (d) the method you used to make the report (preferably, if possible, including the parent in the process of contacting child protection services).

5. When parents directly tell you about engaging in abusive behavior (e.g., punching, bruising, cutting, etc.), maintain empathy by saying something like, "It really sounds like your child is frustrating and that sometimes feel desperate to get her to behave." Then, gently inform the parent that, as discussed at the session's beginning and in the informed consent document, you have a professional obligation to report this information. Working with the parent to call child protective services is usually the best approach. (See the checklist covering the preceding points.)

Checklist for Reporting Child Abuse

☐ Inform parents of confidentiality limits orally and in writing.

☐ When parents tell you of possible abusive situations, maintain an empathic attitude.

☐ If you're uncertain whether you have a reporting obligation, consult with at least two professional colleagues.

☐ Keep written documentation of your decision-making process when reporting or nearly reporting child abuse (including a description of what your professional colleagues recommended).

☐ When possible and appropriate, make the child abuse report with the parent present (or have the parent make the report with you present).

Complications in Child Abuse Reporting

Contrary to the impulses of many professionals, if a parent informs you that the "other parent" or someone else is abusing her or his child, you shouldn't *necessarily* accept the allegation as truth and report it as such to child protective services. Instead, your initial and primary responsibility should be to encourage the parent to make the report and offer to sit with the parent as she or he makes the call. Many times, especially in divorce or shared-parenting situations, one parent will accuse another parent of abuse in a manner that leaves you wondering if the accusation has merit (Ellis, 2000). This situation can be especially confusing because it's not appropriate to simply ignore the allegation or to accuse the parent of lying or exaggeration. Your job is to explore the situation with the parent and gently confront her or him with options. One of several scenarios may then ensue:

1. The parent will agree to jointly make a call to child protective services with you (and you will feel stressed but happy because this is the best outcome).
2. The parent will maintain that abuse has occurred, but refuse to jointly call child protective services. In this situation you should, as firmly and compassionately as possible, inform the parent that you still have an obligation to report and that the report will also include information about the parent's refusal to report. In essence, you're then reporting on both parents.

3. The parent will recant his or her story in a believable way (e.g., "Well, they're not really bruises and I don't really have any evidence that anything is really going on and I'm sorry, but I'm always doing this exaggerating thing because I hate him [her] so much!"). In this case we advise that you tell the parent you need to have a conversation with either an ethics consultant or child protective services to determine if a report is necessary and that you'll get back to him or her.

4. The parent will refuse to make a report and then begin to recant and minimize in such a way that leaves you continuing to suspect abuse has occurred. In this case, it is wise to go ahead and make a report with or without the parent present.

In these scenarios, the big challenge is that you may not know whether you're being pulled into a parent–parent conflict or whether the story is completely true. Your best option is almost always to explain this to the parent while trying to preserve the therapeutic relationship and then help the parent make the call from your office. However, if the parent is unwilling to make a report and you remain concerned that child abuse is occurring, you have an obligation to report. The report would typically include reporting both parents—one for potential abuse and the other for not reporting potential abuse. Finally, one interesting twist in these highly conflicted divorce situations is that, occasionally, the parent who accuses the other parent of physical or sexual abuse is the perpetrator (Ellis, 2000).

WHEN PARENTS BRING THEIR CHILDREN ALONG

Sometimes parents will schedule a parenting session and then bring their children along unannounced. In a recent parent consultation, contrary to instructions provided by the agency, the parent arrived for the appointment with her three-year-old son and eight-month-old daughter. This is not ideal because the parent may not be able to focus or listen due to preoccupation with the children. There is also the strong possibility that the child will act out or misbehave and the likelihood that the parent will display parenting skills that are far short of optimal. You can easily get caught up in doing family therapy when an educational session with parents was the plan.

Nevertheless, this situation may be viewed as necessary and natural for parents of small children who are overwhelmed and unable to find child care. Once the parent has arrived, it may feel dismissive to refuse a stressed-out parent his or her hoped-for educational experience. If you decide to go ahead and see the parent, the following physical accommodations and mental set might help:

- Put toys and blocks and children's books on one side of the room and set your seating up on the other.
- Intentionally overlook intermittent clingy, overactive, and other mildly troubling behaviors.
- Intentionally overlook minor, suboptimal parenting behaviors; instead, focus on having empathy with the parent's challenging situation.

- Specifically notice and make positive comments about any positive parenting behaviors (e.g., a mother gives her 3-year-old son a clear choice).
- Provide positive compliments about the parent's clear dedication to his or her children.
- Provide several very specific and concrete parenting assignments.
- If you have a simple assignment and the situation seems appropriate, you might demonstrate it during the meeting with the child (e.g., demonstrating character feedback with a 3-year-old).
- Support the parent and children by helping clean up the toys and books.

As noted previously, two main problems associated with having children at a parenting appointment include (a) the parent being distracted or preoccupied and therefore unable to hear or process educational information; and (b) the session turning from a more educational experience into a family therapy situation (especially with older children who can hear and understand the conversation).

Given these problems, we strongly recommend that you be clear and up-front with parents as to why children are not included in parent education, consultation, or therapy sessions. Further, although we advocate flexibility, we also recommend that you firmly set limits and reschedule the session if doing so seems to be the best and most professional option.

POST-PARTUM DEPRESSION

In Chapter 6, we discussed the great internal force for positive change. Based on this theoretical position, we make the presumption that, given the right circumstances, nearly all parents will work to improve themselves. However, sometimes mental or physical challenges deplete that internal force. Post-partum depression might be one reason why you see a parent without much internal force for positive change. Based on U.S. studies, approximately 12 to 17 percent of mothers experience post-partum depression within the first three months of motherhood (Horowitz & Goodman, 2005).

Post-partum depression symptoms are similar to major depression. Most often, mothers experiencing depressive symptoms will display a depressed mood, anhedonia (lack of pleasure), changes in sleeping, eating, and weight, feelings of worthlessness, fatigue, and difficulty concentrating. Some of these symptoms are natural during the post-partum period (e.g., sleep difficulties, negative body image or worthlessness, and fatigue) and these natural post-partum symptoms can trigger additional depressive symptoms—especially among mothers with depression in their history.

The initial treatment approach for post-partum depression involves a broad range of non-drug or psychosocial interventions. This is partly due to parent concerns about the transmission of antidepressant medications to infants through breast feeding. To address this issue, Tip Sheet 11 in Appendix B offers a number of evidence-based, non-drug approaches to treating post-partum depression. These "tips" should, of course, be offered verbally and in combination with empathy, emotional validation, and universalization. This tip sheet can also be modified for using with parents who are not post-partum, but who are displaying depressive symptoms.

NOTICING AND HELPING WITH PARENTAL GUILT

Somewhat related to depression, many parents are inclined toward feeling guilty about not being perfect parents. However, it's important to note that for parents, experiencing guilt—and the sad and regretful feelings associated with guilt—is a natural phenomenon. It can be very therapeutic for parents to know that feeling guilty is a relatively universal experience among parents (Yalom & Leszcz, 2005). Samalin (2003) describes this:

> *Before my children were born, I was convinced that I would be patient, kind, and nurturing—the quintessential earth mother. But I failed to live up to the ideal mother image that I had pictured for myself. I was daunted by the enormous gulf between the perfect parent that I wanted to be and the flawed parent that I actually was. Since then, I have learned that such feelings are quite common. Scratch any parent, and you'll find guilt. It's lurking just beneath the surface, ready to spring out when we lose patience with our children, fail to make them happy, feel resentful of their demands, or believe that when they misbehave it's all our fault. (p. 265)*

Guilt is a complex human emotion. For many parents it can be painful to know that perfection is impossible and that mistakes—sometimes daily mistakes—are unavoidable. One of the best solutions for parents tormented by guilt is participation in parenting classes or support groups. Being with other parents who also make mistakes but continue trying to improve themselves can be reassuring and inspiring.

REVISITING BUTTON-PUSHING: SELF-CARE FOR THE PARENTING PROFESSIONAL

If you work with parents frequently, you may find you've grown less reactive to old buttons that, when pushed, used to produce a rather intense emotional response (see Chapter 2, the "Dealing with Emotional Button-Pushing" section). Or, over time, you may find the opposite has happened; perhaps you're having stronger and stronger emotional reactions to what parents say and do. Either way, feeling numb and underreactive or intense and overreactive, can be a signal for engaging in a bit (or a lot) of self-care and personal exploration.

We bring up this topic because the repetitive nature of working with parents sometimes gets to us. For example, we recall seeing five parents in a row on a Monday, all of whom declared some version of this claim: "I was spanked and I turned out just fine." Then, when the sixth parent arrived and made his claim about turning out fine, he didn't receive our most empathic and compassionate response.

If you've worked much with parents, you likely know what we mean. The topics parents bring up and the comments they make begin to feel redundant. This is in part due to the redundant nature of parenting (and children's behavior) as well as cultural factors that train people to think of parenting in rather narrow and colloquial ways. Sometimes this redundancy brings us to the point where we feel like strangling the next parent who says yet another common cruel and inane comment like, "I told my kid, you'd better stop crying or I'll give you something to cry about."

It requires considerable patience to work effectively with parents. It's easy to become jaded and cynical. Nevertheless, we hope you can maintain your compassion and continue this important work. To do so, we strongly recommend that you take very good care of yourself and seek counseling and collegial support to prevent and address a wide range of potential side effects, including feelings of inadequacy, numbness, or over-reactivity, and burnout.

We hope this book has provided you with a few new ideas to help inspire and rejuvenate you. But in the end, it's up to you to creatively implement these ideas within the context of your unique setting and situation. We urge you to take care of yourself as you face the challenge of listening so parents will talk and talking so parents will listen.

CONCLUDING COMMENTS

In this chapter we covered several special issues that can emerge when working directly with parents. Of course, the topics covered are not exhaustive. As parenting professionals, you will undoubtedly face many other compelling issues. Your work with parents may include coping with disabilities, adoption, raising multiples (e.g., twins, triplets, etc.), healthy biracial identity development, religious conflicts, sexuality, and many other issues that emerge during a consultation. This means you will need to review many other books on many other topics—as learning never ends. But also, keep in mind that even though the presenting issues among parents may seem wildly different, their underlying needs may be remarkably similar.

If we had to leave you with only one basic instruction for helping parents, it would be to *listen well.*

And if we can listen with focused attention and intention, it will become progressively clearer that every parent who comes for assistance is a unique human being worthy of our compassion. In a recent parenting consultation a mother reminded us of this. When talking about her 13-year-old son's behavior problems, she said, "He always does better when we listen." This statement is equally true for parents.

Perhaps even more important, if we can drop our personal distractions and listen well, we may recognize that every parenting-related contact, no matter how seemingly inconsequential, is a remarkable opportunity to help move a family in a more positive and healthy direction. To be able to make even a tiny but important difference in the life of the family is an amazing experience. This small difference, if nurtured along, could extend out into the community and forward into the future. All of this brings us to the final conclusion that working directly with parents puts us in a position of great fortune, because it's hard to imagine doing something more meaningful and influential than helping parents create more positive lives for their children.

Checklist for Dealing With Special Issues and Situations

☐ Remember that we're typically better served by practicing cultural humility than by flaunting our cultural competence.

☐ When appropriate, help parents examine and evaluate their own cultural practices.

☐ Be aware of the special sensitivity to judgment that divorced and divorcing parents might feel.

☐ Be aware of your specific state child abuse reporting statutes.

☐ When needed, use the checklist for reporting child abuse.

☐ Be flexible but professional when parents bring their children to their individual appointments.

☐ Offer psychosocial intervention options if you see signs of post-partum depression.

☐ Monitor your reactions to parents and seek collegial or professional help as needed.

☐ Go to the comprehensive intervention checklist in Appendix D and/or the practitioner-support website to gather more ideas about relationship-based interventions parents can use with their children (http://www.familiesfirst montana.org/parenting/John%20Sommers-Flanagan%20Tip%20Sheets.html).

An Annotated Bibliography of Parenting Books

The following is an annotated list of classic, popular, and useful parenting books. We provide this list because we believe it's helpful for parenting consultants to have good general knowledge of the parenting book literature.

There are too many parenting books on the market for us to provide a comprehensive list. We may have even missed your personal favorite. This list was not compiled using a systematic process. Generally, it includes books that are either classics or currently popular. We intentionally avoided a few books, but many others were overlooked simply because we were not familiar with them. We haven't yet read every parenting book on the planet (and never will). If your favorite book isn't on this list, feel free to email us your recommendation (johnsf44@gmail.com).

1. ACKERMAN, M. (1998). *Does Wednesday mean Mom's house or Dad's?* New York, NY: John Wiley & Sons.
   This book is written by a nationally renowned expert on child custody evaluations. It includes broad coverage of how parents can co-parent in a manner that is less confusing and more healthy for children. One of the book's strengths is a chapter on developing parenting and custodial schedules, which is a practical problem often plaguing parents who are divorced or divorcing.

2. BRAZELTON, T. B., & SPARROW, J. D. (2006). *Touchpoints: Birth to 3 (2nd ed.).* Cambridge, MA: Da Capo Press.
   T. Berry Brazelton is one of the most renowned parenting experts in the world. His *Touchpoints* books (there is also a *Touchpoints: 3–6 years*) are packed with critical information about how to deal with parenting challenges. Although you may not agree with every recommendation in the book, it's difficult to find a more comprehensive, balanced, and gentle approach to parenting. The book includes three main sections: Touchpoints of Development; Challenges to Development; and Allies in Development. The breadth and depth of these books are very impressive.

3. CLINE, F., & FAY, J. (2006). *Parenting with love and logic (rev. ed.)*. Colorado Springs, CO: NavPress.

The love-and-logic model for parenting and teaching is extremely popular, particularly among educators. Cline and Fay are master storytellers and they bring home the lesson that parents need to give children increasing responsibility and stand by them (but not in for them) with empathy when they make mistakes or fail. The underlying premise of this model is that children learn best from their own mistakes and natural consequences and that we should all avoid being "helicopter" parents who rescue our children from real-world learning.

4. COLOROSO, B. (2009). *The bully, the bullied, and the bystander: From preschool to high school—How parents and teachers can help break the cycle (rev. ed.)*. New York, NY: Harper.

Barbara Coloroso is a popular parent educator from the Pacific Northwest. She has written several well-received books and this is her latest. It focuses on how parents and teachers can help children cope with bullying. Coloroso paints the bully, the bullied, and the bystander as "three characters in a tragic play." Her focus on the bystander is especially important because of its consistency with research suggesting that the best bullying interventions focus not only on the bully and victim, but also on bystanders, parents, and teachers.

5. DREIKURS, R., & SOLTZ, V. (1991). *Children: The challenge*. New York, NY: Plume.

This is an early parenting classic, originally published in 1964. It's based on Adlerian theory and emphasizes natural consequences and other methods through which parents can encourage, but not spoil, their children. The book provided foundational concepts for many parenting books that followed. For example, it discussed the goals of misbehavior, the family council, and natural consequences—all of which have been used as basic principles and strategies in many different contemporary parenting books.

6. FABER, A., & MAZLISH, E. (1999). *How to talk so kids will listen & listen so kids will talk*. New York, NY: Harper.

This classic book, originally published in 1980, focuses on enhancing parent–child communication and remains immensely popular. As of this writing it was ranked #149 overall and #5 in the parenting book category on Amazon.com. The book includes communication strategies for helping children deal with their feelings, engaging cooperation, and dealing with misbehavior without punishment. It includes cartoons illustrating positive and negative communication strategies.

7. FABER, A., & MAZLISH, E. (2005). *Siblings without rivalry*. New York, NY: Harper.

Originally published in 1988, the latest edition of Faber and Mazlish's second parenting classic begins with an excellent story that helps parents see that sibling rivalry can stem from jealousy similar to the jealousy a spouse might feel if asked to welcome another husband or wife into the home. The book provides clear ideas about how to avoid comparing, assigning roles, or taking sides and suggests specific alternative strategies to avoid conflict and promote more peaceful interactions.

8. FERBER, R. (1985). *Solve your child's sleep problems*. New York, NY: Simon & Schuster.

This is a very distinct approach to helping very young children sleep better. It has been called the "Ferber approach" or the "cry-it-out solution." About a decade ago it was featured on the comedy series, *Mad About You*. Many parents swear by this approach while other parents believe it could be emotionally damaging. Research indicates it is effective in improving sleep onset, but there is no clear evidence about whether "crying it out" causes emotional damage. Sleep is such a common issue that we also recommend you be familiar with the extreme opposite approach (Tine Thevenin's *The family bed*), and a more moderate approach (Pantley & Sears, *The no-cry sleep solution*).

9. FIELDS, D., & BROWN, A. (2009). *Baby 411: Clear answers & smart advice for your baby's first year* (4th ed.). Boulder, CO: Windsor Peak Press.
   This book was recommended to us by a colleague who swears by its authoritative guidance. She raved about the precision of the authors' advice . . . ranging from sleep to teething to illness to feeding. Not surprisingly, we also found it helpful both in terms of comprehensiveness and clarity. It's a practical book designed as a much needed instruction manual for new parents. There are also additional 411 books by the same authors focused on handling pregnancy and parenting your toddler.

10. FISHER, B., & ALBERTI, R. E. (2006). *Rebuilding: When your relationship ends* (3rd ed.). Atascadero, CA: Impact Publishers.
    This book is designed to help adults deal with the emotional side of divorce. It is highly acclaimed as a self-help book for parents and a good recommendation for parents who are suffering emotionally from divorce. As discussed in Chapter 11, many parents struggle deeply with divorce and knowing about a book that can help navigate this process is important.

11. GINOTT, H. G., GINOTT, A., GODDARD, H. W. (2003). *Between parent and child: The bestselling classic that revolutionized parent–child communication (rev ed.)*. New York, NY: Three Rivers Press.
    This is another classic book focusing on parent–child communication. The main emphasis is on respecting and understanding children's emotional states. Like Adler and Dreikurs, Haim Ginott's work was a foundation for many to follow. For example, Faber and Mazlich attribute their approach to their experiences in workshops with Ginott.

12. GLASSER, W. (2002). *Unhappy teenagers*. New York, NY: HarperCollins.
    Glasser developed choice theory and in this book he applies it to raising teenagers. Similar to Dreikurs (and Adler), he believes all children (and teens) strive for love and belonging, but that if they feel excessively controlled or criticized they will rebel and begin seeking freedom and fun as their primary goals. Glasser's approach in this book is very liberal and it may make some parents and consultants uncomfortable, but he provides a worthwhile and stimulating perspective.

13. GORDON, T. (2000). *Parent effectiveness training: the proven program for raising responsible children*. New York, NY: Three Rivers Press.
    Thomas Gordon's Parent Effectiveness Training (PET) was originally published in 1970. You can find many copies of these original editions on used-book shelves. PET quickly became very popular and still has a substantial following. Gordon's PET is a very non-authoritarian approach that emphasizes listening and communication. Gordon is strongly opposed to using force, coercion, or power when parenting children. Instead, he emphasizes using active listening and interactive problem-solving when conflicts arise.

14. GOTTMAN, J. & DECLAIRE, J. (1998). *The heart of parenting: Raising an emotionally intelligent child*. New York, NY: Simon & Schuster.
    John Gottman is a renowned marriage researcher at the University of Washington. Apparently, in his spare time, he produced an excellent book on helping parents deal with their children's emotions. This book emphasizes emotion-coaching, which is a procedure through which parents can teach their children how to cope with challenging

and uncomfortable emotions. Gottman and DeClaire encourage parents to view their children's meltdowns and tantrums as opportunities for positive and educational inter-actions. This book uses Daniel Goleman's concept of *emotional intelligence* as a founding principle.

15. KAZDIN, A. E. (2008). *The Kazdin method for parenting the defiant child*. Boston, MA: Mariner Books.

Alan Kazdin is past-president of the American Psychological Association and a highly respected researcher in the area of behavior therapy for teenagers and families. Not surprisingly, his approach to parenting the defiant child is strongly behavioral. Although behavioral approaches can be overly tedious and impersonal, Kazdin's approach is relatively user-friendly (and perhaps more importantly, child-friendly). His substantial hands-on experience with children and families make this book a reasonable choice for parents and consultants. In particular, he does a fabulous job discussing challenging issues like punishment and provides immensely clarifying com-ments about timeout.

16. KOHN, A. (2006). *Unconditional parenting*. New York, NY: Atria Books.

Alfie Kohn is a well-known and controversial writer who is strongly against using behavioral psychology to control children's behavior. Author of *Punished by rewards*, he emphasizes that children do best with unconditional love, respect, and the opportunity to make their own choices. He also emphasizes that most parents don't really want compliance and obedience from their children in the long run and so they should work more on establishing positive relationships than on controlling their children. He believes controlling and authoritarian parenting methods communicate a destructive message of conditional love.

17. KURCINKA, M. S. (2001). *Kids, parents, and power struggles*. New York, NY: Harper.

Kurcinka's book gives a concise, practical, and engaging account of how to use non-authoritarian approaches to attain children's compliance and cooperation. The focus is on parents as emotion coaches (see Gottman for another resource) and does not offer immediate or magical solutions. Instead, it covers a range of creative techniques for using power struggles as pathways to better parent–child relationships and mutual understanding. There is a strong emphasis on firm guidelines and mutual respect.

18. KURCINKA, M. S. (2006). *Raising your spirited child: A guide for parents whose child is more intense, sensitive, perceptive, persistent, and energetic (rev. ed.)*. New York, NY: Harper.

When we get feedback on books especially designed for parents of children who have very active and challenging temperaments, parents generally rate this as their favorite. Of course, spirited children have been called a variety of less positive names in the literature, including but not limited to: active alert, challenging, difficult, explosive, and strong-willed. These are also children who might be labeled as having attention-deficit/hyperactivity disorder. Kurcinka takes a masterful approach to relabeling and accommodating spirited children in a way that focuses on their personal strengths and avoids unnecessary power struggles.

19. MACK, A. (1989). *Dry all night: The picture book technique that stops bedwetting*. New York, NY: Little, Brown.

There are several different approaches to address bedwetting in children. This is our favorite. The author takes a gentle approach to helping parents work through their own bedwetting reactions (which she refers to as sleepwetting). The book includes two main sections: (a) 10 steps that will help your child become dry all night, and (b) a picture book with a story to read to your child. In contrast to more behavioral and medical approaches, this book offers reasonable guidance that parents are likely to understand and implement without much ambivalence.

20. McKENZIE, R. G. (2001). *Setting limits with your strong-willed child: Eliminating conflict by establishing clear, firm, and respectful boundaries*. New York, NY: Three Rivers Press.

    This book is hailed by many parents as a kinder and gentler approach to being a firm parent and limit-setter. Parents are educated about how they partake in the "dance" of noncompliance, and taking disciplinary action rather than using repeated warnings is emphasized. McKenzie helps parents move beyond using the constant reminders that erode parental authority and teach children to ignore their parents.

21. Nelsen, J., LOTT, L., & GLENN, H.S. (2007). Positive discipline A–Z: 1001 solutions to everyday parenting problems. New York, NY: Three Rivers Press.

    The lead author of this book, Jane Nelsen, is the author of the original, and very popular, "positive discipline" book, published in the 1980s. Like many other parenting authorities, Nelsen bases much of her advice for parents on the theoretical perspective of Alfred Adler and Rudolf Dreikurs. The main emphasis is on mutual respect and helping children learn from the natural consequences of their behaviors.

22. PANTLEY, E., & SEARS, W. (2002). *The no-cry sleep solution: Gentle ways to help your baby sleep through the night*. New York, NY: McGraw Hill.

    This is the middle-of-the-road book for helping parents cope with their young child's sleeping difficulties. Pantley and Sears help parents study their child's sleep patterns and discover how to work with the baby's biological sleep rhythms. They also articulate a "Persistent Gentle Removal System" that teaches babies to fall asleep without the breast, bottle, or pacifier.

23. PHELAN, T. (2004). *1-2-3 magic: Effective discipline for children 2 through 12 (3rd ed.)*. Glen Ellyn, IL: Parentmagic.

    This book and its accompanying video describes and advocates a simple approach for parents to set limits and take back control from children. Phelan coaches parents on avoiding the endless arguments with children. He also does a great job pointing out that one of the best ways to get your child to continue misbehaving is to have an extreme emotional reaction to the misbehavior.

24. POPKIN, M. (2005). *Doc pop's 52 weeks of active parenting*. Kennesaw, GA: Active Parenting.

    Michael Popkin is a popular contemporary parenting expert who has authored most books in the "Active Parenting" series. His approach is highly democratic and, like many parenting authorities, he follows the work of Adler and Dreikurs. In this book (there are many other Active Parenting books you could become familiar with), Popkin provides 52 weekly family activities designed to promote parenting skill development and family bonds. Sample activities include actively listening to children, methods for monitoring and limiting television/computer time, sharing stories from family history, as well as playful activities.

25. REICHLIN, G., & WINKLER, C. (2001). *The pocket parent*. New York, NY: Workman Publishing.

    This is a handy, pocket-sized book filled with tips on how to deal with challenging parenting situations. It's organized in an A–Z format and includes quick, bulleted suggestions on what to try when facing specific behaviors and situations (e.g., anger, bad words, lying, morning crazies, etc.). This book provides direct advice in ways that can help expand the repertoire of parenting consultants.

26. RICCI, I. (1997). *Mom's house, Dad's house (2nd ed.)*. New York, NY: Fireside
Originally published in 1980, this is the classic book for establishing a joint custodial or shared parenting arrangement. Generally, if we recommend only one book for divorcing parents, this is it. The author clearly addresses many biases that our society and individual parents have about divorce and shared parenting. She articulates clear ways parents can modify their thinking and develop more healthy and adaptive post-divorce attitudes. She also includes a sample parenting plan and excellent chapters on how ex-spouses can work to establish a productive business relationship for managing their joint parenting interests more effectively. In 2006, Ricci published a related book, titled *Mom's house, Dad's house for kids*.

27. SAMALIN, N., & WHITNEY, C. (2003). *Loving without spoiling: And 100 other timeless tips for raising terrific kids*. New York, NY: McGraw-Hill.
Nancy Samalin, a well-known parenting expert, includes 100 mini-chapters in this book of tips. Similar to the *Pocket parent*, she covers a wide range of parenting challenges. Her focus often acknowledges the intense love and concern that parents have for their children, which can make it easy for parents to become too lenient, spoil their children, and then end up dealing with repeated bratty behavior. Samalin helps parents recognize how they can give their children responsibility, maintain their authority, and raise well-mannered children.

28. SEARS, W., SEARS, M., SEARS, R., & SEARS, J. (2003). *The baby book: Everything you need to know about your baby from birth to age two (revised and updated ed.)*. New York, NY: Little, Brown.
This is a great resource for parents of very young children. The focus is on developing a strong attachment and raising a healthy baby. It's written by the Sears family, three of whom are physicians and one a registered nurse. William and Martha Sears (the parents) are strong advocates of attachment parenting, a style that emphasizes touch and connection.

29. SIEGEL, D., & HARTZELL, M. (2004). *Parenting from the inside out*. New York, NY: Tarcher.
Daniel Siegel is a child psychiatrist, and Mary Hartzell is an early childhood expert. In this book they explore recent developments in neurobiology and attachment research and discuss how interpersonal relationship patterns can affect brain development. They also address the interesting phenomenon of parents suddenly noticing that they're unintentionally repeating their parents' parenting patterns. This book helps parents look at their own lives in an effort to become parents who provide more optimal levels of love and security for their children.

30. SOMMERS-FLANAGAN, R., ELANDER, C., & SOMMERS-FLANAGAN, J. (2000). *Don't divorce us! Kids' advice to parents*. Arlington, VA: American Counseling Association.
Somewhat surprisingly, this is one of our personal favorites. It focuses almost exclusively on advice that children and adults (who went through divorces as children) would like to give to divorcing parents. We've used it, with some success, to help children of divorce talk about their own experiences during therapy.

31. THEVENIN, T. (1987). *The family bed*. Wayne, NJ: Avery Publishing Group.
Getting babies to sleep well can be challenging. This approach emphasizes that it's natural and nurturing for babies/children and their parents to sleep together. The family

bed is viewed as a very helpful solution to children's sleeping problems. As you may recognize, this approach is in contrast to the Ferber or "cry-it-out" approach described previously (see Ferber). We're not necessarily endorsing either the cry-it-out or the family bed approach (both of which will raise heated emotions from some parents), but believe it's very important for parenting consultants to know the ends of the spectrum when it comes to dealing with sleep problems.

Tip Sheets for Parents

TIP SHEET 1: THE RULES OF SPANKING (*CONTINUED*)

1. Never use a weapon or object to spank or inflict physical pain on children.
2. Never spank when angry because angry spanking can lead to excessive spanking or child abuse.
3. Always spank with an open hand on the child's buttocks.
4. Never pull the child's pants down to spank on bare skin.
5. Always limit yourself to one or two swats because repeated swatting is linked to parents losing control.
6. Always explain, before and after, the reason for the spanking (the negative behavior).
7. Always explain, before and after, how your child might have avoided the spanking (the positive behavior).
8. Whenever possible and reasonable, use alternatives to spanking
9. Remember that because children grow up, spanking can never be a long-term parenting strategy.

Note: For a comprehensive review of corporal punishment research, see: Gershoff, E. T. (2002). Corporal punishment by parents and associated child behaviors and experiences: A meta-analytic and theoretical review. *Psychological Bulletin, 128*(4), 539–579.

TIP SHEET 2: CHOICE THEORY 101

This tip sheet is for parents who get in repeated and destructive power struggles with their children, especially with their preteens or teens.

Choice theory was developed by William Glasser. Glasser wants everyone to understand the first rule of choice theory: *The only person whose behavior we can control is our own.*

Although it's normal for parents and children to occasionally engage in a battle of wills, when these battles become too frequent or too intense, the parent–child relationship usually suffers. According to choice theory, parents who are too invested in controlling their children will begin using unhealthy methods to get control. These controlling behaviors can become what Glasser refers to as the seven deadly habits:

1. Criticizing
2. Blaming
3. Complaining
4. Nagging
5. Threatening
6. Punishing
7. Bribing or rewarding to control

Think about these habits. Are they common in your family? Do you use them more than you'd like? If so, according to choice theory, your children may distance themselves from you and focus instead on freedom, friends, and fun. Unfortunately, when young people react to parental efforts to control them, freedom, friends, and fun usually translates into drugs, sex, and trouble.

To practice choice theory in your family you need to embrace the first rule. But because the cultural norm in the United States is for people to try to control each other, it may help to say this rule out loud: "The only person whose behavior I can control is my own."

You may be wondering: "If I can control only my own behavior, then how can I be a positive influence on my child?" This leads to choice theory's second big rule: *All we can give another person is information.*

Consider the preceding statement. If all you can provide is non-criticizing, non-blaming, non-complaining, non-nagging, non-threatening, non-punishing, and non-rewarding information, what information is left?

You *can* provide your child with information about the world, about what you want, and about your concerns and fears and hopes and dreams. For example, you can say:

- "I need help with the dishes. I'd like it if you'd take some time to help me."
- "I want you to be safe and sober and happy."
- "I am afraid that if you drink too much or use drugs that you'll damage your body."
- "I know if you use drugs you can become addicted for life and it can ruin your chances for a happy and healthy life."
- "I want a good relationship with you."
- "I'm your mother. I can't stop loving you. I can't stop myself from being concerned about your safety. And so I'd like to talk about how you can keep yourself safe tonight."

Some parents complain that choice theory is too soft and takes away parental authority. We believe the opposite. If you focus on what you can control (yourself) and then give your children clear and passionate information about what you want, what you fear, and your personal convictions, you'll be providing them with a strong foundation for positive behavior—and very little reason to rebel.

Tip Sheet 3: Character Feedback

Most parents want their children to develop positive character traits. These traits or virtues typically include things like:

- Honesty
- Self-control
- Respect for others
- Generosity
- Courage

However, in an odd twist of reasoning, most parents use negative feedback to teach children these positive character traits. For example, Marcus wants his son Bruce to be honest and so whenever he notices Bruce bending the truth, he corrects him. He says things like: "Bruce, you know that wasn't the truth" or "You need to stop lying!"

(Continued)

Tip Sheet 3: Character Feedback (*Continued*)

Despite Dad's positive intentions, his negative comments may shape Bruce's character. Bruce may notice his father's displeasure at his dishonesty. Eventually, Bruce's character or identity will take on a negative spin. He may think, "I've got a problem with honesty" or "I'm a guy who doesn't tell the truth."

Character feedback is a means through which parents can help their children recognize and develop positive attributes. It's a strategy that leads children to think of themselves differently, as illustrated in the following example:

> By the time she was six years old, our youngest daughter [Rylee] had developed a passion for sweets. Recognizing this, Rita, John, and Rylee's older sister [Chelsea] all began commenting, "Rylee has a sweet tooth!" Very quickly, Rylee, when eating candy, stuffed it in her mouth, proclaiming, "I've got a sweet tooth!" It didn't take us long to see that labeling Rylee with this character trait was a very bad idea.
>
> Huddling up, we made a new plan. There was, in fact, minor evidence that Rylee liked broccoli. She would eat broccoli dipped in ranch dressing. The three of us adopted a new mantra. We said things like: "Rylee likes her broccoli with ranch dressing. Rylee is the kind of girl who knows she'll grow up strong and smart if she eats her vegetables."
>
> In less than a week, Rylee affirmed our character feedback. While eating broccoli with ranch dressing, she exclaimed, "I'm a girl who eats my broccoli." At the time of this writing, Rylee [now 21 years old] still enjoys her broccoli.

The lesson for parents is that since we make statements about our children's character anyway, we might as well consciously and intentionally make these character statements in a positive and hopeful direction. For instance, in the opening example, what if Marcus had taken a positive approach with Bruce? What if he consistently noticed and commented on Bruce's truth-telling? What if he said things like, "I love it when you tell me the truth" or "You're the kind of son whom I can trust to be honest with me" or "It was so cool when you told the truth about what happened at school."

This doesn't mean that parents should never point out their children's negative behaviors. Sometimes children need direct and critical feedback. The problem is that if we do that too often, we may unintentionally contribute to the development of negative character traits.

Tip Sheet 4: I've Got a *New* Attitude

This tip sheet is for parents who have children or teens who often have tantrums or temper/anger problems.

Here is some crazy-sounding advice: The best first step for stopping your child's tantrums is for you to *begin looking forward to your child's next tantrum*. This advice is true whether you're the parent of a 1-year-old or a 16-year-old.

Children are smart. They can sense your fear and your worries. And if they sense you're worried about their next tantrum, the result will be more and bigger tantrums.

Many parents feel like they're *walking on eggshells* —fearing their child's next tantrum. If this true in your home, then your child has too much power!

Looking forward to your child's next tantrum (or your teen's next angry outburst) is an excellent tool for rebalancing power in your relationship with your child. To deal with your child's tantrums, you must stop feeling afraid of them.

John Gottman, PhD, a great parenting and marriage expert, has explained that children's tantrums are an irreplaceable opportunity to:

- Show empathy and compassion for your child.
- Make an emotional connection with your child.
- Teach your child not to be afraid of her strong emotions.
- Help your child solve his emotional problems.
- Teach your child emotional self-control.

To get over your dread and begin looking forward to your child's next tantrum, you need a clear and positive plan for how you want to deal with the tantrum. Then, you need to practice the plan. And finally, you need to look forward to your chance to implement the plan because you're confident that it's not only okay to face your child's anger directly—it's healthy and good for you and your child.

Consider the message in this tip sheet. Are you willing to try looking forward to your child's next tantrum or your teenager's next angry outburst? Can you really start believing that it's okay for your child to be angry and that it's good to face that anger directly? Can you embrace the positive possibilities linked to your child's anger?

The next time you ask your child to do a chore or to stop playing a computer game, imagine doing it with positive expectations. Imagine facing your child's anger and being strong and showing empathy. And to help with your limit-setting plan, be sure to read Tip Sheet 2.

TIP SHEET 5: THE GOALS OF CHILDREN'S MISBEHAVIOR

Your telephone rings. You answer it. You begin a conversation with a friend. Suddenly, your son, who had been playing quietly, begins pestering you. Or, perhaps, as soon as she recognizes you're on the phone, your daughter climbs into the cupboard where you keep candy.

It's good to think about why children act in the ways they do. At Families First Boston (a parent education center), parents are taught to "Get curious, not furious." If we take time to reflect on why children misbehave, we'll be more understanding and better able to come up with solutions to their misbehavior.

Many years ago, Rudolf Dreikurs identified four main psychological goals of children's misbehavior:

1. To get attention
2. To get power or control
3. To get revenge
4. To display inadequacy (and get help)

(Continued)

TIP SHEET 5: THE GOALS OF CHILDREN'S MISBEHAVIOR (*CONTINUED*)

Dreikurs believed that if children had a sense of belonging and being useful contributors to their families, they wouldn't misbehave much. But, if they didn't feel a sense of belonging and usefulness, they would try to gain attention, power and control, and revenge, or to prove themselves inadequate.

In the opening example, the boy who began pestering his parent after his parent answered the telephone may be seeking attention. Often, attention-seeking behavior causes parents to feel irritated or annoyed.

The girl who climbed up for candy during the phone call may have been waiting all day to exert her power and control. When children seek power and control, parents often react with anger.

Many other examples of misbehavior fit this theory. Children who refuse to get out of bed for school in the morning may be trying to obtain much-needed power. Or, they may be displaying their sense of inadequacy and trying to get their parents to take care of all their needs. When children show inadequacy, parents usually feel desperate, exhausted, and worried.

Consider sibling rivalry. The boy who slaps his sister may be seeking revenge. He's tired of hearing everybody talk about his cute little sister. His parents probably feel scared and threatened; they don't know if their beautiful daughter is safe from her mean brother.

There are no perfect solutions to children's misbehavior. But here are a few ideas:

- If you feel annoyed about attention-seeking, pay positive attention to your child *before* she starts annoying you. Try special time (Tip Sheet 7), pay attention to her positive behaviors, and try ignoring her annoying behaviors.
- If you feel angry and think your child is seeking power and control, find ways to give him power and control. Again, do this *before* the manipulative behavior begins. It's also a good idea to give choices: "Would you rather clean your desk now, or in twenty minutes?"
- If you feel threatened or hurt by your child's revenge behaviors, do what you can to address the roots of her revenge feelings. Active teaching and limit-setting may be needed (see Tip Sheet 2).
- If you feel worried because your child is displaying inadequacy, take less responsibility for him and think about what small things he can do to feel useful. This situation might call for counseling or a consultation with school personnel.

Children don't just misbehave for psychological reasons; they also misbehave for physical reasons. If your children misbehave, check to see whether they're hungry,

TIP SHEET 6: ENHANCING YOUR CHILD'S SENSE OF SECURITY THROUGH ATTACHMENT

A large amount of research suggests that children and adults who feel secure and loved are more likely to be successful in relationships, school, and employment. This statement is nearly universally accepted as both true and important. Just think of the opposite: Children and adults who feel insecure and unloved are more likely to struggle in their relationships, school, and employment.

These statements also reflect basic common sense. If you want your children to do well in the world, you should work to provide them with a secure base and strong foundation. The question for parents is: What can you do to help your child develop internalized feelings of security and of being loved?

The best answer to this question involves general sensitivity and responsiveness to your baby, toddler, child, or teenager. Attachment is enhanced when you:

- Provide encouragement and support when your child leaves your side to explore the world.
- Are welcoming and happy when your child returns from exploring the world for emotional "refueling."
- Are sensitive to your child's unique needs (for example, some children are more comfortable than others with physical affection).
- Learn to read and address your baby and toddler's signals for needing food, rest, and comfort.
- Respond in emotional tune with your child's positive emotions, such as joy, happiness, and satisfaction.
- Use songs, play, rituals, and other consistent patterns for providing a positive emotional environment.
- Are sensitive to what helps your child calm down.

The challenge for parents is to be sensitive to all these signs and signals and issues without being overbearing. Children are often strongly interested in independence and will oppose your efforts to get them to do what's good for them. As a consequence, this dance of tending to your children's needs and mirroring their emotional state, while at the same time letting your children attend to their own needs is one that you'll be doing for many years into the future.

There are many popular resources on attachment in bookstores and on the Internet. Our only warning about this is that you avoid materials that place too much responsibility on mothers for attending to every detail of their children's moment-to-moment emotional needs. Attachment should be a part of what fathers and other caretakers do as well. Always be cautious of parenting approaches that put too much blame on one parent or the other for being unavailable or out-of-sync. After all, children are robustly resilient and can thrive even though their parents are imperfect and not always available. In fact, sometimes children struggle more when their parents try to be too attentive, too available, and too responsive to their children.

TIP SHEET 7: SPECIAL TIME

Special time gives your child brief experiences of having 100 percent of your attention and nearly complete *control*. The rules include:

1. Identify when and how long you'll be doing special time (we recommend 15–20 minutes two to four times a week). Select these times in advance because you cannot and should not provide 100 percent attention during the rest of the day.

(*Continued*)

2. Tell your child you've decided to spend special play time with her. Say something like, "During our play time, you get to decide what we'll do." Set a timer or watch so you both know when the time is up.

3. For more aggressive or impulsive children, you may need to introduce rules by saying, "Even though you're in charge during our play time, there's no hitting or hurting, no breaking things, and no spending too much money or eating candy. If you do any of those things, our special play time will end and we'll try again next time."

4. During special time, practice reflective listening skills and follow your child's lead. If he's playing army and the soldiers get killed, say something like: "It looks like these soldiers all got killed." Do this even if your child behaves unusually (as long as he's following the rules). Avoid making judgments or suggesting feelings, because doing so will lead your child in a particular direction (and there's plenty of time to be a leader during the other 23 hours and 40 minutes of each day). For example, it would be leading to say, "Oh no. I don't like seeing soldiers killed. Aren't their families going to be sad?" This is your child's time to lead and your time to follow.

5. At the end, help your child deal with the fun having ended. Your child may be disappointed or angry or refuse to help clean up. If so, show empathy ("It's hard to stop having fun and I see you're upset"), but be firm in enforcing the end of play. If you have time and want to continue playing, tell her, "Our special time is over. But I still have time to play. So now if we keep playing, we'll just play like we usually do. You won't be in charge anymore." If your child refuses to clean up, don't get into a power struggle. Clean up on your own and act like you're having lots of fun while putting stuff away. Special time is not for active teaching. You can be more forceful during the rest of the day and week. For this 20 minutes, keep an accepting attitude.

6. Special time is guaranteed time and shouldn't be withheld as a punishment. If it's scheduled, don't take it away because of misbehavior.

Observing Your Child During Special Time

Special time is great for observing your child. If you're nondirective during special time, your child may act out her main emotional and behavioral struggles. We remember a six-year-old girl who had her father pretend to be her little brother and run away from home because their parents forced them to clean their room too much and didn't allow them to eat candy. Her father wanted to tell her she had it easy and that she got too many desserts as it was. But to argue would have invalidated her internal experience of struggling with cleaning up and eating healthy foods. By observing children in free play, you can see what issues they're trying to master.

This tip sheet is for separated, divorced, or never-married parents who are considering new romantic relationships or have started becoming a new stepfamily.

Parents should proceed with caution in all new relationships. Consider the following guidelines:

- Don't promise your child that you'll never date again. No one can predict the future. Falling in love can happen when you least expect it (and least plan on it).
- If you're getting serious with a new person, introduce your child slowly. Even though you may be head-over-heels in love, don't rush your child; he or she will probably not be feeling love for this new person.
- Manage your expectations. Your child may never be happy with your new romance or new spouse. Find a way to adjust to reality. Forcing your child to fall in love with your new lover hardly ever works.
- If you get remarried, consider involving your child in the ceremony. Having the new parent make vows to your child can be a nice touch.
- When it comes to discipline or using punishment with children, biological parents should take the lead. Stepparents shouldn't hit or spank stepchildren. If you're wondering why, look no further than the fact that stepparents are 20 times more likely to abuse children than biological parents.
- Discipline will be tricky. It's okay for stepparents to enforce reasonable and established limits, but for the first several years (and possibly forever), all primary discipline should flow from the biological parent.
- Just as you need special time with your new romantic partner, remember you need special time with your child.
- Don't require—or even encourage—your children to call the new parent "Mom" or "Dad." Find an alternative affectionate name (e.g., Bapa, PJ). For obvious reasons, this is an explosive issue.
- You may hope your new engagement, wedding, and marriage will be joyful for everyone, but it's not likely. The reality is that children, in-laws, former spouses, biological parents, neighbors, and virtually everyone on the planet other than you and your new partner are likely to have mixed feelings about your fresh, new romantic relationship.
- Children are likely to show their mixed feelings through tears, withdrawal, or anger. The transition will flow more smoothly if both parent figures can express compassion and understanding for the children's mixed feelings.
- Watch out for taking sides. It will be hard to make it perfectly clear you love your children and your stepchildren and your spouse all at the same time.
- Never stop educating yourself. Read books, consult with friends, take classes, and watch educational DVDs about stepparenting and stepfamilies.

TIP SHEET 9: ANTI-BULLYING TIPS FOR PARENTS

Although some educators and individuals refer to bullying (and being bullied) as a normal part of growing up, for many children (and parents) bullying is quite simply a traumatic nightmare. This tip sheet offers ideas for dealing with this perplexing and persistent social problem in schools and neighborhoods.

1. Encourage your child to communicate openly to you about his or her bullying experiences. This will be difficult because you will instantly want to contact the bully's parents or "beat up" the bully, neither of which is recommended.

(Continued)

TIP SHEET 9: ANTI-BULLYING TIPS FOR PARENTS (*CONTINUED*)

2. Open communication includes empathy and asking your child what she or he has done to try to stop or cope with the bullying. Avoid blaming and avoid taking action on behalf of your child (unless the level of bullying aggression makes an intervention necessary and then only do so with the support of school personnel, law enforcement, or other appropriate community members).

3. Help your child understand that being bullied is not his or her fault. Although sometimes bullies increase their bullying when children react, reacting to bullies should not become a reason to blame the victim for increased bullying.

4. Help your child identify different strategies for dealing with bullies, recognizing that some strategies will work better than others for individual children. Strategies might include (a) avoiding and/or ignoring the bully; (b) hanging out with friends and not being alone and vulnerable (parents can help children develop new social connections); (c) connecting with school or community personnel who can help with bullying; or (d) using humor to defuse bullying situations. Encouraging your child to fight back is not recommended as it usually results in increased bullying frequency and longevity.

5. Use your child's school as an ally and resource. Although you should be careful about approaching the school without your child's permission, often school personnel will have ways to address bullying, in general, that don't identify you or your child (and thereby increase bullying likelihood). Also, encourage your child to speak with trusted school personnel (school counselors or school psychologists are a good start).

6. Become more present and available in your child's life. This might mean volunteering at school and even having casual, face-to-face contact with the bully (not to confront the bully, but to help make your presence in your child's life a reality to the bully and bystanders).

TIP SHEET 10: TEN TIPS FOR PARENTING THROUGH DIVORCE

To parent well through divorce and into the future, you should educate yourself about the unique challenges you're likely to face and how to manage them. The following short list is a beginning. Additional resources are listed in Appendix A.

1. *Make a commitment to good self-care.* There are two big reasons why this is good advice. First, divorce is emotionally painful and stressful. If you don't take care of yourself physically, emotionally, and spiritually, you may suffer. Second, if you're suffering, your children will suffer right along with you.

2. *Cultivate a support system for your children.* You can't do it all. Therefore, when you're feeling exhausted your children will need other healthy adults with whom they can spend time. Identify who these adults are and ask them for help and support.

3. *Listen to your children, even when it's hard.* Your children may or may not want to talk about the divorce or their feelings. In most cases, they'll suddenly become angry, irritable, or sad and possibly direct those feelings at you. If so, listen and comfort, even if what they're saying is hard to hear.

4. *Set limits for your children.* Sometimes during and after a divorce parents will start letting their children do whatever they want. This isn't healthy. Children need limits; they need you to be a firm and loving parent.

5. *Work on communicating respectfully with your child's other parent.* Practice positive communication skills. It can also help to change your language and not call your former spouse, "My ex," but instead, "My daughter's father" or "My son's mother." See Ricci's book, *Mom's house, Dad's house,* for more information on this.

6. *Develop smooth transitions from one home to another.* Child exchanges can be traumatic for everyone. Having a regular and positive routine when you get your children ready to go to their other home can help. Also, avoid conflicts with the other parent during child exchanges. Exposing your child to parent–parent conflict is very unhealthy. Consider finding an outside person to help you establish a positive exchange.

7. *Set limits with your child's other parent.* Consider establishing guidelines for parent–parent meetings. Don't meet for long hours alone or make yourself spontaneously available anytime the other parent wants to talk. Instead, set up official meetings at a safe and pleasant (but not intimate) location.

8. *Educate yourself.* Consider taking a class or reading a book or watching an educational DVD on divorce and shared parenting.

9. *Educate yourself II.* Consult with legal and mental-health professionals as appropriate. Neither legal nor mental health professionals should be used in an effort to manipulate or punish the other parent or the children.

10. *Embark on a healthy new life.* Give your child's mom or dad privacy and maintain your own. Encourage your children to have good times with the other parent (never make your children feel guilty about having a good time with their mom or dad). Establish new family rituals to help you and your children adjust to your new lives.

TIP SHEET 11: NON-DRUG OPTIONS FOR DEALING WITH DEPRESSION

The following options can be very effective for relieving depression symptoms. Although antidepressant medications are also an option, because they're so widely marketed and many parents are reluctant to take them, only non-drug alternatives are listed and described here.

1. **Psychotherapy:** Going to a reputable and licensed mental-health professional who offers counseling or psychotherapy for depression can be very helpful. This may include marriage, couple, or family therapy.

2. **Vigorous aerobic exercise:** Consider initiating and maintaining a regular cardiovascular or aerobic exercise schedule. This could involve a specific referral to a personal trainer and/or local fitness center (e.g., YMCA).

3. **Herbal remedies:** Some individuals benefit from taking herbal supplements. In particular, there is evidence that omega-3 fatty acids (fish oil) and St. John's Wort are effective in reducing depressive symptoms. Consult with a health-care provider if you're pursuing this option.

(Continued)

Tɪᴘ Sʜᴇᴇᴛ 11: Nᴏɴ-Dʀᴜɢ Oᴘᴛɪᴏɴs ꜰᴏʀ Dᴇᴀʟɪɴɢ Wɪᴛʜ Dᴇᴘʀᴇssɪᴏɴ (*Cᴏɴᴛɪɴᴜᴇᴅ*)

4. **Light therapy:** Some people describe great benefits from light therapy. Specific information on light therapy boxes is available online and possibly through your physician.

5. **Massage therapy:** Research indicates some patients with depressive symptoms benefit from massage therapy. A referral to a licensed massage therapy professional is advised.

6. **Bibliotherapy:** Research indicates that some patients benefit from reading and working with self-help books or workbooks. *The Feeling Good Handbook* (Burns, 1999) and *Mind over Mood* (Greenberger and Padesky, 1995) are two self-help books used by many individuals.

7. **Post-partum support:** There is evidence suggesting that new mothers with depressive symptoms who are closely followed by a public-health nurse, midwife, or other professional experience fewer post-partum depressive symptoms. Additionally, new moms and all individuals suffering from depressive symptoms may benefit from any healthy and positive activities that increase social contact and social support.

8. **Mild exercise and physical/social activities:** Even if you're not up to vigorous exercise, you should know that nearly any type of movement is an antidepressant. These activities could include, but not be limited to, yoga, walking, swimming, bowling, hiking, or whatever you can do!

9. **Other meaningful activities:** Never underestimate the healing power of meaningful activities. Activities could include (a) church or spiritual pursuits; (b) charity work; (c) animal caretaking (adopting a pet); and (d) many other activities that might be personally meaningful to you.

Parent Satisfaction and Counselor Reflection Inventory

SAMPLE PARENT SATISFACTION INVENTORY

Parent Consultation Satisfaction Questionnaire

Please help us improve our parent consultations by completing the following questionnaire. We're interested in your honest opinions, whether positive or negative. *Please answer every question.* **We also welcome your comments and suggestions. We appreciate your help. Thank you.**

Circle your answer:

1. How would you rate the overall quality of services you received at our agency?

1	2	3	4	5
Excellent	Good	Neutral	Poor	Very Poor

2. How satisfied are you with the help you received?

1	2	3	4	5
Very satisfied	Mostly satisfied	Neutral	Mostly dissatisfied	Dissatisfied

3. Did the consultation help improve your relationship with your child?

1	2	3	4	5
Yes, it helped a great deal	Yes, it helped	Neutral (No effect)	No, it really didn't help	No, it seemed to make things worse

4. If you need help again, would you schedule another consultation?

1	2	3	4	5
Definitely	I think so	Maybe	I don't think so	Definitely not

What did your consultant do or say, if anything, that you found helpful?

What did your consultant do or say, if anything, that you found unhelpful?

Please give us any further feedback about your consultation on the back of this sheet.

CONSULTANT REFLECTION INVENTORY

Rate each item on the following Likert-type scale:

1	2	3	4	5
Completely false	Somewhat false	Neutral	Somewhat true	Completely true

1. _____Before the session, I took time to mentally and emotionally prepare.
2. _____I greeted the parent with warmth and positive expectations.
3. _____I told the parent about confidentiality and its limits.
4. _____I told the parent that she or he could ask for more advice or tell me to be quiet and listen.
5. _____I responded non-defensively to questions about my competence or parental negativity.
6. _____I experienced a sense of empathy for what it might be like to be the parents with whom I was working.
7. _____I understand the term "radical acceptance" and practiced it during the consultation.
8. _____I made a clear effort to *collaborate with* the parent, rather than being an expert who knows best.
9. _____I listened well and paraphrased back to the parent as she (he) described her (his) concerns.
10. _____I asked for and got a reasonably thorough problem description.
11. _____I discussed child problems *without* using diagnostic terminology.
12. _____At some point, I directly told the parent that she (he) was the best expert on her (his) child or family.
13. _____I listened for positive motives or goals of the parent.
14. _____I provided specific compliments and reassurance to the parent several times.
15. _____At least once I asked the parent permission before starting a goal list or offering advice.
16. _____I observed for backward behavior modification and discussed what I noticed with the parent.
17. _____I asked about and found out about what solutions the parent had already tried.

18. _____I used scientific-mindedness to avoid coming to premature conclusions about the parent.

19. _____I asked the parent to tell me about his (her) best explanation for the child's misbehavior.

20. _____I linked the parent's best explanation to my primary problem formulation.

21. _____When I offered suggestions, I did so using an experimental attitude and mindset.

22. _____I wrote out a list of ideas and handed this "prescription" to the parent at the end of the meeting.

23. _____I provided tip sheets.

24. _____I felt calm and centered during the consultation.

25. _____At least several times during the meeting, I empathized with the parent's challenges.

26. _____I felt positive feelings toward this parent.

27. _____I feel this consultation was very helpful for the parent and expect a positive outcome.

Answer the following to the best of your ability:

28. How many "stories" did you share about your own child/children or parenting experiences?

29. What specific tip sheets or assignments did you provide that you believe will be most helpful?

Master List of Attitudes, Strategies, and Interventions

I. Attitudes to Have Toward Parents (from Chapter 1)
   a. Empathic understanding
   b. Radical acceptance
   c. Collaboration

II. General Strategies to Use With Parents (from Chapter 2)
   a. Focus on parent strengths using compliments and validation.
   b. Understand parallel process and use it to be an active and positive role model.
   c. Practice goal-alignment or collaborative goal-setting.
   d. Embrace the primacy and power of social interaction.

III. Specific Techniques to Use When Working With Parents (from Chapters 4–6)
   a. Collaborative role induction
   b. Honoring parents as experts
   c. Obtaining a problem description
   d. Empathy, support, and problem universalization
   e. Goal-setting
   f. Uncovering what parents have tried previously
   g. Using experience-near language
   h. Using scientific-mindedness
   i. Asking for the parents' best explanation
   j. Brief empathy stories
   k. Problem-and-solution formulation
   l. Activating the great internal force
   m. Writing out recommendations as you take notes
   n. Asking permission to give advice
   o. Offering suggestions humbly and respectfully
   p. Using tentative and gentle language

    q. Affirming previous problem-solving efforts

    r. Modifying recommendations based on parent feedback

    s. Writing out a prescription and giving it to parents

    t. Using tip sheets and homework assignments with parents

IV. Techniques to Teach Parents (briefly described in Chapters 4–6)

    a. Grandma's Rule

    b. Establishing preset rules

    c. Generating behavioral alternatives

    d. Consequential thinking

    e. Four questions of choice theory

    f. Child-generated rules

    g. Encouragement

    h. Storytelling

    i. Wagering, racing, and giving audience

    j. Everyday connection

    k. Spontaneous and genuine statements of affection

    l. Asset flooding

    m. Favors and IOUs

    n. Shared teaming

    o. Honest expressions of negative emotions

V. Big Interventions to Teach Parents (from Chapters 7–9)

    a. Special time

    b. Dealing with parental anger

    c. Helping parents honor children's emotions

    d. Choice theory communication training

    e. Using praise, mirroring, character feedback, and solution-focused questions

    f. Mutual problem-solving

    g. General rules for chores (teaming)

    h. Backward behavior modification

    i. Behavioral simulations and role modeling

    j. A new attitude and limit-setting

    k. A new and improved timeout from reinforcement

    l. Natural and logical consequences

    m. Backing out of power struggles

Chapter Checklists

Chapter 1
Checklist for Being With Parents

- ☐ Be aware that parents are a distinct and unique population.
- ☐ Recognize that parents typically want immediate and direct guidance to help solve their children's problems (and that it's important to listen and understand the parents and parenting situation before attending to that desire).
- ☐ Recognize that parents tend to be knowledgeable, critical, and demanding consumers.
- ☐ Recognize that, especially when seeking help, parents are often both defensive and vulnerable.
- ☐ Develop and hold an attitude of empathy for parents and the parenting challenges they face.
- ☐ Experience and to some degree express radical acceptance.
- ☐ Develop and hold a collaborative or "not knowing" attitude toward working with specific parents.

Chapter 2
Checklist for Preparing to Work With Parents

- ☐ Explore and examine your attitudes toward parents.
- ☐ Prepare to deal with emotional button-pushing.
- ☐ Know the literature on child/adolescent development, child/adolescent problems, and parenting.
- ☐ Prepare to respond non-defensively to questions about your competence.
- ☐ Create an informed consent form, and work out an informed consent process for working with parents.
- ☐ Take time to mentally and emotionally prepare for each session.
- ☐ Practice describing child problems without using diagnostic terms.
- ☐ Prepare to practice using the four therapeutic strategies: (a) focusing on parent strengths, (b) parallel process and role modeling, (c) goal alignment, and (d) acknowledging and embracing the primacy of social interaction.

Chapter 3
Checklist for Thinking About What Parents Want

☐ Recognize that to some extent most parents want to be and to exert a positive influence on their children.

☐ Develop an understanding of the four approaches to parental influence or social power.

☐ Recognize that all behavioral approaches to influence and change are forms of direct power where a person in authority is in control of rewards and punishments.

☐ Recognize that problem-solving power is a strategy for helping children activate their inner personal problem-solving skills.

☐ Recognize that indirect power involves modeling or manipulating and framing situations so that parents can indirectly get children to comply with parental wishes.

☐ Recognize that without relationship power, parents will often be unsuccessful in having positive influence with their children.

☐ Do your best to help parents be aware that they should use direct power only when necessary and the other forms of power more often.

Chapter 4
Checklist for Initial Contact and Assessment

☐ Meet, greet, normalize, and comfort.

☐ Discuss confidentiality.

☐ Describe the therapy or consultation process (use a collaborative role induction).

☐ Honor the parent as expert.

☐ Listen for the positive motives and provide sincere compliments and reassurance.

☐ Check with the parent or ask permission as you begin a goal list.

☐ Avoid getting caught up in criticism, negativity, or hopelessness (watch out for your countertransference).

☐ Get a reasonably thorough problem description.

☐ Take time out from your problem-description task to join with and empathize with the parent.

☐ Ask: "What else happened?" or "How did things get better?"

☐ Help the parent identify goals and solutions that are within their control.

☐ Make empathic-validating-universalizing statements when possible and appropriate.

☐ Watch for backward behavior modification.

☐ Find out everything the parent has already tried.

☐ Begin watching and listening for child and parent behavior patterns.

Chapter 5
Checklist for Problem Formulation With Parents

☐ Keep a broad range of theoretical perspectives in mind when working with parents.

☐ Remember, get the theory to fit the parent and not the parent to fit the theory.

☐ Use "experience-near" language with parents.

☐ Use scientific-mindedness to avoid coming to premature conclusions about parents.

☐ Ask parents to tell you about their best explanation for their child's misbehavior.

☐ Tell brief empathy stories to let parents know you "get" how challenging children's behavior can be, even if it is relatively normal behavior.

☐ Find a way to link the parent's best explanation to your primary problem formulation.

☐ Think about behavioral contingencies and teach parents to be aware of behavioral contingencies, but avoid mechanistic, tedious, and conditional intervention approaches.

Chapter 6
Checklist for Providing Guidance, Advice, and Solutions

☐ Remember to never blame the parent for rejecting your advice.

☐ Identify and align with the Great Internal Force for Positive Change.

☐ Use principles and strategies from Chapters 3 and 4 to resonate with parents' positive intentions.

☐ As you listen, express empathy, and formulate the problem, clearly and legibly begin writing down your intervention ideas.

☐ Before offering advice, ask permission.

☐ Offer suggestions using an experimental attitude and mind set.

☐ Use tentative and gentle language.

☐ Use storytelling.

☐ Compliment the parent and affirm previous problem-solving efforts.

☐ Modify your recommendations based on interactive feedback from parents.

☐ If you're planning additional sessions, write the date and time and topics to be discussed during the second or next session on the "prescription."

☐ Hand the prescription to the parent.

☐ Provide tip sheets or home activity projects as appropriate.

☐ Reflect on and evaluate the parent intervention outcomes.

Chapter 7
Checklist for Relationship-Based Approaches and Resources

☐ When children need a regular dose of attention and control, consider teaching parents about special time.

☐ Remember that special time can be both a non-directive play therapy approach and a conceptual approach where high-quality parent–child time is emphasized.

☐ Help parents see that it's normal to feel angry toward their children.

☐ If parent anger is a significant issue, help parents develop a clear and realistic plan for dealing with their anger.

☐ Help parents recognize that it's possible and desirable for them to simultaneously have empathy for their children's emotions while setting limits on their children's behavior.

☐ Help parents learn how to make it clear that they love their children, but that despite their love, some behaviors are inappropriate or unacceptable.

☐ Go to the comprehensive intervention checklist and/or the practitioner support website to gather more ideas about relationship-based interventions parents can use with their children.

Chapter 8
Checklist for Indirect and Problem-Solving Interventions and Resources

☐ To help parents communicate directly while not activating their child's or teen's opposition or resistance, discuss and suggest the possibility of *giving information and then backing off*.

☐ Depending on the parent's level of sophistication and understanding of parenting nuances, it may be helpful to teach the differences between praise, mirroring, character feedback, and solution-focused questions.

☐ Mutual problem-solving is often a useful recommendation, especially when parents are taking more responsibility for their child's behavior than is ideal.

☐ Help parents develop plans for handling chores and any other issues where an emphasis on teamwork and communication and simple strategies can make onerous tasks more palatable.

☐ Remember to recommend Grandma's Rule as a direct communication technique for assigning and completing less pleasant tasks first before engaging in more pleasant tasks.

☐ Go to the comprehensive Master List of Attitudes, Strategies, and Interventions in Appendix D and/or the practitioner-support website to gather more ideas about indirect and problem-solving interventions parents can use with their children.

Chapter 9
Checklist for Direct Approaches to Power and Influence

☐ Watch for parent examples of backward behavior modification and then gently help parents understand how easy and natural it is to use basic behavioral principles (e.g., such as how paying too much attention to negative behavior can serve as a positive reinforcement) in a way that's contrary to their own goals.

☐ Help parents set up situations where they can actively teach positive behaviors to their children using active role-modeling and behavioral simulations.

☐ Help parents develop a new attitude toward misbehavior—an attitude characterized by confidence in their ability to handle whatever misbehavior happens.

☐ Help parents develop a plan for setting limits and handling misbehavior—so that their new attitude of confidence is bolstered by an actual plan.

☐ Describe and identify how parents can understand and implement new-and-improved approaches to timeout from reinforcement.

☐ Remember to remind parents that natural and logical consequences provide their children with better and more realistic learning experiences than large and illogical consequences (this is also a good justification for why parents should plan ahead for how they want to respond to misbehavior, rather than responding spontaneously when angered).

☐ Help parents discover and apply the art of backing out of counterproductive power struggles.

☐ Go to the comprehensive Master List of Attitudes, Strategies, and Interventions in Appendix D and/or the practitioner-support website to gather more ideas about direct power and influence interventions parents can use with their children.

Chapter 10
Checklist for Ongoing Contact

☐ Be clear up-front with parents about your time limits and consultation model.

☐ Bring your recommendation list from session-to-session.

☐ Keep the comprehensive intervention master list (provided in Appendix D) with you in case you need it.

☐ After the initial session, ask the three recall questions and one follow-up.

☐ Reflect and highlight positive parental efforts, insights, abilities, and outcomes.

☐ If parents are negative and critical, avoid being negative, critical, and defensive in return.

☐ When parents are disappointed or critical, use empathic-validating-universalizing statements.

☐ Apologize, take responsibility, and move on if your recommendations didn't work.

☐ If recommendations are implemented incorrectly, but there's a positive outcome, support the positive outcome.

(Continued)

- ☐ In complex or confusing situations, use your best clinical judgment to guide your response.
- ☐ Listen for differences between the recommendations that worked and those that didn't.
- ☐ Offer new recommendations as needed and tailor them to fit parental quirks and strengths
- ☐ Before making referrals, find out what (and whom) the parents already tried.
- ☐ Consider whether, when, and how you want to contact parents if they miss an appointment.

Chapter 11
Checklist for Dealing With Special Issues and Situations

- ☐ Remember that we're typically better served by practicing cultural humility than we are by flaunting our cultural competence.
- ☐ When appropriate, help parents examine and evaluate their own cultural practices.
- ☐ Be aware of the special sensitivity to judgment that divorced and divorcing parents might feel.
- ☐ Be aware of your specific state child abuse reporting statutes.
- ☐ When needed, use the checklist for reporting child abuse.
- ☐ Be flexible but professional when parents bring their children to their individual appointments.
- ☐ Offer psychosocial intervention options if you see signs of post-partum depression.
- ☐ Monitor your reactions to parents and seek collegial or professional help as needed.
- ☐ Go to the comprehensive intervention checklist in Appendix D and/or the practitioner-support website (http://www.wiley.com/go/sommers-flanagan) to gather more ideas about relationship-based interventions parents can use with their children.

Parent Homework Assignments

Parent Homework Assignment 7-1

Creating Special Family Times

Special time for families can be formal (as described in Tip Sheet 7) or less formal. This homework assignment is for parents who want to work on creating spontaneous special time for family connection.

Idea 1: Be a keen observer of what your child loves. This can be as simple as noticing when and why your child smiles. If you watch for these happy or joyful moments, you'll undoubtedly be able to generate ideas for how to help create more happiness and joy.

Idea 2: Ask yourself some questions to get even more in touch with how you might create more special times. These questions might include:

1. "What do you and your child naturally do for fun together?"
2. "When do you and your child find yourselves enjoying each other?"
3. "What would be a fun or interesting activity that you and your child could do together?"
4. "What does your child like to do on his or her own or with friends?" "Is it possible for you to be involved in any of these . . . even as a supportive person to create the situation?"
5. "Do you play any family games together with your child?"
6. "What did you do for fun when you were younger?" "Is there any way to smoothly (without big expectations) introduce your child to something you love to do? (for example, playing cards, fly-fishing, second-hand shopping, arts and crafts, etc.)

(Continued)

Idea 3: Sometimes when your child seems to need your time and attention, drop everything and focus on your child. Although it's not healthy for you to "be there" for your child and cater to his or her every desire, it's important to occasionally stop whatever you're doing to give your child your undivided attention. This might involve turning off the television, closing your laptop, putting down the newspaper, or powering down your telephone. The point is that you want to, at least occasionally, give your child the clear message that she or he is your number one priority. This message will help you put a deposit in your child's emotional bank account.

Idea 4: Speak up about your positive feelings. It's not unusual to forget to consistently express your love for your child. As a consequence, you should try to say "I love you" to your child on a regular basis. However, perhaps even more important are spontaneous statements about how you "like" your child. Try that out. When you see something you like in your child's personality or behavior, just say, "I like who you are" or "I like it when you do that." Interestingly, saying you like your child can convey even more important meaning to them than saying "I love you." In addition, be clear about wanting to spend time with your child by saying things like, "I want to spend some time with you," and then scheduling it if you need to.

These are four simple ideas for creating special time in your family. Take a minute to think about these ideas and then improve on them by creating new and better ideas that fit your family and help you intentionally have more fun and more special times together.

Parent Homework Assignment 7-2

Sample Anger Management Homework

We give the following assignment to parents interested in controlling or managing their anger.

Step 1: Before starting, make a clear commitment. Think about it. Do you really want to express your anger differently? If so, make a list of the top five or ten reasons why you want to change your anger behaviors. Also, make a list of the benefits you'll experience from changing this behavior.

Step 2: Get curious before you get furious. Take time to contemplate the "buttons" or "triggers" that, when pushed or pulled, result in an angry reaction. Draw some big buttons on a sheet of paper and label them. Common parent buttons include: (a) child disobedience, (b) children having a "smart mouth," (c) children who lag behind when you're in a hurry. Try to identify a reasonably long list of the main child behaviors that trigger your anger. Remember, when it comes to dealing with anger constructively, knowledge is power.

Step 3: Identify the signs and symptoms of your increasing anger. Some people say they become angry very quickly and that it's hard to identify the signs. This may be the case for you. If so, study your anger patterns and ask for feedback from someone who knows you well. Your anger signals may include (a) feeling hot; (b) muscular tension; or (c) thinking angry thoughts. The purpose of knowing your anger signs is so you can begin derailing the process as soon as possible.

Step 4: Think prevention and self-care. We're all more likely to get angry when stressed or when short on sleep. For some parents, prevention will help you move from having anger flareups to anger sparks. Prevention ideas include:

- Regular time to work out at home or at the gym (e.g., yoga, dance, or kick-boxing)
- Hot baths or hot-tubbing
- A regular date night for Mom and Dad
- Getting a therapeutic massage
- Regular meditation

Many other self-care strategies are available. Make your own best prevention and self-care list and then incorporate your unique self-care strategies into your life on a regular basis.

Step 5: Make an excellent plan for what you want to do instead of engaging in negative anger behaviors. Excellent plans are specific, clear, and easy to immediately implement. For example, you might decide—because music is a natural emotional shifter—that you'll take a three-minute break to listen to one of your favorite calming songs if you feel yourself getting angry. To accomplish this, it will help to have a preplanned statement to make ("Daddy needs a quick break") and a prerecorded playlist on your iPod or other music device to immediately listen to.

Step 6: Practice your plan. The best-laid plans aren't likely to happen unless you practice them. Brain research suggests that whatever we practice (even as adults) generates changes in our brains to make us better at whatever we're practicing (Jenkins, Merzenich, Ochs, Allard, & Guic-Robles, 1990). This also makes good common sense. Whether you repeatedly bite your fingernails or repeatedly get very angry and yell, you've developed neural pathways in your brain that make these patterns more likely. The best way to address this neural pattern is to develop a new neural pattern by practicing new anger behaviors. For example, if your plan is to use your spouse as a partner and for one of you to tag the other when you get too stressed and need a break, don't just say, "How about if we tag each other when we're stressed?" Instead, say it and then physically practice it like you're preparing to perform in an upcoming drama production. It will feel silly, but practicing or rehearsing is one of the best ways to change an undesirable repeating behavior pattern.

Step 7: Reward yourself. Many people make the mistake of thinking they should be able to change pesky, habitual behavior patterns solely on the basis of willpower.

(Continued)

If that were the case, most of us would be practically perfect. Instead of completely relying on willpower, develop a reward system for yourself. For example, if you make it an hour or a day or a week without an undesirable anger explosion, give yourself a reward. Your reward can be as simple as thinking a positive thought ("I'm doing very well at this"), or a much more elaborate system of awarding yourself points for handling life's challenges calmly and taking them away when you blow up. If you have a spouse or romantic partner, the two of you can develop a program for supporting and rewarding each other. Self-behavior management is one of the best uses for behavioral techniques.

Parent Homework Assignment 7-3

Why Is Listening to Children Such a Big Deal?

Listening to children—really listening to what they have to say—can be a major pain. Thus the well-known saying, "Children should be seen and not heard." Sometimes listening to children can seem like too much trouble, too time consuming, and of little value.

On the other hand, when you listen closely to children, you often experience surprisingly nice outcomes. The purpose of this assignment is for you to consider the benefits of listening to your children and reflect on whether you want to work on becoming a better listener for your children's sake.

A big problem with listening to children is that they frequently have a lot to say. We recall with fondness a 10-year-old girl who conversed with such breathless intensity that even a huge mid-sentence belch didn't slow her down. If adults are interested in listening, even just a little, children are often ready to talk. Although sometimes teenagers are more reluctant to talk with adults, given the right place, time, and an interested ear, many teens become open and talkative.

Here are some benefits of listening to your children:

- If you consistently listen to your children, they'll be more likely to listen to you.
- If you listen to your children, they'll behave more cooperatively.
- Children will feel respected if you listen to them; this respect helps build healthy self-esteem.
- Listening can slow you down; if you listen to your child before reacting, it can help you be more calm, thoughtful, and moderate in your discipline.

Can you think of additional benefits of listening to your children? If so, consider making a list in case you need reminders.

It's both impossible and unnecessary for parents to always listen to their children. In fact, children don't need total attention (or total perfection) from their parents. Children profit when parents try to listen well; your effort can count as much as your accuracy. The point of this handout is not to convince you to listen perfectly all the time, but instead to convince to you learn to listen well at least some of the time.

Evaluating Your Listening Habits

Read the following questions, take a few minutes to reflect on your answers, and then write down your responses.

1. Do you ever "drop everything" and listen to your child or children? What happens when you do? Would you like to do that more often? Do you do it too often?
2. Do you ever listen to your child as he or she talks about a personal activity in which you have absolutely no interest? For example, do you listen as he talks with you about his video/computer game conquests, even though you really don't like video/computer games?
3. Rate how available you are as a listener for your children on a scale from 0 to 10 (0 = Not at all available; 10 = Always available).
4. Rate how skilled you believe you are at listening to your children (0 = I have absolutely no listening skills; 10 = I am the best listener ever).
5. Think about whether you'd like to become more available for listening and/or more skilled at listening to your children. If you want to become a better listener, what can you do to improve yourself?

Parent Homework Assignment 8-1

Choice Theory Communication Skills Training: How to Provide Information and Then Back Off, Instead of Trying Too Hard to Control Your Child's Decision Making

As a loving parent, if you're concerned about your children's behaviors, you'll probably have a strong and nearly irresistible impulse to tell them how to live their lives. After all, you're the adult and they should listen to your excellent advice. You may feel the urge to say:

- You need to clean your room **now** because being disorganized and undisciplined is a bad habit that will make your life miserable.
- Alcohol and drugs are illegal and so if you go out and behave illegally, I'll call the police and have you ticketed.
- You need to start caring about your grades at school and that means scheduling time for homework and studying for tests.
- Swearing is unacceptable in this house and if you do it again, I'll wash your mouth out with soap.

Unfortunately, as you may recall from your own childhood, when parents are bossy and insistent about how things should be, children often become more

(Continued)

stubborn and resistant. Then parents begin to nag and lecture and the pattern of advice-giving and advice-rejection deepens. This assignment is designed to help you communicate important information to your children without starting an all-out power struggle or negative nagging pattern. The following suggestions are appropriate only if the situation isn't dangerous and you don't need to jump in and directly and forcefully protect your children:

1. **Ask permission.** If you have a strong opinion that you'd like your child to hear, try asking permission to share it. Say something like, "Can I share my opinion on this with you?" Then, either your child will say "yes" and you can share your opinion or she'll say "no" and then you'll need to accept her boundary (in response to a "no," you might say, "Okay. Thanks for being honest with me. Let me know if you change your mind" and then walk away).

2. **Express your intention not to express your opinion.** You could try telling your child, "I have an opinion on this, but I trust that you can work it out, or that you'll ask me for help if you need it. So I'm going to try to keep my mouth shut for now." This gives your child the message that you're trying to respect his ability to work out his own problems. You can also add humor into this or other power-sharing techniques by adding: "You should really appreciate this, because you know how hard it is for me to keep my mouth shut and not give you advice."

3. **Provide your information or opinion and then back off.** If you can't resist giving your opinion, just do it and then back off and let your child consider your input. The key to this strategy is patience. Undoubtedly, you'll provide excellent advice and then your child will look like she's not considering your advice and so you'll have the urge to repeat your advice over and over until you see action. Instead of falling into this pattern, try saying, "Look. I've got an opinion, which you probably already know. But instead of staying quiet, I'm just going to say it and then let you make your own decision on how to handle your situation. It's your life. You have to make your own decisions. But I love you and can't stop myself from telling you what I think, so here it is."

As you probably already know, if you express your opinion you may get a strong emotional response (e.g., "I'm fifteen years old and I can make my own decisions!"). Although this seems weird, if you give lots of advice, your children may see your ideas and opinions as evidence that you don't believe they're competent to make their own decisions. This is why you should always express your advice with love and concern; avoid sounding as if your main goal is to control your child's behavior.

Finally, if the situation is dangerous or potentially so, skip the less direct parenting recommendations listed above and instead think strategically about how to deliver direct advice that will be heeded. You'll probably need to use a more direct approach than is described here, and you may need to consult with a professional.

Parent Homework Assignment 8-2

Exploring the Differences Between Praise, Mirroring, Character Feedback, and Solution-Focused Questions

If you've been given this homework assignment, you're probably already using many good parenting techniques with your child. This assignment will help you refine your parenting approach to intentionally include even more ways of being positive with your child.

Imagine that a father is busy taking care of household chores while he's parenting his 5-year-old daughter. She's creating some excellent 5-year-old crayon art and approaches her daddy with a finished product and a beaming smile. Dad looks up and takes a break from his chores to admire his daughter's artwork. He returns her grin and says one of the following:

- "This is beautiful!" (An example of **praise**—a form of direct power)
- "Thanks for showing me your drawing. You look very happy with your picture." (An example of **emotional mirroring or encouragement**—a form of indirect power)
- "You love doing artwork!" (An example of **character feedback**—another form of indirect power)
- "How did you manage to create this beautiful drawing?" (An example of a **solution-focused question**—a form of problem-solving power)

If you can increase your awareness of these different strategies, you'll feel more capable of being intentional and positive when interacting with your children. The result usually includes fewer power struggles and more positive parent–child relationship dynamics.

Using Praise

Using praise is simple. For example, praise includes statements like: "Great work," "I'm proud of you," and "Look at what a good job you've done cleaning the bathroom!" When you use praise, you're clearly communicating your expectations and your approval to your child. Praise is best when it's behaviorally specific.

Think about how much praise you use with your children. Are you being clear enough with them about what you want and are you letting them know when they've done well? As a part of this homework assignment, consider increasing how much you praise your child and then see how your child reacts.

Using Mirroring

Sometimes children don't have a clear sense of how their behaviors look to others (which can also be true for adults). The purpose of mirroring is to help children see themselves through your eyes. After seeing (or hearing) their reflection, children become more aware of their behavior and may choose to make changes.

(Continued)

For now, we recommend that you practice using mirroring only to reflect your child's positive behaviors. For example, if your daughter has a play date and shares her toys with her friend, you could say, "I noticed you were sharing your toys." Or if your son got home on time instead of breaking his curfew, you might say, "I noticed you were on time last night." The hard part about using mirroring is to stay neutral, but staying neutral is important because mirroring allows your children to judge of their own behaviors. If you want to be the judge, you can use praise.

Using Character Feedback

Character feedback works well for helping your children see themselves as having positive character traits. For example, you might say, "You're very honest with us," or "You can really focus on and get your homework done quickly when you want to," or "You're very smart."

Usually, as parents, instead of using character feedback to focus on our children's positive qualities, we use it in a very negative way. Examples include: "Can't you keep your hands to yourself?" "You're always such a big baby," and "You never do your homework."

For your homework assignment, try using character feedback to comment on your children's positive behaviors, while ignoring the negative. You can even use character feedback to encourage a new behavior—all you have to do is wait for a tiny sign of the new behavior to occur and then make a positive character feedback statement: "You're really starting to pay attention to keeping your room clean."

Using Solution-Focused Questions

Problem-focused questions include: "What's wrong with you?" and "What were you thinking when you hit that other boy at school?" In contrast, solution-focused questions encourage children to focus on what they're doing well. For example, "How did you manage to get that puzzle together?" "What were you thinking when you decided to share your toy with your friend?" and "What did you do to get yourself home on time?"

Solution-focused questions require us to look for the positive. For practice, try asking your child questions designed to get him or her to think about successes instead of failures. After all, it's the successes that you want to see repeated. Of course, when you ask these questions, don't expect your child to answer them well. Instead, your child will most likely say, "Huh? I don't know." The point is that you're focusing on the positive and **eventually** these questions get your children to focus on the positive as well.

Parent Homework Assignment 8-3

Mutual Problem-Solving

Mutual problem-solving brings family members together to solve problems collaboratively. It works best if your child is at least four years old. It also works well with strong-willed children who like to challenge parental authority. It includes five steps.

Step 1: Identify the problem together. Present the situation in a way that your child will agree that something is a problem.

Let's say your 6-year-old is very stubborn and won't share his toys with other children and so they don't want to play with him. Here's how you could proceed: (a) Discuss this behavior with your child when he's in a good mood, like when you're drawing or eating ice cream together; (b) describe the situation in a way that makes it so your child will likely agree that the situation presents a problem for him (e.g., "I noticed that when you play with Matt sometimes he gets mad when you don't share your toys, and then he stomps off and goes home, and then you're usually upset, because you like playing with Matt. Don't you hate it when that happens?"). Your child will probably agree and say something like, "Yeah, I don't like him doing that," and then you're free to problem-solve together.

Step 2: Identify potential solutions. Say something like, "Okay, since we both agree that you don't like it when Matt gets mad and leaves, let's come up with some ideas to solve this problem."

When coming up with solutions, let yourself (and your child) be creative. Encourage him to take the lead, but if he doesn't, throw out suggestions to get things rolling. Examples include: "We could send Matt home," or "We could practice how to deal with Matt before he comes," or "I could pay Matt one dollar to stay and play with you," or "I could be toy-keeper and time-keeper and keep track of who gets to play with which toy for what length of time," or "If you guys fight over the toy, the toy goes in timeout."

Track all ideas on paper. Be prepared for your child's first idea to be very bad. Even if he suggests something ridiculous, "He should pay me to share!" just nod your head, repeat what he said, and write it down. Don't criticize his suggestions or he might stop giving them.

As you generate possible solutions, remember that eventually you'll have to agree to try out one of these potential solutions.

Step 3: Rate and rank potential solutions. After you've generated at least three or four options (hopefully more) rank the possible solutions. Together, select one to try out for a while. This procedure is mutual and you should agree to check back on how well the solution is working. That way, you can let him try out a less-than-perfect strategy, knowing you'll get to talk about it and

(Continued)

encourage a better solution next time. With a 15-year-old daughter who is violating her curfew, your solution list might look like this:

Angie's Rank	Possible Ideas if Angie Violates Curfew	Mom/Dad Rank
#1	Nothing should happen; Angie's parents are so uncool.	#10
#6	Angie is grounded for two weekend nights.	#1
#5	Angie loses her weekly allowance.	#5
#4	Angie has to help cook dinner and do dishes for a week.	#2
#7	Angie loses her telephone privileges for a week.	#3
#8	Angie is fined $1.00 for every minute she's late.	#9
#3	Angie writes an apology note.	#6
#10	Next time, Angie's mom (dad) goes out with her and her friends.	#8
#9	Angie's and mom (dad) go for family counseling.	#7
#2	Angie gets 15 extra minutes out if she gets home on time.	#4

To calculate the most agreeable solution, add the rankings and select the lowest number. In this case, there's a tie between having Angie cook dinner and do dishes for a week (total = 6) and giving Angie 15 extra minutes out for getting home on time (total = 6). If there's a tie, you can try both solutions at once.

Step 4: Try out the most agreeable solution. Do this for a predetermined period of time. After agreeing on a proposed solution, say, "Let's try this out for three weeks and then meet again to talk about how things went."

Step 5: Evaluate how well the solution worked. The solution may work perfectly or you may have to go back and try this again, but either way, stay positive. It's nice to have your original brainstorming sheet to use as a reference for what you thought of last time.

Mutual problem-solving probably won't produce magical solutions. The process is more important than the outcome. The main goal is to give your child the message: "We work on our problems together as a family." This message models the continuous use of a positive problem-solving family strategy.

Parent Homework Assignment 8-4

Brightening up the Chore List

As a parent, when it comes to getting your child to do chores, your response may range from "*Ugh*" to "It's easier and simpler if I just do them myself." Whatever your response, this homework assignment is designed to help you develop new strategies and a positive attitude toward assigning and doing chores.

The first step toward joyful chore completion (we're joking about the joyful part) is to adopt a positive attitude. If you hate chores and you expect your children to hate chores and you approach them with dread, the outcome will likely be negative. In contrast, if you pair chore activities with something pleasant, you may inspire a more positive attitude in your children. Try some of the following strategies:

1. Play fun music while doing chores.
2. Schedule the chores about 30 minutes before your children's favorite television show and tell them if they get the chores done, they can watch the television.
3. Do chores together (and act happy).
4. Give your children frequent compliments for their involvement in chores (even if their efficiency or outcome isn't perfect).
5. Have a family meeting where the children get to select two or three chores from a menu and a small reward for completing their chores from a menu of rewards.
6. Schedule pizza and a movie for a family reward after completing chores and then be supportive of and realistic about your children's efforts; but if they fail to complete their chores, let them experience the natural consequence of left-overs (instead of pizza) and an early bedtime (while the chore completers watch the movie).

Parent Homework Assignment 9-1

Backward Behavior Modification

One amazing thing about parenting is how easy and natural it is to do things backward. For example, imagine your 7th-grader comes home with a report card that has five A's, one B, and one C. If you're like most parents, you'll take a quick look and say something like, "Why'd you get that C?" or, "How can you raise that B up to an A?"

Even though these questions make excellent sense, they're in direct violation of a very basic principle of human behavior. That principle is: **Whatever you pay the most attention to will tend to grow and whatever you** ignore **will tend to shrink.** Despite this powerful principle, our human and parental tendency is almost always

(*Continued*)

to pay close attention to the F's and C's in life, while only offering a passing glance at the A's.

Another version of the same problem happens with parents who have two or more children. Your children may coexist very nicely together 60 percent of the day and fight like cats and dogs for the other 40 percent. Unfortunately, in that situation the natural tendency is to give **almost all** your attention to your children when they fight and **very little** attention to them when they're playing nicely.

The consequence of violating this basic principle is:

- Your 7th-grader feels his efforts are underappreciated and becomes less motivated.
- Your children, sensing that they can get more of your attention by fighting than from playing together nicely, may begin fighting even **more**.

Our **first** point with this homework assignment is to reassure you that it's perfectly natural to pay more attention to "bad" behavior than "good" behavior. But, it's equally true that even though paying too much attention to bad behavior is natural—it's **not** helpful because it can become a reward for bad behavior.

Our **second** point is that you should work very hard to:

Pay more attention to your children when you like what they're doing than you do when you don't like what they're doing.

Or, better yet, try this:

When giving out consequences, be boring, but when giving out rewards, be passionate.

I had this lesson driven home to me many years ago. While doing therapy with teenagers who were in trouble for delinquent behavior, they started telling me how much satisfaction they got from making their parents angry. When I asked about this, they said things like, "I love it when my dad's veins start sticking out of his neck" or "It's cool when I can get my mom so mad that she spits when she talks."

Keep these images in mind the next time your child does something that gets under your skin. Then, instead of a long lecture complete with bulging veins and spitting, be short and boring. Use a monotone to say something like: "I don't like it when you do that."

Then, when your child comes home on time, or gets an A, or plays nice with her brother, or makes an intelligent comment about virtually anything—that's when you should launch into a passionate and positive lecture—complete with bulging veins and spittle.*

---

*These rules may not hold perfectly for your unique child. Some teens may not like much positive attention. That's why you're the best judge of whether a particular parenting strategy will work with your child. We're also kidding about the spittle; that's hardly ever a good thing to see.

Parent Homework Assignment 9-2

Intentional Role Modeling

In this handout, we outline a strategy for intentionally, but indirectly, teaching children positive behaviors through role modeling. This strategy works best if you have at least one other adult available to help. Even for single parents—it helps if you can recruit an aunt or uncle or good friend to help with indirectly delivering educational messages.

Most children don't have skills for dealing with conflict. This may be partly because they just haven't had a chance to see two adults or two children resolving their differences politely. Your goal with this homework assignment is to actively demonstrate to your child or children how to politely disagree and how to respectfully manage or resolve conflict. If you'd like to help your children learn this important skill, you'll need to enact a scenario or conflict situation.

Get your spouse, partner, sibling, or friend to help you with a minor conflict scenario. Be sure to plan it in advance. One of the following situations might help you demonstrate polite conflict and successful resolutions:

- You and your partner disagree on what to have for dinner, on what movie to watch, or on what to do for a recreational outing.
- You and your partner disagree during a political discussion.
- You and your partner discuss a fair balancing of chores in the home.

During your intentional role-modeling, you and your partner should express a disagreement. For example:

You: "I want to go to the lake on Saturday."
Partner: "I'd rather stay home and watch football."
You: "How are we gonna figure this out?"

At this point, you and your partner can choose to illustrate your preferred conflict negotiation and management approaches. What you choose will depend on what you want to role-model or teach. You can teach domination–submission—where one person pushes hard for her or his position and possibly dismisses the other person's perspective. In this situation, the weaker party gives in and a lesson (perhaps not an ideal one) is learned. Or you could teach conflict avoidance where both of you consistently avoid talking about anything you might disagree about.

You can also teach communication and conflict negotiation, where each person makes his or her case and the other party uses active listening (e.g., "Jodie, I hear you saying this particular football game is very important and that's why you'd rather not go to the lake this particular Saturday"). You might choose this approach if your goal is to teach your children how to engage in respectful communication—even during disagreements.

(Continued)

However, you might also decide to demonstrate to your children that couples, partners, or families can also apply a variety of problem-solving strategies to conflict situations. For example, you might decide to illustrate "turn-taking." If so, one of you could offer something like, "How about we do football this weekend and go to the lake next weekend?"

In addition to turn-taking, you could model "compromise." With compromise, each party gets "part" of what she or he wants. For example, the final decision (after modeling a respectful communication process) might be: "Okay, we'll go to the lake and bring the television."

The most important point in this intentional role-modeling activity is for you, as a parent, to become more aware of the fact that your children are almost always watching and listening and learning from you. As a consequence, rather than spontaneously erupting into conflict (and perhaps modeling less-than-positive communication), you can intentionally show your children how two people can communicate constructively and respectfully even when minor disagreements arise.

One complaint parents sometimes offer about this assignment is that it feels fake or manipulative. Our response is to ask you to reflect on your parenting goals and to decide whether you want to intentionally and actively teach your children positive social behaviors or whether you want to unintentionally and passively teach negative social behaviors. What you decide to teach your children is really up to you—we just recommend that you do it intentionally.

Parent Homework Assignment 9-3

A Practical Guide to Setting Limits

Unfortunately, children are not born knowing how to deal with frustration, anger, and disappointment. This means it's our job to teach them how to deal with these difficult and sometimes unpleasant emotions.

One way to teach your child about how to handle frustration and other difficult emotions is through limit-setting. If you let your child do whatever she wants anytime she wants to, she'll have trouble learning to cope with frustration. This can happen if you always give your children whatever they want.

Many parents mistakenly think that when they set limits, they need to be mean or especially tough. Don't make that mistake. Good limit-setters are firm, but kind and compassionate. Try to be the kind of boss you'd like to have yourself.

An effective limit-setting strategy includes the following:

1. Set a clear limit or clear expectation.
2. If your child appears upset or resistant, show empathy for your child's frustration, disappointment, or anger.
3. Repeat the limit in clear language (you could also have your child repeat the limit or plan back to you).

4. Give your child a reasonable choice or timeline (this is especially important with strong-willed children; see the following for examples).
5. Show more empathy by joining in with your child's unhappiness (this might include telling a story, if there's time).
6. Enforce the limit on time and with a logical consequence.
7. Stay positive and encouraging.

A Limit-Setting Example

1. **Set a clear limit:** "Dinner will be ready in five minutes, so it's time to turn off your computer game."
2. **Show empathy** by using feeling words: "I know it's hard to stop doing something fun and you're feeling very upset."
3. **Repeat the limit:** "But you know it's time to stop playing computer games."
4. **Give a choice and a timeline:** "Either you can stop playing in the next two minutes, or I'll unplug the computer."
5. **Show more empathy** by joining in with your child's unhappiness: "I hate it when I have to stop doing something I love."
6. **Enforce the limit** on time and with a logical consequence. (Say what you'll do and then do what you said: If you said it will be two minutes, wait two minutes and enforce the limit; don't wait three minutes or one minute).
7. **Stay positive and encouraging:** "Even though I had to turn off your computer in the middle of your game tonight, I'm sure you'll be able to plan for this and turn it off yourself tomorrow."

Remember, although it's your job to teach your child how to become more responsible and how to cope with the life frustrations, you won't be able to do this perfectly; no one does this perfectly. Just keep the principles in this homework assignment in mind and practice them when you can.

Parent Homework Assignment 9-4

Following the Rules for a New-and-Improved Timeout
From Reinforcement

Most parents use timeout like punishment, but punishment and timeout are really two different parenting techniques. Timeout is a less-aversive and more compassionate alternative to punishment.

- Punishment is the application of something aversive or painful (spanking or scolding).
- Timeout is the taking away of something positive (children are removed from opportunities to have fun or receive positive reinforcement).

(Continued)

The differences between punishment and timeout are subtle but important. When using timeout from reinforcement properly, children should be calmly taken from their usually rich and rewarding environment, but they should not be punished through pinching, squeezing, slapping, scolding, or yelling.

There are two main types of timeout: behavioral timeouts and emotional timeouts. **Behavioral** timeouts are used in response to inappropriate misbehavior. **Emotional** timeouts are used to help with emotional de-escalation or calming.

Tips for Behavioral Timeouts

- Timeout effectiveness is based on how much fun and good stuff is happening during time-in. If your child has lots of fun during time-in, timeout will be powerful.
- Timeout should be used in a boring and matter-of-fact manner. Avoid yelling and lecturing.
- The first minute (or two) of timeout is the most important. Don't extend timeout beyond 10 minutes.
- There should be no pushing, holding down, or aggressive touch during timeout. Timeout is not a physical intervention.
- Don't use timeout as "thinking time" or demand an apology from your child at the end.
- Don't do more than about two timeouts a day or continually threaten timeout.
- Teach your child about timeout through practice or rehearsals.
- Praise your child for going to timeout.
- Practice, simulate, discuss, and educate your child about what behaviors cause a timeout.
- Praise your child for completing his or her timeout.
- Stay quiet during your child's timeout.

A behavioral timeout is used immediately after your child has misbehaved. When misbehavior happens, consider saying: "Uh-oh. That's not okay. You need to go to timeout." The timeout location should be a chair or pillow or other location where your child can be separated from the social or family activity. Maintain silence (other than praising your child for going to timeout). Set a timer for between 1 and 10 minutes. Two minutes is appropriate for most children. If your child refuses to go to timeout, don't get physical; simply shift the consequence to something you can control (e.g., turn off the television or computer, send the friend home, end the family outing, assign a "when you/then you" chore, etc.). If you've rehearsed your timeout procedure, it should go smoothly. When timeout is finished, praise your child for completing the timeout and verbally release him or her. Explain the reason for timeout as needed.

Your child shouldn't be required to stay silent during timeout. Many parents incorrectly assume that timeout should continue until children calm down.

Calming down and completing a timeout are two different issues. If your child is angry or crying, a consequence has **already been delivered** and so there's no need to continue the scene until he or she is quiet. If your goal is a quiet child, timeout may not be the appropriate consequence. Instead, you may need to implement a quiet time in the child's room or remove him or her from a social or public situation.

Tips for Emotional Timeouts

If your child has trouble calming down after one or two minutes, you may need to approach and comfort him or her. This is okay. After one or two minutes you can release your child from timeout. At that point, the behavioral timeout has ended and an emotional timeout may begin.

During an emotional timeout children need soothing and comforting. They still may be angry or upset about not getting what they wanted and you shouldn't give in and give them their desired outcome. Instead, give empathy, comfort, and support. Life is hard and most adults don't like not getting what they want, either. Help them know this. Help them breathe deeply and think about happier times. Help them move past their distress and into a calmer and more comfortable place. This can be a powerful and positive experience for both parent and child. Behavioral timeouts are about limit-setting. Emotional timeouts are about parent–child bonding and emotional regulation.

Parent Homework Assignment 9-5

The Beauty and Power of Natural and Logical Consequences

Life is not easy and children (and adults) learn through struggles, failures, and disappointments. Your goal, as a parent, is to create a reasonable, consistent, and loving home and then let your child struggle with the demands of life. These demands include very basic things like:

- Not getting to watch television after a certain time
- Participating in housecleaning
- Not getting attention 100% of the day
- Having to get ready and get to school on time
- Having to wait your turn to get served dessert or to play with an especially fun toy
- Not getting to eat your favorite food for every meal
- Having to tie your own shoes

(Continued)

As you might gather from the preceding list, even little things in life can be hard for a growing child; but to learn, children need to directly experience frustration and disappointment.

Natural or logical consequences are a necessary part of learning. They help your child get better at surviving disappointments in the world and in your family home. Natural and logical consequences are always related in some way to the misbehavior and are not given out with anger or as "punishment."

Here are some examples:

1. Your children leave toys in a public area of the house, even though they've been told to put toys away when done playing. **Logical consequence:** Use a "Saturday box" or put the toys in timeout. This involves picking up the toys and putting them in a box and storing them away until the next Saturday (or whatever day), when they're given back. This logical consequence avoids the overreaction ("If you don't put your toys away, then I'll give them away to someone else") and the attention-giving lecture ("Let me tell you about when I was a child and what would happen if I left my toys out. . . . ") and instead provides children with a clear, consistent, and reasonable consequence.

2. Your children argue with you about a consequence or about you being unfair. **Logical consequence:** You let your children know, "I don't feel like arguing about this" and leave the area. You may want to go to the bathroom to take time away to further develop your planned response. While remaining friendly, another important message to give is, "I know you'd like things your way, but we have rules and consequences for everyone in our family." Of course this may trigger another argument and you can walk away again and tell your children, "I know you can figure this out and not have this consequence next time."

3. You cook dinner, but your children don't show up on time. **Reasonable rules and logical consequences:** If you cook dinner, everyone needs to show up on time and be respectful about the dinner-eating process. That doesn't mean everyone has to eat every bite or provide you with lavish praise for your most excellent meal, but respectful attendance is a reasonable expectation. If your child is late for dinner, one reminder is enough. No drama or excess attention is needed. Just sit down and start eating and enjoying the mealtime process. Possible logical and natural consequences include: (a) Your child prepares the next meal; (b) you put away foods after you dish yourself up and so the child has to get them out and serve himself; (c) you got there early and prepared the food and so your child gets to stay afterward and clean up; (d) no special rewards (e.g., eating dinner in front of the television); instead, your child eats alone at the table.

To do logical and natural consequences, it's helpful to work on the following:

1. *Take the "punishing" quality out of your voice and the interactions.* This is not about punishment; it's about what's logical, reasonable, and natural. You can even be friendly and positive.

2. **Prepare in advance.** Because you'll be emotional when your children are non-compliant, it's critical that you have a list of logical and reasonable and natural consequence ideas in your head. Otherwise, you will overreact. Going to parenting classes or talking with other parents can help you identify a wider range of reasonable consequences.
3. **Use small consequences.** Your purpose is to teach your child. Your purpose is not to hurt or humiliate. Learning occurs best if children are not emotionally overwhelmed by large consequences. Small consequences provide plenty of feedback.
4. **Use mirroring and encouragement.** Reflect back to your children what they're feeling ("It's very upsetting that you can't play with your toys for the rest of the week"). Let your child know that you think things will go better the next time around ("I know, if you want to, you'll be able to remember to put your toys away next time").
5. **Don't lecture or shame.** Let the small consequence do its work.

Parenting Homework Assignment 9-6

Problem Polarization: Backing out of a Power Struggle

Families often show peculiar dynamics, especially when it comes to motivation. For example, if your daughter loves computer games and plays them all day, sooner or later you may begin hating computer games. Your daughter probably has enough love for computer games in her little pinky to accommodate the whole family. Similarly, if your son shows no motivation to do homework, you may suddenly find you've got all the motivation for his homework while he has none. This particular family dynamic is called **problem polarization**.

Problem polarization is a tough nut to crack. This is because it's perfectly natural for parents to become obsessed with the very responsibilities that their children avoid. For example, when your child stops showering, you will undoubtedly become more committed to his personal hygiene. The same is true when children neglect virtually any basic responsibility (think about keeping rooms clean, writing thank-you notes, etc.).

The solution to this problem always involves getting your children to take more responsibility for their basic family and personal responsibilities. Of course, you've probably already tried twisting yourself into pretzel shapes trying to get your child motivated to perform these basic tasks. And if you're reading this information, you may be semi-permanently pretzel-shaped and yet your children are still unconcerned about their personal hygiene, homework, chores, and grades.

(Continued)

Although you probably want to deliver one more lecture to get your message across, the truth is you need to let go of your motivation to get your child to behave appropriately. Your best new approach is to get more carefree about your child's personal responsibilities than your child. This is, of course, easier said than done. After all, you're a wise and conscientious adult and you know all too well the dangers of irresponsibility.

The answer to your dilemma is wrapped up in the following question: How can you (without using lectures or punishments) get your child to experience greater distress over his or her personal irresponsibility?

A direct approach might include saying something like this:

> You're a perfectly intelligent young person and so I'm going to stop nagging you about your homework. My new policy is to remind you one time every evening and then I'll go off and have some fun myself. Then, if you flunk, it's all you. If you want help, I'm there for you, but I'm not getting hung up on this anymore. I'm a new-and-improved parent who knows you'll do better with your homework if you take more responsibility for it yourself.

After making your "I'm backing off" speech, you should sit down, relax, and see what happens. Even better, you might need to distract yourself with something fun and interesting because, no doubt, your child will have a greater tolerance for a few failures than you.

References

Achenbach, T. M., & Edelbrock, C. S. (1978). The classification of child psychopathology: A review and analysis of empirical efforts. *Psychological Bulletin*, *85*(6),
1275–1301.

Adler, A. (1927). *Understanding human nature*. Garden City, NY: Garden City
Publishing.

Adler, A. (1958). *What life should mean to you*. New York, NY: Capricorn.

Ainsworth, M. S. (1989). Attachments beyond infancy. *American Psychologist*, *44*(4),
709–716.

Alderman, G. L., & Craver, J. R. (August 1999). Difficult to manage students:
A model of school consultation and in-service. *Annual Convention of the American
Psychological Association*, Boston.

American Psychological Association. (2002). Ethical principles of psychologists
and code of conduct. *American Psychologist*, *57*, 1060–1073.

Anderson, H. (1993). On a roller coaster: A collaborative language systems approach to therapy. In S. Friedman (Ed.), *The new language of change: Constructive
collaboration in psychotherapy* (pp. 323–344). New York, NY: Guilford Press.

Anderson, H., & Goolishian, H. (1992). The client is the expert: A not-knowing
approach to therapy. In S. McNamee, & K. J. Gergen (Eds.), *Therapy as social
construction* (pp. 25–39). Thousand Oaks, CA: Sage Publications.

Anthony, W. (2003). Expanding the evidence base in an era of recovery. *Psychiatric
Rehabilitation Journal*, *27*(1), 1–2.

Aucoin, K. J., Frick, P. J., & Bodin, S. D. (2006). Corporal punishment and child
adjustment. *Journal of Applied Developmental Psychology*, *27*(6), 527–541.

Axline, V. M. (1964). *Dibs in search of self*. New York, NY: Ballantine Books.

Bandura, A., Ross, D., & Ross, S. A. (1963). Imitation of film-mediated aggressive
models. *Journal of Abnormal & Social Psychology*, *66*, 3–11.

Bandura, A., & Walters, R. H. (1963). *Social learning and personality development*.
New York, NY: Holt, Rinehart, & Winston.

Barkley, R. A., Robin, A. L., & Benton, C. M. (2008). *Your defiant teen: Ten steps to
resolve conflict and rebuild your relationship*. New York, NY: Guilford Press.

Battino, R. (2007). Expectation: Principles and practice of very brief therapy. *Contemporary Hypnosis, 24*(1), 19–29.

Baumrind, D. (1975). The contributions of the family to the development of competence in children. *Schizophrenia Bulletin, 14*, 12–37.

Beck, A. T. (1976). *Cognitive therapy and the emotional disorders*. New York, NY: New American Library.

Berg, I. K., & DeJong, P. (2005). Engagement through complimenting. *Journal of Family Psychotherapy, 16*(1–2), 51–56.

Biel, L., & Peske, N. (2009). *Raising a sensory smart child*. New York, NY: Penguin.

Bitter, J. R. (2004). Two approaches to counseling a parent alone: Toward a Gestalt-Adlerian integration. *Family Journal: Counseling & Therapy for Couples & Families, 12*(4), 358–367.

Bitter, J. R. (2009). The mistaken notions of adults with children. *The Journal of Individual Psychology, 65*(2), 135–155.

Bitter, J. R., Christensen, O. C., Hawes, C., & Nicoll, W. G. (1998). Adlerian brief therapy with individuals, couples, and families. *Directions in clinical and counseling psychology* (pp. 95–111). New York, NY: Hatherleigh.

Bowlby, J. (1988). *A secure base: Parent-child attachment and healthy human development*. New York, NY: Basic Books.

Bratton, S. C., Landreth, G. L., Kellam, T., & Blackard, S. R. (2006). *Child-parent relationship therapy (CPRT) treatment manual: A 10-session filial therapy model for training parents*. New York, NY: Routledge/Taylor & Francis Group.

Bratton, S. C., Ray, D., Rhine, T., & Jones, L. (2005). The efficacy of play therapy with children: A meta-analytic review of treatment outcomes. *Professional Psychology: Research and Practice, 36*(4), 376–390.

Brazelton, T. B., & Sparrow, J. D. (2006). *Touchpoints birth to 3: Your child's emotional and behavioral development (2nd ed.)*. Cambridge, MA: Da Capo Press.

Breggin, P. R. (2000). *Reclaiming our children: A healing plan for a nation in crisis*. New York, NY: HarperCollins.

Brown, D., Pryzwansky, W. B., & Schulte, A.C. (2006). *Psychological consultation and collaboration* (6th ed.). Upper Saddle River, NJ: Pearson.

Bryant, J. K. (2009). School counselors and child abuse reporting: A national survey. *Professional School Counseling, 12*(5), 333–342.

Burns, D. D. (1999). *The feeling good handbook*. New York, NY: Plume.

Cline, F. & Fay, J. (1992). Parenting teens with love & logic. Colorado Springs, CO: Pinon Press.

Coloroso, B. (1995). *Kids are worth it*. New York, NY: Harper.

Conroy, E., & Mayer, S. (1994). Strategies for consulting with parents. *Elementary School Guidance & Counseling, 29*(1), 60–66.

Costello, E. J., Egger, H., & Angold, A. (2005). Ten-year research update review: The epidemiology of child and adolescent psychiatric disorders: I. Methods and public health burden. *Journal of the American Academy of Child & Adolescent Psychiatry, 44*(10), 972–986.

Costello, E. J., Mustillo, S., Erkanli, A., Keeler, G., & Angold, A. (2003). Prevalence and development of psychiatric disorders in childhood and adolescence. *Archives of General Psychiatry, 60*(8), 837–844.

Covey, S. (1990). *The seven habits of highly effective people*. New York, NY: Free Press.

Croake, J. W. (1983). Adlerian parent education. *The Counseling Psychologist, 11*(3), 65–71.

de Shazer, S., Dolan, Y., Korman, H., McCollum, E., Trepper, T., & Berg, I. K. (2007). *More than miracles: The state of the art of solution-focused brief therapy*. New York, NY: Haworth Press.

Dennis, T. (2006). Emotional self-regulation in preschoolers: The interplay of child approach reactivity, parenting, and control capacities. *Developmental Psychology, 42*(1), 84–97.

Dinkmeyer, D., & Dinkmeyer, J. (1979). A comprehensive and systematic approach to parent education. *American Journal of Family Therapy, 7*(2), 46–50.

Dreikurs, R. (1950). The immediate purpose of children's mis-behavior, its recognition and correction. *Internationale Zeitschrift für Individual-Psychologie, 19*, 70–87.

Dreikurs, R. (1958). The cultural implications of reward and punishment. *International Journal of Social Psychiatry, 4*, 171–178.

Dreikurs, R., Gould, S., & Corsini, R. J. (1974). *Family council: The Dreikurs technique for putting an end to war between parents and children (and between children and children)*. Oxford, England: Henry Regnery.

Dreikurs, R., & Soltz, V. (1964). *Children: The challenge*. New York, NY: Duell, Sloan, & Pearce.

Duncan, B. L., Miller, S. D., Wampold, B. E., & Hubble, M. A. (Eds.) (2010). *The heart and soul of change: Delivering what works in therapy* (2nd ed.). Washington, DC: American Psychological Association.

Dunst, C. J., Trivette, C. M., & Thompson, R. B. (1994). Supporting and strengthening family functioning: Toward a congruence between principles and practice. In C. J. Dunst, C. M. Trivette & A. G. Deal (Eds.), *Supporting & strengthening families: Methods, strategies, and practices* (pp. 49–59). Cambridge, MA: Brookline Books.

Edwards, C. D. (1999). *How to handle a hard-to-handle kid*. Minneapolis, MN: Free Spirit Press.

Eisenberg, N., Spinrad, T. L., & Eggum, N. D. (2010). Emotion-related self-regulation and its relation to children's maladjustment. *Annual Review of Clinical Psychology, 6*, 495–525.

Ellis, E. M. (2000). *Divorce wars: Interventions with families in conflict*. Washington, DC: American Psychological Association.

Erchul, W. P. (1987). A relational communication analysis of control in school consultation. *Professional School Psychology, 2*(2), 113–124.

Faber, A., & Mazlish, E. (1987). *Siblings without rivalry*. New York, NY: W.W. Norton.

Ferber, R. (2006). *Solve your child's sleep problems* (rev. ed.). New York, NY: Fireside.

Fields, D., & Brown, A. (2010). *Toddler 411: Clear answers & smart advice for your toddler*. Boulder, CO: Windsor Peak Press.

Fischer, C. T. (1979). Individualized assessment and phenomenological psychology. *Journal of Personality Assessment, 43*(2), 115–122.

Fischer, C. T., & Finn, S. E. (2008). Developing the life meaning of psychological test data: Collaborative and therapeutic approaches. In R. P. Archer & S. R.

Smith (Eds.), *Personality assessment* (pp. 379–404). New York, NY: Routledge/ Taylor & Francis Group.

Gershoff, E. T. (2002). Corporal punishment by parents and associated child behaviors and experiences: A meta-analytic and theoretical review. *Psychological Bulletin, 128*(4), 539–579.

Gershoff, E. T. (2008). Report on Physical Punishment in the United States: What Research Tells Us About Its Effects on Children. Columbus, OH: Center for Effective Discipline.

Glasser, W. (1998). *Choice theory: A new psychology of personal freedom.* New York, NY: HarperCollins.

Glasser, W. (2000). *Reality therapy in action.* New York, NY: HarperCollins.

Glasser, W. (2002). *Unhappy teenagers.* New York, NY: HarperCollins.

Glasser, W. (2003). *Warning: Psychiatry can be hazardous to your mental health.* New York, NY: HarperCollins.

Goldfried, M. R. (2007). What has psychotherapy inherited from Carl Rogers? *Psychotherapy: Theory, Research, Practice, Training, 44*(3), 249–252.

Goldstein, N. J., Martin, S. J., & Cialdini, R. B. (2008). *Yes! Fifty scientifically proven ways to be persuasive.* New York, NY: Free Press.

Gottman, J., Notarius, C., Gonso, J., & Markman, H. (1976). *A couple's guide to communication.* Champaign, IL: Research Press.

Gottman, J. M., & DeClaire, J. (1997). *The heart of parenting.* New York, NY: Simon & Schuster.

Gottman, J. M., & DeClaire, J. (2001). *The relationship cure: A five-step guide for building better connections with family, friends, and lovers.* New York, NY: Crown.

Greenbaum, P. E., Dedrick, R. F., & Lipien, L. (2004). The Child Behavior Checklist/4-18 (CBCL/4-18). In M. J. Hilsenroth, & D. L. Segal (Eds.), *Comprehensive handbook of psychological assessment, vol. 2: Personality assessment* (pp. 179–191). Hoboken, NJ: John Wiley & Sons.

Greenberg, L. S., Watson, J. C., Elliot, R., & Bohart, A. C. (2001). Empathy. *Psychotherapy: Theory, Research, Practice, Training, 38*(4), 380–384.

Greenberger, D. & Padesky, C. A. (1995). *Mind over mood.* New York, NY: Guilford.

Greene, R. W., & Ablon, J. S. (2006). *Treating explosive kids: The collaborative problem-solving 1 approach.* New York, NY: Guilford Press.

Greene, R. W., Ablon, J. S., Goring, J. C., Raezer-Blakely, L., Markey, J., Monuteaux, M. C., . . . Rabbitt, S. (2004). Effectiveness of collaborative problem solving in affectively dysregulated children with oppositional-defiant disorder: Initial findings. *Journal of Consulting and Clinical Psychology, 72*(6), 1157–1164.

Grosshans, B. A., & Burton, J. (2008). *Beyond time-out: From chaos to calm.* New York, NY: Sterling.

Guerney, L. (2001). Child-centered play therapy. *International Journal of Play Therapy, 10*(2), 13–31.

Guerney, L., & Guerney, B. (1989). Child relationship enhancement: Family therapy and parent education. *Person-Centered Review Special Issue: Person-Centered Approaches with Families, 4*(3), 344–357.

Hays, P. A. (2008). *Addressing cultural complexities in practice: Assessment, diagnosis, and therapy* (2nd ed.). Washington, DC: American Psychological Association.

Hirschland, D. (2008). *Collaborative intervention in early childhood: Consulting with parents and teachers of 3- to 7-year-olds*. New York, NY: Oxford University Press.

Hogg, T., & Blau, M. (2006). *The baby whisperer solves all your problems*. New York, NY: Atria.

Holcomb-McCoy, C., & Bryan, J. (2010). Advocacy and empowerment in parent consultation: Implications for theory and practice. *Journal of Counseling and Development, 88*, 259–268.

Horowitz, J.A., & Goodman, J.H. (2005). Identifying and treating postpartum depression. *Journal of Obstetric, Gynecological, and Neonatal Nursing, 34*(2), 264–273.

Hughes, D. (1998). *Building the bonds of attachment: Awakening love in deeply troubled children*. Northvale, NJ: Jason Aronson.

Hutchinson, J., & Pretelt, V. (2010). Building resources and resilience: Why we should think about positive emotions when working with children, their families and their schools. *Counselling Psychology Review, 25*(1), 20–27.

Jenkins, W. M., Merzenich, M. M., Ochs, M. T., Allard, T., & Guic-Robles, E. (1990). Functional reorganization of primary somatosensory cortex in adult owl monkeys after behaviorally controlled tactile stimulation. *Journal of Neurophysiology, 63*(1), 82–104.

Kagan, J. (1998). *Three seductive ideas*. Cambridge, MA: Harvard University Press.

Kaminski, J. W., Valle, L. A., Filene, J. H., & Boyle, C. L. (2008). A meta-analytic review of components associated with parent training program effectiveness. *Journal of Abnormal Child Psychology: An Official Publication of the International Society for Research in Child and Adolescent Psychopathology, 36*(4), 567–589.

Kampwirth, T. J. (2006). *Collaborative consultation in the schools* (3rd ed.). Upper Saddle River, NJ: Pearson.

Katz, L. F., Wilson, B., & Gottman, J. M. (1999). Meta-emotion philosophy and family adjustment: Making an emotional connection. In M. J. Cox, & J. Brooks-Gunn (Eds.), *Conflict and cohesion in families: Causes and consequences* (pp. 131–165). Mahwah, NJ: Lawrence Erlbaum Associates.

Kazdin, A. E. (2008). *The Kazdin method for parenting the defiant child: With no pills, no therapy, no contest of wills*. Boston, MA: Houghton Mifflin.

Kohn, A. (1993). *Punished by rewards: The trouble with gold stars, incentive plans, A's, praise, and other bribes*. Boston, MA: Houghton-Mifflin.

Kohn, A. (2005). *Unconditional parenting: Moving from rewards and punishments to love and reason*. New York, NY: Atria.

Kohut, H. H. (1984). *How does analysis cure?* Chicago, IL: University of Chicago Press.

Kuhn, B. R., & Elliott, A. J. (2003). Treatment efficacy in behavioral pediatric sleep medicine. *Journal of Psychosomatic Research, 54*(6), 587–597.

Kurcinka, M. S. (1991). *Raising your spirited child*. New York, NY: HarperCollins.

Kurcinka, M. S. (2001). *Kids, parents, and power struggles*. New York, NY: HarperCollins.

Lambert, M. J., & Barley, D. E. (2002). Research summary on the therapeutic relationship and psychotherapy outcome. In J. C. Norcross (Ed.), *Psychotherapy relationships that work: Therapist contributions and responsiveness to patients* (pp. 17–32). London, England: Oxford University Press.

Lambert, M. J., & Bergin, A. E. (1994). The effectiveness of psychotherapy. In A. E. Bergin, & S. L. Garfield (Eds.), *Handbook of psychotherapy and behavior change* (4th ed., pp. 143–189). New York, NY: John Wiley & Sons.

Landreth, G. L. (2002). *Play therapy: The art of the relationship (2nd ed.)*. New York, NY: Brunner-Routledge.

Latham, G. P., & Locke, E. A. (2007). New developments in and directions for goal-setting research. *European Psychologist, 12*(4), 290–300.

Lazarus, A. A. (1997). *Brief but comprehensive psychotherapy: The multimodal way.* New York, NY: Springer.

Levenson, H. (2004). *Time-limited dynamic psychotherapy: Formulation and intervention.* Washington, DC: American Psychiatric Publishing.

Linehan, M. (1993a). *Cognitive behavioral therapy of borderline personality disorder.* New York, NY: Guilford Press.

Linehan, M. (1993b). *Skills training manual for treating borderline personality disorder.* New York, NY: Guilford Press.

Linehan, M., & Schmidt, H. I. (1995). The dialectics of effective treatment of borderline personality disorder. In W. O'Donohue, & L. Krasner (Eds.), *Theories of behavior therapy* (pp. 553–584). Washington, DC: American Psychological Association.

Locke, E. A., & Latham, G. P. (2006). New directions in goal-setting theory. *Current Directions in Psychological Science, 15*(5), 265–268.

Loyd, B. H., & Abidin, R. R. (1985). Revision of the parenting stress index. *Journal of Pediatric Psychology, 10*(2), 169–177.

Luborsky, L. (1984). *Principles of psychoanalytic psychotherapy: A manual for supportive-expressive treatment.* New York, NY: Basic Books.

Maslow, A. H. (1970). *Motivation and personality* (2nd ed.). New York, NY: Harper & Row.

May, R. (1969). *Love and will.* New York, NY: Norton.

McCrea, S. M. (2008). Self-handicapping, excuse making, and counterfactual thinking: Consequences for self-esteem and future motivation. *Journal of Personality and Social Psychology, 95*(2), 274–292.

McEwan, E. K. (2005). *How to deal with teachers who are angry, troubled, exhausted, or just plain confused.* Thousand Oaks, CA: Corwin Press.

McVittie, J., & Best, A. M. (2009). The impact of Adlerian-based parenting classes on self-reported parental behavior. *Journal of Individual Psychology, 65*(3), 264–285.

Merenda, P. F. (1996). BASC: Behavior Assessment System for Children. *Measurement and Evaluation in Counseling and Development, 28*(4), 229–232.

Merikangas, R. R., He, J. P., Burstein, M., Swanson, S. A., Avenevoli, S., Cui, L., . . . Swendsen, J. (2010). Lifetime prevalence of mental disorders in U.S. adolescents: Results from the National Comorbidity Survey Replication-Adolescent Supplement (NCS-A). *Journal of the American Academy of Child and Adolescent Psychiatry, 49*(10), 980–989.

Metcalf, L. (2008). *Counseling toward solutions: A practical solution-focused program for working with students, teachers, and parents* (2nd ed.). San Francisco, CA: Jossey-Bass.

Miller, W. R., & Rollnick, S. (2002). *Motivational interviewing: Preparing people for change* (2nd ed.). New York: Guilford Press.

Mullis, F., & Edwards, D. (2001). Consulting with parents: Applying family systems concepts and techniques. *Professional School Counseling, 5*(2), 116–123.

Murphy, J. J. (2008). *Solution-focused counseling in middle and high schools.* Alexandria, VA: American Counseling Association.

Neimeyer, R. A., & Mahoney, M. (Eds.). (1995). *Constructivism in psychotherapy.* Washington, DC: American Psychological Association.

Norcross, J. C., Beutler, L. E., & Levant, R. F. (Eds.). (2006). *Evidence-based practices in mental health: Debate and dialogue on the fundamental questions.* Washington, DC: American Psychological Association.

Ohan, J. L., Leung, D. W., & Johnston, C. (2000). The parenting sense of competence scale: Evidence of a stable factor structure and validity. *Canadian Journal of Behavioural Science/Revue Canadienne Des Sciences Du Comportement, 32*(4), 251–261.

Pekarik, G., & Guidry, L. L. (1999). Relationship of satisfaction to symptom change, follow-up adjustment, and clinical significance in private practice. *Professional Psychology: Research and Practice, 30*(5), 474–478.

Pekarik, G., & Wolff, C. B. (1996). Relationship of satisfaction to symptom change, follow-up adjustment, and clinical significance. *Professional Psychology: Research and Practice, 27*(2), 202–208.

Pickhardt, C. E. (2010). *Keys to successful stepfathering.* New York, NY: Barron.

Prochaska, J. O. (1995). An eclectic and integrative approach: Transtheoretical therapy. In A. S. Gurman, & S. B. Messer (Eds.), *Essential psychotherapies* (pp. 403–440). New York, NY: Guilford.

Prochaska, J. O., & DiClemente, C. (2002). *Transtheoretical therapy.* Hoboken, NJ: John Wiley & Sons.

Prochaska, J. O., & DiClemente, C. C. (2005). *The transtheoretical approach.* New York, NY: Oxford University Press.

Ramos, K. D., & Youngclarke, D. M. (2006). Parenting advice books about child sleep: Cosleeping and crying it out. *Sleep: Journal of Sleep and Sleep Disorders Research, 29*(12), 1616–1623.

Reynolds, C. R., & Kamphaus, R. W. (2002). *The clinician's guide to the Behavior Assessment System for Children (BASC).* New York, NY: Guilford Press.

Ricci, I. (1997). *Mom's house, Dad's house: A complete guide for parents who are separated, divorced, or remarried* (2nd ed.). New York, NY: Simon & Schuster.

Rice, D. (2006). Psychotherapy for oppositional-defiant kids with low frustration tolerance and how to help their parents, too. Psychotherapy.net. Retrieved from http://www.psychotherapy.net/article/oppositional-defiants-kids.

Richardson, B. G., & Wubbolding, R. E. (2001). Five interrelated challenges for using reality therapy with challenging students. *International Journal of Reality Therapy, 20*(2), 35–39.

Rogers, C. R. (1942). *Counseling and psychotherapy.* Boston, MA: Houghton Mifflin.

Rogers, C. R. (1961). *On becoming a person*. Boston, MA: Houghton Mifflin.

Rogers, C. R. (1980). *A way of being*. Boston, MA: Houghton Mifflin.

Rosemond, J. (2007). *Parenting by the book*. New York, NY: Howard Books.

Samalin, N. (2003). *Loving without spoiling*. New York, NY: McGraw-Hill.

Searles, H. F. (1955). The informational value of the supervisor's emotional experiences. *Psychiatry: Journal for the Study of Interpersonal Processes, 18*, 135–146.

Sharp, W. G., Reeves, C. B., & Gross, A. M. (2006). Behavioral interviewing of parents. In M. Hersen (Ed.), *Clinician's handbook of child behavioral assessment* (pp. 103–124). San Diego, CA: Elsevier Academic Press.

Sheridan, S. M., Erchul, W. P., Brown, M. S., Dowd, S. E., Warnes, E. D., Marti, D. C., . . . Eagle, J. W. (2004). Perceptions of helpfulness in conjoint behavioral consultation: Congruence and agreement between teachers and parents. *School Psychology Quarterly, 19*(2), 121–140.

Sheridan, S. M., & Kratochwill, T. R. (2008). *Conjoint behavioral consultation: Promoting family-school connections and interventions* (2nd ed.). New York, NY: Springer Science + Business Media.

Shneidman, E. S. (1996). *The suicidal mind*. New York, NY: Oxford University Press.

Shure, M. B. (1992). *I can problem solve: An interpersonal cognitive problem-solving program*. Champaign, IL: Research Press.

Sicher, L. (1991). A declaration of interdependence. *Individual Psychology, 47*(1), 10–16.

Sklare, G. B. (2005). *Brief counseling that works: A solution-focused approach for school counselors and administrators* (2nd ed.). Thousand Oaks, CA: Corwin Press.

Skovholt, T. M., & Starkey, M. T. (2010). The three legs of the practitioner's learning stool: Practice, research/theory, and personal life. *Journal of Contemporary Psychotherapy, 40*(3), 125–130.

Sommers-Flanagan, J. (2007). Single-session consultations for parents: A preliminary investigation. *The Family Journal, 15*(1), 24–29.

Sommers-Flanagan, J., & Campbell, D. G. (2009). Psychotherapy and (or) medications for depression in youth? An evidence-based review with recommendations for treatment. *Journal of Contemporary Psychotherapy, 39*(2), 111–120.

Sommers-Flanagan, J., & Sommers-Flanagan, R. (2001). The three-step emotional change trick. In H. G. Kaduson, & C. E. Schaefer (Eds.), *101 more favorite play therapy techniques* (pp. 439–444). Northvale, NJ: Jason Aronson.

Sommers-Flanagan, J., & Sommers-Flanagan, R. (2004a). *Counseling and psychotherapy theories in context and practice: Skills, strategies, and techniques*. Hoboken, NJ: John Wiley & Sons.

Sommers-Flanagan, J., & Sommers-Flanagan, R. (2004b). *The challenge of counseling teens: Counselor behaviors that reduce resistance and facilitate connection*. [Video/DVD]. North Amherst, MA: Microtraining Associates.

Sommers-Flanagan, J., & Sommers-Flanagan, R. (2007a). Our favorite tips for interviewing couples and families. *Psychiatric Clinics of North America, 30*(2), 275–281.

Sommers-Flanagan, J., & Sommers-Flanagan, R. (2007b). *Tough kids, cool counseling: User-friendly approaches with challenging youth* (2nd ed.). Alexandria, VA: American Counseling Association.

Sommers-Flanagan, J., & Sommers-Flanagan, R. (2009). *Clinical interviewing* (4th ed.). Hoboken, NJ: John Wiley & Sons.

Sommers-Flanagan, R., Elander, C., & Sommers-Flanagan, J. (2000). *Don't divorce us!: Kids' advice to divorcing parents*. Alexandria, VA: American Counseling Association.

Sommers-Flanagan, R., & Sommers-Flanagan, J. (2007). *Becoming an ethical helping professional: Cultural and philosophical foundations*. Hoboken, NJ: John Wiley & Sons.

Spinrad, T. L., Stifter, C. A., Donelan-McCall, N., & Turner, L. (2004). Mothers' regulation strategies in response to toddlers' affect: Links to later emotion self-regulation. *Social Development, 13*(1), 40–55.

Spivack, G., Platt, J. J., & Shure, M. B. (1976). *The problem-solving approach to adjustment*. San Francisco, CA: Jossey-Bass.

Steenbarger, B. N. (2004). *Solution-focused brief therapy: Doing what works*. Washington, DC: American Psychiatric Publishing.

Sue, D. W., & Sue, D. (2008). *Counseling the culturally diverse: Theory and practice* (5th ed.). Hoboken, NJ: John Wiley & Sons.

Sue, S. (1998). In search of cultural competence in psychotherapy and counseling. *American Psychologist, 53*(4), 440–448.

Sutton, S. (2005). Another nail in the coffin of the transtheoretical model? A comment on West (2005). *Addiction, 100*(8), 1043–1045.

Sweeney, T. J. (2009). *Adlerian counseling and psychotherapy: A practitioner's approach* (5th ed.). New York, NY: Routledge/Taylor & Francis Group.

Thevenin, T. (1987). *The family bed*. New York, NY: Perigee.

Vargas, L. (2004). Reflections of a process-oriented contextualist. In J. Sommers-Flanagan, & R. Sommers-Flanagan (Eds.), *Counseling and psychotherapy theories in context and practice* (pp. 428–429). Hoboken, NJ: John Wiley & Sons.

Wampold, B. E. (2005). Establishing specificity in psychotherapy scientifically: Design and evidence issues. *Clinical Psychology: Science & Practice, 12*, 194–197.

Wampold, B. E. (2010). *The basics of psychotherapy: An introduction to theory and practice*. Washington, DC: American Psychological Association.

Watson, J. B. (1924). *Behaviorism*. Chicago, IL: University of Chicago Press.

Watson, J. B., & Watson, R. R. (1928). *Psychological care of infant and child*. New York, NY: W. W. Norton.

Webster-Stratton, C. (2007). Tailoring the Incredible Years Parent Programs according to children's developmental needs and family risk factors. In J. M. Briesmeister, & C. E. Schaefer (Eds.), *The handbook of parent training* (pp. 305–344). Hoboken, NJ: John Wiley & Sons.

Webster-Stratton, C., & Reid, M. J. (2003). The Incredible Years Parents, Teachers and Children Training Series: A multifaceted treatment approach for young children with conduct problems. In A. E. Kazdin, & J. R. Weisz (Eds.), *Evidence-based psychotherapies for children and adolescents* (pp. 224–240). New York, NY: Guilford Press.

Webster-Stratton, C., & Reid, M. J. (2010). Parents, teachers, and therapists using child-directed play therapy and coaching skills to promote children's social and emotional competence and build positive relationships. In C. E.

Schaefer (Ed.), *Play therapy for preschool children* (pp. 245–273). Washington, DC: American Psychological Association.

West, R. (2005). Time for a change: Putting the transtheoretical (stages of change) model to rest. *Addiction*, *100*(8), 1036–1039.

Whitaker, R. (2010). *Anatomy of an epidemic: Magic bullets, psychiatric drugs, and the astonishing rise of mental illness in America.* New York, NY: Crown/Random House.

Wood, M. (1996). *Developmental therapy-developmental teaching: fostering social-emotional competence in troubled children and youth* (3rd ed.) Austin, TX: Pro-Ed.

Wubbolding, R. E., & Brickell, J. (2000). Misconceptions about reality therapy. *International Journal of Reality Therapy*, *19*(2), 64–65.

Wubbolding, R. E., Brickell, J., Loi, I., & Al-Rashidi, B. (2001). The why and how of self-evaluation. *International Journal of Reality Therapy*, *21*, 36–37.

Yalom, I. D., & Leszcz, M. (2005). *The theory and practice of group psychotherapy* (*5th ed.*). New York, NY: Basic Books.

Zimmerman, T. S., Jacobsen, R. B., MacIntyre, M., & Watson, C. (1996). Solution-focused parenting groups: An empirical study. *Journal of Systemic Therapies*, *15*(4), 12–25.

Zuckerman, B., Zuckerman, P. M., & Siegel, D. J. (2005). Promoting self-understanding in parents—for the great good of your patients. *Contemporary Pediatrics*, *22*(4), 77–90.

Author Index

A

Abidin, R. R., 108
Ablon, J. S., 144
Achenbach, T. M., 109
Adler, A., xii, 81, 98, 195
Ainsworth, M. S., 72
Al-Rashidi, B., 43
Alderman, G. L., 34
American Psychological
    Association, 18
Anderson, H., 10
Angold, A., 3
Anthony, W., 27
Aucoin, K. J., 37
Axline, V. M., 183

B

Bandura, A., 44
Barkley, R. A., 142
Barley, D. E., 6
Battino, R. 23
Baumrind, D., 35
Beck, A. T., 62
Benton, C. M., 142
Berg, I. K., xii, 25, 60
Bergin, A. E., 6

Best, A. M., 81
Beutler, L. E., 7
Biel, L., 21
Bitter, J. R., 23, 81, 108
Blackard, S. R., 108
Bodin, S. D., 37
Bohart, A. C., 8
Bowlby, J., 72
Boyle, C. L., 6
Bratton, S. C., 108, 183, 202
Brazelton, T. B., 8
Breggin, P. R., 50
Brickell, J., 43
Brown, D., 11
Bryan, J., 6
Bryant, J. K., 202
Burton, J., 34, 47

C

Campbell, D. G., 27
Christensen, O. C., 23
Cialdini, R. B., 60
Cline, F., 49, 169
Coloroso, B., 113
Conroy, E., 23
Corsini, R. J., 44

Costello, E. J., 3
Covey, S., 47, 48, 117
Craver, J. R., 34
Croake, J. W., 44

D
de Shazer, S., xii, 60
DeClaire, J., 34, 129, 142
Dedrick, R. F., 109
DeJong, P., 25
Dennis, T., 129
DiClemente, C., 94, 96, 141
Dinkmeyer, D., 81
Dinkmeyer, J., 81
Dolan, Y., 60
Donelan-McCall, N., 129
Dreikurs, R., xii, 19, 24, 36, 44, 81
Duncan, B. L., 59
Dunst, C. J., 7

E
Edelbrock, C. S., 109
Edwards, C. D., 144
Edwards, D., 8
Egger, H., 3
Eggum, N. D., 37
Eisenberg, N., 37, 129
Elander, C., 125
Elliot, R. 8
Ellis, E. M., 203, 204
Erchul, W. P., 7
Erkanli, A., 3

F
Faber, A., 21
Fay, J., 49, 169
Ferber, R. 49, 90, 91
Filene, J. H., 6

Finn, S. E., 86, 102
Frick, P. J., 37

G
Gershoff, E. T., 37, 68
Glasser, W., xii, 28, 36, 43, 50, 67, 98, 134
Goldfried, M. R., 8
Goldstein, N. J., 60
Gonso, J., 182
Goodman, J. H., 205
Goolishian, H., 10
Gottman, J., 34, 129, 142, 182
Goring, J. C., 144
Gould, S., 44
Greenbaum, P. E., 109
Greenberg, L. S., 8
Greene, R. W., 144
Gross, A. M., 63
Grosshans, B. A., 34, 47
Guerney, L., 183, 202
Guerney, B., 202
Guidry, L. L., 109

H
Hawes, O. C., 23
Hays, P. A., 198
Hirschland, D., 6
Holcomb-McCoy, C. 6
Horowitz, J. A., 205
Hubble, M. A., 59
Hughes, D., 49
Hutchinson, J., 129

J
Jacobsen, R. B., 42
Johnston, C., 109
Jones, L., 202

K

Kagan, J., 41

Kaminski, J. W., 6, 7

Kamphaus, R. W., 109

Kampwirth, T. J., 11

Katz, L. F., 129

Kazdin, A. E., 36, 48, 68, 76, 86, 142, 163, 165

Keeler, G., 3

Kellam, T., 108

Kohn, A., 3, 38, 87, 103

Kohut, H. H., 77

Korman, H., 60

Kratochwill, T. R., 8, 108

Kuhn, B. R., 90

Kurcinka, M. S., 105, 106

L

Lambert, M. J., 6

Landreth, G. L., 108, 114

Latham, G. P., 26, 27

Leszcz, M., 66, 206

Leung, D. W., 109

Levant, R. F., 7

Levenson, H., 177

Linehan, M., 9, 66

Lipien, L., 109

Locke, E. A., 26, 27

Loi, I., 43

Loyd, B. H., 108

M

MacIntyre, M., 42

Mahoney, M., 77

Markey, J., 144

Markman, H., 182

Martin, S. J., 60

May, R., 98

Mayer, S., 23

Mazlish, E., 21

McCollum, E., 60

McCrea, S. M., 85

McEwan, E. K., 18

McVittie, J., 81

Merenda, P. F., 109

Merikangas, R. R., 3

Metcalf, L., 42

Miller, S. D., 59

Miller, W. R., 13

Monuteaux, M. C., 144

Mullis, F., 8

Murphy, J. J., 41, 60, 95

Mustillo, S., 3

N

Neimeyer, R. A., 77

Nicoll, W. G., 23

Norcross, J. C., 7

Notarius, C., 182

O

Ohan, J. L., 109

P

Pekarik, G., 109

Peske, N., 21

Pickhardt, C. E., 125

Platt, J. J., 43

Pretelt, V., 129

Prochaska, J. O., 94, 96, 141

Pryzwansky, W. B., 11

R

Raezer-Blakely, L., 144

Ray, D., 202

Reeves, C. B., 63

Reid, M. J., 114

Reynolds, C. R., 109

Rhine, T., 202

Ricci, I., 21

Rice, D., 25

Richardson, B. G., 43

Robin, A. L., 142

Rogers, C. R., xii, 3, 7, 9, 13, 57, 72, 98, 113, 134

Ross, D., 44

Ross, S. A., 44

S

Samalin, N., 206

Schmidt, H. I., 66

Schulte, A. C., 11

Searles, H. F., 25

Sharp, W. G., 63

Sheridan, S. M., 6, 108

Shneidman, E. S., 42

Shure, M. B., 42, 43

Sicher, L., 75

Siegel, D. J., 24

Sklare, G. B., 66

Skovholt, T. M., 75

Soltz, V., 19, 24

Sommers-Flanagan, R., 5, 9, 18, 27, 32, 39, 60, 61, 66, 72, 98, 125, 177, 195

Sommers-Flanagan, J., 5, 7, 9, 18, 27, 39, 60, 61, 66, 72, 98, 104, 108, 125, 177, 195

Sparrow, J. D., 8

Spinrad, T. L., 37, 129

Spivack, G., 42

Starkey, M. T., 75

Steenbarger, B. N., 41

Stifter, C. A., 129

Sue, S., 77

Sutton, S., 97

Sweeney, T. J., 27

T

Thevenin, T., 90

Thompson, R. B., 7

Trepper, T., 60

Trivette, C. M., 7

Turner, L., 129

V

Valle, L. A., 6

Vargas, L., 195–196

W

Walters, R. H., 44

Wampold, B. E., 6, 59

Watson, J. B., 91

Watson, J. C., 8, 42

Watson, R. R., 91

Webster-Stratton, C., 114, 155–156

West, R., 97

Whitaker, R., 28

Wilson, B., 129

Wolff, C. B., 109

Wood, M., 34, 35

Wubbolding, R. E., 43

Y

Yalom, I. D., 66, 206

Z

Zimmerman, T. S., 42

Zuckerman, B., 23

Zuckerman, P. M., 23

Subject Index

A

Abuse:
   reporting, 202–204
   sexual, 47
   substance, 47
Acceptance, radical. 8–10, 13, 23, 196
Achenbach Child Behavior Checklist, 109
Action-discipline, 185–186
Action, taking, 94, 97
ADD/ADHD, 28, 85
Adlerian perspective, problem formulation and, 76, 81–84
Advice:
   helping parents accept, 94–98
   modifying, 180
   offering, 99–104
   tailoring, 186–190
   writing, 104–109
   see also Homework, Interventions, Outcomes
Affection, expressions of, 48
American Psychological Association, 18, 201

Anger, 50, 120–124
Appointments. See Sessions
Assessment:
   backward behavior modification, 68–70
   problem formulation, 63–66
   setting goals, 66–68
   strategies already tried, 70–71
   universalization, 66
   watching for patterns, 71–72
Asset flooding, 49
Attachment theory, 49, 77
Attachment-collectivism, 90
Attention, as a goal of misbehavior, 81
Attitude, therapists' towards parents, 8–12, 19–20
Audience, giving, 46–47
Authority, parents', 34–35. *See also* Expert

B

Backtalk, 157
Bedtime, 87–91, 189–190
Behavior Assessment System for Children, 109

Behavior modification, backward, 68–70, 153–156

Behaviorism, 36, 37–41

   problem formulation, 63, 76, 86–91

   see also Limit-setting

Behaviors, kids' negative, 157–161

Biomedicine. *See* Medicine

Bipolar, 28

Biting, 157

Body language, 35

Books, parenting, 21–22

Boundaries, with parents, 200–203

Brainstorming, 42

   during second sessions, 186–187

Buddhism, 9

Bullying, 186–188

C

Cancellation, 192–193

Caretaking, 49

Case examples:

   problem formulation, 87–89

   cultural sensitivity, 196–197

   divorce, 199–200

   first meeting, 4, 5–6

   follow-up session, 188–189

   goal alignment, 29–31

   limit setting, 161–163

   mutual problem solving, 144–148

   natural consequence, 169–172

   power sharing, 135–136

   precontemplation, 95–96

   prejudice, 78

   problem formulation, 64–65, 84–86

   radical acceptance, 12–14

role modeling, 158–161

self-esteem, 138–141

tailoring recommendations, 189–190

timeout, 166–169

Change, stages of, 94–99

Character feedback:

   modifying advice, 180

   teaching parents about, 28, 138–142

   prescribing, 189

   as an indirect power strategy, 45, 52

Child abuse, 202–204

Child custody, 201

Child protective services, 202–204

Child therapy, 201–202

Child-directed play. *See* Special time

Child-generated rules, 42–44

Children:

   at appointments, 204–205

   backward behavior modification, 154–157

   chores, 148–152

   feelings, 125–130

   setting limits with, 161–163

   struggle for power, 172–175

   therapists', 22–23

   See also Special time

Choice theory:

   definition, 67

   natural consequences, 169–172

   problem formulation, 76–77

   See also Magic words

Choices, giving to children, 45–46

Chores, 148–152

Clinician. *See* Therapist

Closing session, 108–109

Co-sleeping, 90

Coercion. *See* Direct power

Collaboration, 10–12, 23

    goal alignment, 26–27

    between parents and children, 42

    establishing, 59–60

    on homework, 107, 117–118

    parents and children, 144–148

    power sharing, 133–134

    problem formulation, 78–80

Collaborative parents, 1

Commands, 36, 40

Communication, 173, 187–188

Compassion. *See* Empathy

Complimenting, 24–25, 49, 61–62, 101

Conditional parenting, 87

Conditions of worth, 8

Confidentiality, 59–60, 202–204

Consequences, 37–41, 154–155

    modification, 173–174

    natural, 169–172

Consequential thinking, 42–43

Constructive perspective, 41, 76

Consultant, xi. *See also* Therapist.

Consultation. *See* Sessions

Contemplation stage, 94, 96

Control, 34, 67

Cooperation. *See* Action, Collaboration

Corporal punishment. *See* Physical punishment

Counselor Reflection Inventory, 109

Criticism, 24–25, 182

Cultural sensitivity, 6, 195–198

Custody, 201

D

Defensiveness, 13, 19. *See also* Insecurity

Depression, 205–206

Dialectical behavior therapy, 9

Direct power, 35–36, 52

    behavioral psychology, 37–41

    Grandma's Rule, 39–40, 145

    lecturing, 134

    physical punishment, 36–37

    versus child-generated rules, 43

    See also Physical punishment

Disappointment, expressing, 50

Discipline, 36–37. *See also* Physical punishment

Diversity, 20, 60, 195–198

Divorce, 199–202

Doormat parents, 1

E

Eclecticism, 84

Educating parents, 5, 200

Ego, 98

Email, 193

Emotions

    children's, 125–130

    therapists, 20–21, 206–207

Empathic statement, 182

Empathy:

    contemplation and, 96

    for parents, 7–9, 23, 66

    parent openness, 14

    parents' for children, 113–114

    problem formulation, 80–81

Empowerment, of children, 134
Enabling, 49–50
Encouragement, 45
Ethics, preparation, 18
Everyday connection, 48
Evidence-based common
    factors, 6
Expectations, parents', 6
Experience-near, 77
Expert:
    parent as, 60–61, 78–80, 195
    therapist as, 60, 99
    see also Collaboration,
        Problem-solving power
External control psychology, 36
External learning. *See* Direct power
Extinction, 36, 39, 90
Extratherpeutic factors, 6
Eye contact, 35

F
Facial expression, 35
Factors, common to positive
    outcomes, 6
Familiesfirstmontana.org, 121, 123,
    130
Family bed, 90
Family meetings, 44
Family practice model, 178
Family system, problem
    formulation and, 63, 76.
    See also Polarization principle
Family therapy, 5
Favors, 49
Feedback:
  constructive, 25
  negative, 181–183
  positive, 180–181

Feelings:
  children's, 125–130
  therapists', 20–21, 206–207
Ferberization, 90
First contact, 58–59
Follow-up, 108, 178–179.
    See also Session
Four Big Questions of Choice
    theory, 42, 43
Friendship, between children and
    parents, 47

G
Generating behavior alternatives,
    42
Giving audience, 46–47
Giving choices, 45–46
Goal alignment, 26–27
Goal setting, 66–68
Goals of misbehavior, 81
Grandma's Rule, 36, 39–40, 145
Guidance. *See* Advice, Interventions
Guilt, parental, 206

H
Helicopter parents, 49
Hitting, 157, 185–186. *See also*
    Physical punishment
Homework, for parents:
  anger, 122–124
  giving to parents, 104–109
  honoring children's emotions,
    129–130
  natural consequences, 170–172
  power sharing, 136–138, 142–144
  problem polarization, 174–175
  role modeling, 159–161
  setting limits, 163–164

special time, 117–120

timeout, 167–169

See also Advice

Homophobia, 9, 195–198

Human services provider, xi.
  See also Therapist.

Humility, therapists', 195–198

Hypocrisy, 196–197

Hypothesis, scientific mindedness
  and, 77–78

I

Ideal self, 98

Identity formation, 28

Ignoring behavior, 36, 39, 90

Inadequacy, 81, 96

Incredible Years curriculum, 155

Indirect power, 44–47

  asking permission, 135–136

  character feedback, mirroring,
    and solution-focused
    questions, 138–142

  role modeling 158–161

Influence, parents' on children, 34

Initial contact, strategies, 57–62

Insecurity:

  parents', 8, 26

  therapists', 17, 23

Insensitivity, parents', 9

Integrative approach, 84

Internal learning, 134

Intervention, 11

  experience-near, 77

  length of, 193

  on parent-child relationship, 6–7

  options, 5

  importance of specificity, 6–7

  limitations of, 23–24

premature, 13–14

specific psychological, 6

strategies for facilitation,
  24–29

see also Advice, Homework,
  Sessions

IOUs, 49

J

Judgment, 11, 19–20. *See also*
  Empathy, Collaboration,
  Defensiveness

L

Language, 77, 100

Leaderlessness, 11. *See also*
  Collaboration, Power sharing

Length, of intervention, 191–193

Likability. *See* Relationship power

Likert scale, 109

Limits, setting, 36, 161–165

List of ideas, 104

Listening, 207

  goal alignment and, 27

  importance of, 207

  nonjudgmental, 14

  to children, 129–130

  to parents, 70–71

Literature, parenting, 21–22

Love-and-logic, 169

Love, 61, 63, 91–92, 97. *See also*
  Relationship, Special time

Loving statements, 48

M

Magic words, 172–173

Maintenance, of parents' change,
  94, 97–98

Manipulation, 46–47.
    See also Indirect power
Manualized approach, 7
Media, influence on parents, 8,
    21–22
Mediation, 201
Medicine, 28, 85, 190
Mental disorders, 1
Minorities. *See* Multiculturalism
Mirroring, 138–142, 155
Misbehavior, motivations for
    (goals of), 81
Missed appointments, 192–193
Modeling. *See* Role modeling
Models, for sessions, 177–179
Motivational Interviewing, xii
Multiculturalism, 20, 60, 195–198
Mutual problem solving, 42,
    144–148
    second session, 181–183
    see also Collaboration

N
Natural reinforcement, 38
Natural teaming, 50
Negative feedback:
    for parents, 24–25
    from parents, 181–183
Negative reinforcement, 36–37, 39
Non-directive play, 114–120
Nonjudgment. *See* Empathy
Nonreaction, 9. *See also* Ignoring

O
Objectivity 19–21
Ongoing contact:
    feedback, 179–184

mixed results, 185–190
    nature of relationship, 191–193
Opening statement, 59–60
Outcomes:
    mixed, 185–190
    positive or negative, 180–184

P
Parallel process, 25–26
Parenting:
    conditional, 87
    consultation, 5–6
    education, 5, 200
Parenting Influence Model, 34,
    50–52
Parenting Sense of Competence,
    108–109
Parenting Stress Index, 108
Parents:
    anger, 120–124
    doormat, 1
    as experts, 11, 78–80, 195
    backward behavior modification,
        154–157
    building a relationship with, 7–12
    collaboration with children,
        144–148
    cultural influences, 195–198
    developing trust, 8
    difference from other clinical
        populations, 4–5
    divorced or never married,
        199–202
    empathy for children, 113–114
    goals of, 33–34
    limit setting, 161–163
    motivation for change, 94–99

non-attendance, 192–193

power struggles with children, 172–175

remembering session information, 179

respecting children's feelings, 125–130

sharing power with, 133–134

therapists' attitudes towards, 19–20

see also Advice, Intervention

Passive-aggressive behavior, 182

Patterns, 71–72

Pediatrician, 5

Permission, asking, 99

Persistence coaching, 155

Person-centered approach, 7, 8, 10, 61, 113

Philosophy, personal, 59

Physical punishment, 35–37, 165

Play, 114–120. *See also* Special time

Polarization principle, 51, 85, 174–175

Positive feedback:
  for parents, 24–25
  from parents, 180–181

Positive outcomes, 6–8 180–184

Positive reinforcement, 36, 38, 102–103

Positive working relationship, 6

Post-partum depression, 205–206

Power-sharing, mutual problem solving, 144–148

Power:
  as a goal of misbehavior, 81
  direct, 35–41, 50
  indirect, 44–47

problem-solving, 35, 41–44

relationship, 47–50

sharing, 97, 133–134

sources of parental, 35

struggles, between children and parents, 172–175

Practitioner, xi. *See also* Therapist.

Praise, 86, 138–142

Precontemplation, 94–96

Preparation:
  parents', 94, 96–97
  therapists', 18

Prescription, parenting, 104–109. *See also* Advice

Preset rules, 36, 40–41

Problem formulation:
  Adlerian perspectives on, 81–84
  assessment and, 63–66
  getting parents' perspective, 78–80
  multi-theoretical, 84–86
  theoretical perspectives, 76–77

Problem polarization, 51, 85, 174–175

Problem-solving power, 35, 41–44

Prompts, 36, 40

Provider, xi. *See also* Therapist.

Psychiatric diagnosis, 28

Psychoanalysis, 25

Psychologist, 5. *See also* Therapist

Punishment:
  as external learning, 134
  backward behavior modification, 68
  effectiveness, 40–41
  physical, 36–37

Q

Questions:
parents', 22
previous session recall, 179–180

R

Race, 9, 46–47, 195–198
Radical acceptance, 8–10, 13, 23, 196
Reactions, to parents, 9
Readiness to change, 94–98
Reality therapy, 67, 76–77
Rebellion, 34, 41
Recall, of session information, 179–180
Recommendations, modifying, 180
Records, 59–60
Referrals, 190–191
Reflection, 45, 185
Relationship bank account, 47
Relationship power, 47–50
Relationship:
parent-child, 27–28, 47–48
parent-therapist, 4–7, 191–193
see also Sessions
Religious influences, 195–198
Remembering, previous session, 179–180
Reassurance, 61–62
Resistance, parental. *See* Precontemplation
Respect, 96, 113, 173. *See also* Expert
Response cost, 36, 38, 165–169
Revenge, as a goal of misbehavior, 81

Rewards, 87, 154–155. *See also* Positive reinforcement
Role induction, 60
Role modeling:
apology, 174
as indirect power strategy, 44–45
case example, 158–161
parallel process, 25–26
Role-playing, 42–43
Rules, 36, 40–41
child-generated, 42, 43–44
(*see also* Special Time)

S

Satisfaction ratings, 109
Scheduling, 108, 177–178
School counselor, 5. *See also* Therapist
Science-individualism, 90
Scientific mindedness, 77–78
Self-actualization, 98
Self-awareness, 20
Self-care, 206–207
Self-evaluation, 108–109
Separation, 200
Sessions:
children's presence at, 204–205
feedback, 179–184
format, 177–178, 191–193
mixed results, 185–190
Seven Habits of Highly Effective People, 47
Sexism, 9. *See also* Multiculturalism
Sexual abuse, 47
Sibling rivalry, 21
Silence, 9
Single parents, 199–202

Single-session consultations, 178

Sleep problems, 87–91, 189–190

Social interaction, 27–28

Social power, 34

Social pressures, 8

Socialization, of client, 60

Solution talk, 42

Solution-focus, 25, 41, 61, 76, 94

   questions, 138–142

   strategies, 155

Solutions, 66–68

   generating alternatives, 42

   see also Advice, Intervention

Spanking. *See* Physical punishment

Special time, 48, 102, 114–120, 183

Stages of change, 94–99

Star Wars, 98

Stepparents, 125–128

Storytelling, 46, 69, 100–101

Strategies:

   intervention, 24–29

   listening, 207

   See also Intervention

Stress, related to childrearing, 96

Substance abuse, 39, 47, 196–197

Suggestions. *See* Advice

Support, for parents, 8, 21, 26

Surprise rewards. *See* Behavior
   modification, backwards

Systematic Training in Effective
   Parenting, 81

T

Talking with parents, 77

Teacher-student interaction,
   34

Teaming, natural, 50

Teenagers:

   backward behavior modification,
     154–157

   chores, 150

   honoring emotions, 129

   natural teaming, 50

   rebellion, 69

   sharing power, 135

   special time, 118

Therapeutic process, 23–34

Therapist:

   advice for parents (*see* Homework)

   attitude towards parents, 19–20

   necessary skills, 11

   personal emotions, 19–21

   power, 133–134

   receiving feedback, 180–183

   role in divorce, 201

   scientific-mindedness, 77

   self-care, 206–207

   self-disclosure, 22–23

   self-evaluation, 108–109

   see also Advice

Therapy, child, 201–202

Threats, 35

"Tiger" parents, 1

Time constraints, 177–178.
    See also Sessions

Time, 48

Timeout, 158, 165–169

Tip sheets, 104–109

Tolerance. *See* Multiculturalism

Training. *See* Sessions

Transtheoretical change model, 94

Treatment. *See* Interventions.

Triangulation, 200

Two-session consultations, 178

U
Underachievement, 84
Universalization, 66, 182

V
Validating statement, second
    session, 182
Validation, 21, 24–26, 61–62, 134

Variable-ratio reinforcements,
    155
Verbal abuse, 35
Voice tone, 35

W
Wagering, 46–47
Whining, 157